ALAN EASTON

★

50 NORTH

AN ATLANTIC

BATTLEGROUND

★

with a foreword by

REAR-ADMIRAL K. L. DYER

D.S.C., C.D., R.C.N.

1963

EYRE & SPOTTISWOODE

LONDON

First published in 1963 by
Eyre & Spottiswoode (Publishers) Ltd
22 Henrietta Street, Covent Garden, WC2
© 1963 by Alan Easton
Printed in Great Britain by
Cox & Wyman Ltd, London, Fakenham & Reading
Catalogue No. 6/2475/1

To

the Officers and Men

who served with me

Author's Note

This is a factual account. The whole episode was recorded in 1945 while it was still fresh in my mind. All I have done recently is to put it into more readable form, eliminating inevitable repetition and some technical aspects.

The dialogue is, of course, drawn from my memory and imagination and, I hope, will not be thought by those to whom the words are attributed to be far from what was actually said.

To some people I have appended fictitious names. My only purpose in this has been to identify individuals more clearly from among the many titles used.

A. E.

Contents

Illustrations

Foreword

The Atlantic Battle against Hitler's U-boats occupied the energies and resources of the Allies for over four and a half years. Canada and Canadians contributed a major share of the overall effort towards ultimate victory. Other than in official histories, little has been written of, or by, individual Canadians concerning their personal exploits during the long battle.

Alan Easton's story allows us to relive a small fragment of the whole piece, and for those of us who served with him and shared in some of his exploits, it is a vivid account of those days. Those who experienced the loneliness of command on the high seas can readily remember the suspense and strain, the agony almost, of wondering whether a decision made would be right. For the Atlantic Convoy battle was unlike the swift moving surface engagements, although it had its moments of dramatic action. Visual contact with the enemy was fleeting, play of the individual pieces on the vast chequerboard might not result in any reaction for days or even weeks. At times, especially when the weather was a mutual enemy, to us and the U-boats, the whole battle took on the recurring unreality of a nightmare.

Alan Easton has told us his story with a depth of feeling, modesty and factual accuracy which we, who know him, would expect. However, even for those of us who are his friends, it is with astonishment that one concludes this account, realizing from all that is left unsaid, what amazing powers of endurance and fortitude he possessed. There were not many who held a record comparable to his, or who commanded continuously at sea in corvette, frigate and destroyer over those four wearying years.

It is appropriate then that he has led the way in telling Canadians and others of our part. Perhaps this will encourage more to come forward and help complete our wartime saga at sea.

K. L. DYER
D.S.C., C.D., *Rear-Admiral*, R.C.N.
Flag Officer Atlantic Coast

9

1. The Knave

The corvette lay stopped. We had reached our rendezvous and were waiting to identify the vessel whose smoke we had seen on the horizon fifteen minutes before. Her hull was now visible but we could not yet make her out clearly enough with binoculars to be sure that she was the troop transport we were to meet. We had made a fine passage to the Gulf and were well into the St Lawrence off Cap Chat, two hundred miles below Quebec.

It had been an extraordinary trip in a way. Since it was foggy we came round Cape Breton instead of taking the shorter route through the Gut of Canso. We used radar, which was the curiosity that made the voyage extraordinary. It had actually picked out the coast! It was hard to believe but the operator said he was sure it was the coast. Then he reported a vessel ahead and eventually we overtook her. The radar was right! In my ignorance of modern science I had not believed it possible, but who in the summer of 1941 knew much or anything about radar? I became for the first time aware of its possibilities and saw all the dangers of fog magically disappearing. Life in the Atlantic, I misguidedly thought, was going to be almost rosy.

'That's the trooper,' the navigator announced five minutes later. 'I'd know those ships anywhere.' He was looking over the canvas dodger on the weather side of the bridge beside me. 'It's almost 1400*,' he continued, 'which was our Estimated Time of Arrival.'

He handed me the binoculars. They were ghastly ones. We had only one pair and they had been given to me by the commander's staff officer at Halifax after I had found none in the naval stores.

Glasses had been so scarce that an appeal had been made to the public to give any they might have to the navy. This pair was one of those donated and I felt very grateful to the anonymous person who had so generously turned over his treasured binoculars to the State. But there were differences between the use we had for them

* 2 p.m. The Navy always omits the word 'hours'.

and the purpose to which their original owner had put them – bird-watching perhaps, or the races.

When my squint settled down I was able to agree with the navigator. Even at this distance her lines spelled out pleasure, affluence, a life of cruising in tropical waters.

As she came closer she reported her name, *Lady Rodney*, and we replied saying we would take station ahead of her. I hoped that we looked as though we were worth having as an escort with our four-inch gun poised in readiness for action.

'Ask her the speed she wants to make, Signalman,' I said. 'It'll be thirteen or fourteen knots, I expect,' I remarked to the navigator. 'Don't think they can do much more.'

As we turned and passed close under the trooper's stern, we saw her rails lined with soldiers, most of whom waved and hailed us cheerfully.

'They won't be so happy when they get out into the Gulf to-night,' the navigator prophesied.

'Fifteen knots he says, sir,' shouted the signalman from his lamp.

Fifteen! Why had I dawdled about and gone under her stern! It took us two hours to take up a position a mile or so ahead of her. Her captain, for a time at least, might have wondered if I had changed my mind about the station we were going to keep. And why, on this first opportunity, did we have to force the ship along at fifteen knots?

The wind was blowing moderately from the sou'-sou'-east, but there was hardly a chop on the water for we were protected by the hills of the South Shore. It was a dull afternoon with low clouds scudding by overhead. Travelling fast with the ebb tide and the natural current of the great river, sixty miles wide at this point, we soon passed the little French settlement of Sainte Anne des Monts with its seemingly out-sized parish church standing sentinel, tall and white, over the dwellings of farmers and fishermen. Presently we came up to Cape Magdalen where the wooded slopes of the coast began to turn away. By supper time we had passed Fame Point.

Then the ship began to roll. For the first time in her two month commission we really heard the tune of the wind.

. . . . .

She was resting on the blocks of a deep drydock in a shipyard farther up the river when I first saw her. I had stood on the wall and looked down at her sturdy features, the brand new vessel which was to take me many miles over the ocean. H.M.C.S. *Baddeck* was mine; we were to share at least a part of our lives together.

I was elated at being given command. I could not thank anybody because the news came in a naval signal, one of those pieces of paper rather like a telegram but without the advertising at the top. I just had time to catch the night train from Halifax to Quebec.

When anyone is given an appointment which places him in charge of something which he thinks is pretty important, it generally makes him feel he has been singled out as being above the crowd. But it was not so in my case; the authorities who selected me probably had no alternative. There was no one else handy. In the Royal Canadian Navy during the first half of the war, there were not enough people to go round. Often you got the job whether you deserved it or not.

I could see now that the ship had been built mainly after the fashion of a big steam trawler but with a longer and sharper bow. From drawings I had seen I knew she was 204 feet long and had a thirty-three-foot beam. Her appearance fitted these dimensions and in her nakedness her fat belly seemed to bulge over the floor of the dry-dock suggesting an ample capacity for, among other things, a large engine. Her rounded stern was inclined to turn up like a duck's tail.

The term 'corvette' had fallen into disuse with the disappearance of sail. Since it had been introduced by the French in the early eighteenth century, the three-masted, flush deck corvette with her single tier of guns, had served as a vital support to the fleets of all the great maritime nations. Now she was reborn.

In 1915, William Reed, employed by Smith's Dock Company on the East Coast of England, designed a little ship, a modified whaler, which he thought the Admiralty could use as a submarine chaser. But it took more than two decades and the threat of a new war for the Admiralty to adopt the design. In the summer of 1939 Reed's whaler was accepted and put into production in Britain, and in Canada the following year.

But the First Lord of the Admiralty, Winston Churchill, did not like the name 'whaler'; it was not going to catch whales.

'I would like some suggestions about this,' he wrote to his subordinates. The term submitted delighted him.

The first sight of a ship in which one is going to sail is always exciting, that first intensely interesting glimpse which creates an immediate impression, perhaps of size or strength or just lowlinesss and a sense of curiosity – sometimes of disappointment.

I had viewed many, perhaps a score, in my earlier days – days before I had given up the sea, for ever as I thought – with all those first feelings. Most had proclaimed their character loudly and had made me glow – or shudder. The hundred-year-old ship-of-the-line, a naval cadet ship, which I had joined at fourteen with a mixture of pride and trepidation; the great liners which were as romantic as they were luxurious. But some had been deceptive; the bluff-bowed tramps which seemed humble but were hard-bitten.

This time I was not disappointed. And as I stood on her deck, I felt alone with her in the silence of the deserted yard. It was Sunday and everything was quiet – no hammering or riveting, no trail of steam drifting up from the machine shop. What was her character? Was her spirit yet born? Would she stay young like this or grow old quickly? I was glad it was quiet because this was my private introduction and she would try to show me herself – before our exploits began.

Exploits? That was the trouble. She might never be involved in a fight. A corvette, after all, was designed for coastal patrol work. And Canada had a long coastline. The war was on the other side of the Atlantic.

It was a month or more before I had an opportunity to try out her promises of performance on the broad reaches of the St Lawrence below Quebec. She had been fitted out, her crew had come on board and she had been duly commissioned into the Royal Canadian Navy.

Many men felt strange. But this alien environment was what a good many expected, even sought, when they joined the navy. Stokers looked into the furnaces and felt the burners they would be tending. They looked for a quiet spot in the mess deck to sling their hammocks. They did not know then there would be no quiet spot. Most of them – for most were new to this – felt a twinge of concern and a little ache of homesickness. But these were hidden by an extra swing of the shoulder and more noise than necessary.

14

There had been no fanfare on leaving. No 'off to the war' business. Just a farewell hoot of the whistle as we pulled out into the river and headed down-stream for the coast.

Our first operational job was to carry out patrols off Halifax; these usually lasted a week. A number of ships were engaged in this tedious assignment. You simply went in a straight line from A to B and along to C and back to A. Then you started all over again, most of the time in sight of land. Or, at night, from 1 to 2 and back to 1. It should have been extremely easy, but it was not. Few of the men knew how to go about their duties; there had not been time to acquire the easy familiarity of routine.

Of the three officers only the navigator had been in a ship before. He had been twenty-five years at sea in all sorts of small vessels. He had started to sea in fishing vessels when he was twelve, and had gone on from schooners to small steamers to become master of a coastal tanker. He was a rough and ready little man and a rule-of-thumb navigator, I suspected; not that I was disinclined to be one myself. Of the fifty men, about five had been professional seamen or fishermen and, below, no more than six were experienced with engines and boilers. So with more than three-quarters of the complement as fresh to the sea as the ship herself, it was hard to perform our simple task; hard to keep steam up, avoid the shoals or even to steer a straight course. Had anything warlike occurred there would have been a shambles.

Thus, while we were on patrol, the few who knew their profession taught the others. The principles had been explained to them ashore and our specialists had been well instructed, but when they came to supply their knowledge in the ship, a place where discomfort alone had a dazing effect on the mind as well as the stomach, it did not always work out as expected.

We went at it systematically. I had been back at sea almost continuously since the beginning of the war. I was, therefore, in a fair position to know what was needed to develop the crew.

Boats were lowered many times and rowed and then hoisted; men swung the hand lead for soundings; they put out fires; they were taught lookout-keeping; they learned to read a swinging compass and compensate with the wheel; to stoke the furnaces without belching smoke; to handle the guns in a choppy sea and to throw a heaving line. But all this was not learned easily.

15

Coming in from one of the patrols we were going alongside a jetty which was overlooked by the admiral's office; the admiral was known to be fond of observing his ships docking. A strong offshore wind was blowing. It was now or never with the heaving line as the bow of the ship drew parallel to the jetty at a nice throwing distance. An able seaman heaved but his line went up like the first act of the Indian rope trick instead of across the gap. It came down in the water on the lee side. The gap widened but another man standing by with a spare coiled line, in case the first man missed, heaved. It reached the jetty and was caught but the thrower was empty-handed. The end of the rope had gone too! The ship drifted away. And the admiral looked down from his window on the performance.

The two new officers, the first lieutenant and the sub, were trying hard to learn their practical seamanship a step ahead of the men. Their initial training ashore had given them the edge but it was all terribly new. They probably felt as strange on the bridge with their duty before them as they had when they first stood on the parade ground in their new uniforms.

So the navigator and I split the watches between us, and gave them the beginnings of what was to be almost a war-long course. They took it well and as the weeks went by they began to feel more comfortable; though we were all tired.

But my mind was never at peace. There was much to do, so little time. I was afraid of going far afield with such inexperience; we had to become more efficient. And then I became worried about the speed of the ship. When we came within two knots or so of her maximum of sixteen the chief engine room artificer would appear; we had a hot bearing, could we slow down?

Just as I felt we were getting on but still wanted time and more engine testing we were recalled.

In harbour I found the authorities had decided to fit the ship with radar and as she was to be the first corvette to be so equipped, it was to be done on a trial-and-error basis and would take about six weeks. This would be long enough for the men to forget at least half of what they had learned at sea.

As the work of this installation progressed a vague understanding of the function of radar began to dawn on me. There were no books or pamphlets about it. In fact, I was not informed how to

A corvette similar to H.M.C.S. *Baddeck*, Lieutenant-Commander
Easton's first command.

H.M.C.S. *Sackville*, corvette. Her camouflage was two shades of green and white.

use it at all. It was more or less secret. The warrant officer in charge of the installation work said it would 'see' another vessel in the dark as far as four miles away. This sounded ridiculous.

I was really more anxious about the crew at this time. Also it seemed to me that, with this new gadget, the technical people might want the ship put back on the local patrol job to see how it worked out. Despite my misgivings about the degree of our efficiency I did not want that. I wanted to get away and do something which I imagined could be more useful than the protection of the approaches to the harbour of Halifax which at this time was a long way from the enemy. I decided to speak to my superior officer about it.

This was the Commander in the dockyard who had charge of the auxiliary vessels and, therefore, the power of selection when ships of his force were needed elsewhere. Whenever I went to see him I sought the opportunity of saying something about getting into more vital spheres when we were ready to go. I did not have many chances of expressing myself along these lines but I thought the occasional remark from time to time might sink in.

When the ship was almost ready, the final tests being made to the new radar, and I was becoming fidgety, I was called to the Commander's office.

He was a short man, stocky, with a jovial face. He always stood when he talked to anyone. A chair probably irked him. 'I think you've told me several times you wanted to get away from here.'

'Yes sir,' I replied, hopefully.

'Well, you're going.'

He smiled pleasantly, then led the way into the operations room and over to the staff officer who seemed to be deeply engrossed in a batch of signals.

'This is the C.O.,' the Commander announced.

The staff officer glanced up, and thumbed through numerous pink sheets while my curiosity grew. At last he found the signals which apparently had to do with this operation.

'Here's the job,' he said. 'You're to escort a troop ship from Quebec to Newfoundland for two trips, then take her to Jamaica and back.'

'I see, sir,' I said. Then turning to the Commander. 'Thank you, sir. Thank you very much.'

Secrecy of movement was naturally a cardinal principle, particularly where troops were involved; but next day when we were taking the final complement of stores aboard, a hand-cart, which had wended its way through the dockyard, arrived on the jetty heaped to overflowing with white sun helmets. The rating in charge of delivery shouted up to the petty officer on deck, 'Sun hats for the crew, mister. Guess you're going somewhere hot. Will you send some hands down to take 'em aboard?'

Then heads appeared at the side and the word sped around. We were going South. Everyone knew.

2. A Lee Shore

Now, as we cleared the Gaspé Peninsula with the *Lady Rodney* a mile astern, we lost the lee of the land and felt the full force of the wind and sea. The ship rolled and pitched, sending sheets of spray over the superstructure. She could not keep a high speed in a rough sea like this, two or three points before her beam. Her bows were leaping out of the water and pounding down on the next wave. I saw we were losing position and before long would hardly be able to keep ahead of the trooper.

By 1900 we had fallen back to a position on her quarter and were doing more speed than we really should under such sea conditions. It was squally with occasional rain and the visibility had decreased to about two miles. I knew the Gulf of old and was aware that when it blew it could be very dirty with its short, steep sea. I stood debating whether I should tell the captain of the *Lady Rodney* to ease down.

But I was sure he would not want to do that. I also had the feeling that he probably did not think there was any danger from the enemy, anyway – which I would not have been prepared to dispute strenuously. And if the navy could not send him a ship that would keep up with him, why should he stick around and wait for her? The navy, of course, did not have a faster ship to spare.

Then I heard a tinkle from below. The engine room had rung 'stop'.

I called to the signalman to pass the message to the troop ship that we were stopping because of engine trouble, but before he had flashed more than three words, our friend faded from sight in the misty dusk.

Some of my high hopes faded too. I did not inquire of the engine room what their trouble was; they would not have stopped without warning the bridge unless there was a real urgency and in that case matters below would not be improved by my asking questions immediately. I would be notified as soon as the chief engineer had a clear report to make.

The ship began to roll more and pitch less. The pounding of her keel ceased, her wild rearing and shuddering fell away into a wallowing motion.

The whistle on the engine room voicepipe sounded; I turned up the lid and shouted, 'Bridge – Engine Room.'

'Is that the captain?' a voice asked.

'Yes, Chief.'

'Bottom end gone, sir.'

'Was it very hot?' I shouted, my mouth against the pipe.

'Yes, it was very hot when we got it,' came the reply. 'I'll have to take it down and examine it.'

'Surely it's not as bad as that, Chief!'

'Quite bad, sir. Metal may have run and if it has, I'll have to use the spare.'

'Good God! How long will that take you?'

'About three hours, anyway, in this, sir.' The Chief's voice seemed to come from a long way off.

'All right. Thanks, Chief, but don't waste any time.'

As he assured me he would not, I clapped the lid on the voice-pipe again.

'Well, Number One,' I said to the first lieutenant, 'I'm quite sure the trooper won't hang about for us and I wouldn't want her to. Send for the navigator, will you?'

I thought of the predicament below. A thoroughly nasty job. Though I still did not know the chief engineer very well, he seemed to have assurance, which was comforting. He had served probably fifteen years in the navy and, as a chief engine room artificer, was a very senior rating. He rarely made an observation unless he considered he had good reason to do so, and his responses were brief unless he was trying to be convincing. The situation was in his hands now.

I inquired of the quartermaster how the ship's head was by compass. He told me N 85° E, which would be about N 60° E true. I went to the weather side of the bridge and watched the sea. It was getting quite dark, but the running sea could be seen easily. It was the direction of the wind I was looking for. The direction from which the sea broke, the way the wave crests curled and the spindrift flew would determine it.

It was still sou'-sou'-east and I also concluded that it was blowing at force 7 – a moderate gale, about thirty-five miles an hour. As all ships do when they are stopped, she was lying more or less beam on to the sea and was consequently rolling quite heavily – often thirty degrees on the roll to leeward.

When the navigator came up we went into the asdic house, which occupied the centre of the bridge and which served also as the chart house, and automatically fell to gazing at the chart.

'We stopped at 1920, Pilot. Now where are we?' I asked.

The navigator worked out the distance we had run from the last accurate fix off Fame Point, while I checked the effect of the tide. In a few minutes we had our position marked on the chart.

'Not the most desirable position, is it?' I remarked, looking at the black cross he had marked. I tapped the dividers on the chart.

'No, it isn't. I noticed as I came up the wind seemed to be blowing harder.'

This was true. 'Same direction though. The visibility isn't likely to improve while it holds in this quarter.'

He was looking up at the barometer on the bulkhead, rising a little on his toes, his hands on the small chart table supporting his weight. The navigator was short and rather stout. 'Still falling.'

I knew I had to do something about notifying the authorities. I could not leave it any longer. I had lost my charge. I had lost my job. I hated to say so.

Finally I wrote out a signal to the Commander-in-Chief briefly describing the situation. Then, telling the officer-of-the-watch to keep a good lookout, I went down to my cabin.

After I had thrown off my wet things, I went down to the wardroom for supper and found only the sub-lieutenant there, finishing his meal. Collins was one of the few with a strong stomach. The quarters were in a shambles. They had not been prepared for severe rolling, probably because this was our first experience of really rough weather. The wardroom pantry was more or less all right, although some china had been broken. The two stewards were experienced hands, which was a blessing. One, Auclair, a Cape Breton Frenchman, had been a steward in the Canadian National Steamships and had fished in trawlers out of Halifax. He was destined to stay with me for three years. The other steward originally hailed from England, and by his accent his birthplace could be identified as Liverpool. A small man with a large voice when the rum was in him, he had been a bell boy on a liner in which I was serving years before and had learned his stewarding in the hard, good service of those days.

So their pantry was comparatively all right. But there seemed to be innumerable objects sculling about, both in and between the officers' cabins – personal belongings mixed up with books, boxes and other oddments which had probably been stowed away neatly enough but not secured against this kind of weather. With practice this would be overcome. But I was disturbed to see water swishing about the deck. We would have to find out where it was coming from. We never did. Nor, as far as I knew, did those in other corvettes who found that water entered the officers' quarters as well as the communications mess ahead of it in bad weather.

The wardroom carpet had been taken up, as was the way in all small naval ships at sea, and the chairs lashed to the bolted-down table legs or convenient posts. Other moveables were wedged into corners or locked in cupboards where they banged about but at least did not come out. Fiddles were not fitted to the table but instead the steward had poured water over the table cloth, to which dishes invariably stuck.

The sub-lieutenant told me there was much seasickness among the crew. This movement was a test for anyone unaccustomed to the sea.

'On the rail, I suppose,' I remarked.

'No, not many of them. They haven't been able to get that far.'

I felt sympathy. Twice in the past year I had been a victim myself. I could still remember the cold sweat and the weakness in my knees.

After supper, I went down to the engine-room. The engineers were bending over the bottom-end bearing as it rested on the plates. I was wearing rubber seaboots and was scarcely able to keep my feet on the oily platform. There was a reek of stale steam and lubricating oil in the place. Something clanged as the ship rolled over. Bilge water spouted up when the engine-room started to come back from its steeply slanted angle. The bare electric globe in its wire cage hanging over the casting threw great shadows of the piston rods on the white-painted side of the ship.

They had a hard job in front of them. To remove the upper half of the bearing, and perhaps the lower half, was difficult enough while the ship was passing through an arc of fifty or sixty degrees; but to fit the spare would be much more so and dangerous, too. They could easily lose control of a heavy steel casting like that. When the chief saw me he straightened up and, holding on to the rail in front of me, wiped his face with the sleeve of his free arm.

'How's it going, Chief?' I asked hopefully.

'Not so bad, sir.' But he was frowning.

'Running into difficulties?'

'Not yet; but it's mighty hard working in these conditions. We had the devil's own job taking the bearing off. Have a look at it.'

I did and it was not a pleasing sight. It was lashed so that it could be examined without taking charge.

'The metal has run badly,' I said. It had become so hot that the white metal on the inner side of the bearing had melted and run into the oil grooves, almost obliterating them. 'You can't use that one again.'

'No, I can't. We're going to get the spare down.'

'Where is it?'

'Over here.' The chief took a few careful steps and pointed to a spot on the after bulkhead near the platform above. There, abaft the generator, was the spare bearing securely bolted into its position.

'We're going to bring it down in a few minutes.' The chief spoke in a rather matter-of-fact sort of way. 'If all goes well we'll have it on in two hours.'

'Can you set it up in that time?'

'I'll try, sir, but you can never tell – the journal's scored a bit, I'm afraid.'

'Chief,' I said, taking him aside a little but still holding on. 'How in the world was that bearing allowed to become heated so badly?'

'Sorry, sir, I don't know.' He shook his head. 'Hands aren't experienced, you know, and when the engine is turning that fast some of these men are scared to feel into it, and I don't blame them with their lack of practice. It needs some skill, anyway, to feel when a bearing's hot at 160 revs. And more still when the ship's pitching and rolling at the same time.'

That was most of the answer; but he had not mentioned

23

seasickness. I just said, 'All right, Chief, let me know in an hour how it's going, or before if you run into a snag.'

I went up the engine-room ladder, climbing cautiously between each roll, waiting while she heeled over, and then taking another upward step or two as she righted herself. On the grating above I looked back into the eerie cavern. The bare backs were bending over the casting again.

Sub-Lieutenant Collins was standing watch when I came on to the bridge a few minutes later. He was wedged by the side of the asdic house and said he had just asked the navigator to swing the boat in as it had become insecure when a wave had hit its bottom while the ship was rolling down. It had lifted the boat in the davits and so loosened the griping. Normally one boat at least was kept swung out at sea so that it could be readily lowered in an emergency. But this was impracticable in anything more than a moderate sea; a corvette was too lively.

The weather had worsened. The gale had become stronger although the sea was still doing no damage on deck to speak of, high though the combers were. I looked over the after part of the bridge and saw a few hands gathered on the boat deck. I recognized the little navigator, his round form swathed in an oilskin which was glistening from its wetness, galvanizing the men to the task of turning the boat in. 'Call yourself a sailor!' I heard him shouting. I could leave it to him with confidence although he did lose his temper occasionally. But I could not blame him.

It was always my fear with inexperienced hands that they would be either washed overboard or hurt. They did not know when to hold on or what swinging object to avoid. This time it was the boat and how easily, if it were not kept under control, could a man be squashed between the boat and the casing around the funnel if he did not stand clear as the davits were turned in and the boat not yet on its chocks.

When the job was done, I shouted to the navigator to come up. We studied our position again.

We were now drifting before the gale at about three miles an hour and we were on a lee shore. Our position when we had stopped was about twenty-five miles sou'-sou'-east of South West Point, Anticosti Island, so that the gale was blowing the ship directly towards it. More than two hours had passed since then and I reckoned we were now about twenty miles from the land. If the gale continued – and there was no immediate sign of it abating, although southerly gales did not usually blow for long in this region – we would drift that distance in seven hours. But on examining the chart carefully, we found that a reef extended along the south coast of Anticosti at a distance of about three miles offshore. Thus it was evident that we would have to be underway in less than six hours.

It was quite reasonable to assume that repairs would be completed well within this time, but it would be unwise to count on it.

'It's 2130 now,' I finally said to the navigator. 'We'll give them an hour and then see what progress they've made.'

We went out on to the bridge to look at the weather again. The wind was shrieking dismally and the low clouds raced northward overhead. It was not a very dark night but you could not see far; a light would not have been visible at a greater distance than about a mile and a half. Though spray and spindrift often flew over the ship with stinging force, the waves did not come aboard. The ship caught their progression and rolled easily, though far over, particularly to leeward. A driving rain squall came over every now and then cutting into the faces of the men on deck. I went below again, wet and disconsolate. At 2230 a leading stoker knocked on my cabin door.

'The Chief says, sir, that he's sorry he can't come up himself, but that the job's going along fairly good.'

'Is that all?'

'Yes, sir. That's all he said to tell you.'

'All right, thank you.'

The lad waited a moment while the ship swung more or less upright, to gain a firmer footing and then stepped into the cross passage and out the lee door to the upper deck.

I sat and thought. The back of my armchair was against my bunk and I had one foot against the edge of the settee to keep the chair from tipping or sliding. I began to wonder what they had meant in the official description of the corvette, as reliable and highly manœuverable. What would stop the drift? One or two things suggested themselves but I had never heard of anybody using them. Well – time enough yet.

I got up, put the chair in the bunk and went up to the bridge again. Here the officer-of-the-watch told me that the barometer seemed to have ceased falling.

A little after 2300 the chief groped his way on to the bridge. He held his jacket collar tight around his neck.

'Captain, sir?' he inquired, peering through the darkness.

'Yes, Chief.' I stood beside him, ready to seize his next words.

'I've run into trouble, I'm afraid, sir.'

'What is it?'

'I can't get the new bearing to fit.'

'Well, what's the matter with it?' I asked, although his answer might be Greek to me.

'We've been struggling with it for half an hour and it seems that the bolt holes aren't square to one another. I've got it down now and I'm trying to ream them out."

'This means a big delay?' If it did, where was I?

'There will be a delay, but I'm working as fast as I can.'

The chief's oily boots slipped as the wet deck canted steeply but his grip on the stanchion tightened and he righted himself nimbly.

'I'm sure you are, Chief. Would you care to estimate how long you'll be now?'

'Wouldn't like to say, sir. I'll do it as quick as I can.'

'Yes, I know you will, Chief. But will it be two hours or ten hours?'

'I don't know for sure. Perhaps five hours,' the chief said at last, reluctantly.

'Well, here's the situation. We're drifting towards the shore pretty fast and, while I may be wrong, I reckon we're likely to be on the reefs in four hours.'

'I won't let you do that,' the chief said quickly. 'I'll disconnect the H.P. engine and work her on three cylinders if necessary.

In my concern I was glad to grab at anything.

'Could you do that quickly?'

'No, but I'll do it in time if I can't fit the bearing.'

'Then if it's not fixed by one, disconnect the H.P. We'd be underway by three, wouldn't we?' I lapsed into the use of civil time; we varied it.

'Hardly, sir, but I'll let you know in good time. I'll go right down and get on with it again.'

26

'All right, Chief. Let me know in an hour how it's going.'

'I will, sir.' The chief moved towards the ladder. 'I won't let you go on that reef,' he threw back as he started down.

I went to the voicepipe and told the messenger in the wheel-house to ask the first lieutenant to come to the bridge. In less than five minutes he was up.

'You wanted me, sir?'

'Yes, Number One.'

He was standing bare-headed but with oilskins and seaboots on. His face and hair were already wet with spray. He was a handsome fellow of about twenty-six with a very pleasant manner and presence. He had not been in the ship long – three weeks or so. The original first lieutenant had already been sent to another appointment.

'I want to try to lessen the leeway,' I explained. 'You've got to do two things. First pay out two shackles of cable, then rig a sea anchor.'

'What's a sea anchor?' he asked.

'I'll show you when you've done the first job. And I'll be with you as soon as you have the men on the fo'c'sle head.'

He went off. I passed word to the engine-room to put steam on the windlass. Then my head instinctively turned to leeward and my eyes looked into the murky darkness.

There was a lighthouse on South West Point whose flash had a range of fifteen miles. Although I knew I could not see much more than a mile in the clearer intervals between the squalls I periodically glanced in its possible direction. Not that I wanted to see it. I would have hated to. In fact, we would have been fast aground before its rays could have penetrated the thick, wet atmosphere; fast aground and breaking up. I looked now and then involuntarily, just the same.

Conditions now warranted a further signal to C-in-C giving him the miserable picture – briefly, of course, since there was the coding and decoding to be done. I did not want to send a signal, but had to. In such a position you were inclined to hesitate before creating a 'flap' in the admiral's 'Ops', and you were only too aware that if things turned out well the message need never have been sent. But I sent this signal – jagged rocks and all – not that it could do any good.

When I saw several men go on to the fo'c'sle head I went forward. The steam was already coming through in cracking noises and I explained to the first lieutenant why I wanted him to lower the anchor with the windlass in gear rather than letting it go in the usual way and fetching the cable up with the brake. If it were just let go in deep water without a bottom to catch the anchor, the whole cable would run out and be lost.

The slip holding the cable was released and the weight taken on the windlass and as the order was given to lower away, it was put in reverse, the steam turned on and the anchor moved slowly down the hawse pipe and into the water. Two shackles – thirty fathoms – were paid out, the steam turned off and the big slip hooked on to a link on deck to take part of the strain. Now we had an anchor and 180 feet of cable beneath us, just hanging, so that the ship would be held up in her drift at any rate to some extent.

Now to rig a sea anchor. I had never heard of such a thing being used in a steamer, never in any craft larger than a lifeboat, but I was determined to leave nothing untried to retard the ship's drift towards the reef.

Merchant navy lifeboats were always equipped with a sea anchor, which had been responsible for saving many lives for years back. It consisted of a cone-shaped canvas bucket on the end of a rope about twenty fathoms long. It had the effect, when streamed over the bow in heavy weather, of acting as a drogue. Lying just beneath the surface it pulled the drifting boat around head to wind and lessened the likelihood of it being swamped or capsized. It naturally stopped most of its drift to leeward.

A number of seamen were still too sick to take any interest in the proceedings, but there were enough to do what I wanted. The largest single piece of canvas in the ship was a black-out curtain which hung at the break of the fo'c'sle to prevent light coming out of the seamen's mess. It measured about seven feet by twelve. This was taken down amid much flapping and banging in the gale, and heavy iron bars laced along one edge and to the other edge were secured three lifebuoys. Meanwhile ropes were got up from below and flaked out on deck. The canvas was then brought on to the fo'c'sle head and the ends of two four-inch ropes secured to the upper corners away from the weighted edge.

When all was ready, this odd looking sea anchor was launched over the weather bow, albeit with some difficulty against the wind and sea and the constant heave of the ship. But when the water caught it, I saw the sea hold it while we drifted away. As we paid out the two lines, I saw the canvas was hanging vertically, weighted down by the iron bars and supported by the buoys. The lines were belayed with about forty fathoms out and I assumed, or trusted, that the canvas still hung vertically, though I really did not know. Of course, I did not expect such a drogue to turn the ship's head to windward; it was far too light for that.

But how much our drift was reduced by these measures I could not tell. I liked to think it was at least a knot and a half.

By 0030 nothing definite had been reported from the engine-room and at 0115, sitting wedged in my cabin with a mug of cocoa, I felt a decision one way or the other must be made, though we had some spare time now as a result of our probable reduced drift. I put on my wet oilskin again and struggled up the steep ladders to the bridge.

Coming out of the comforting warmth and brightness of my cabin the chill bleakness which struck me, the shock of the gale and slash of the sea, suddenly made the night seem a shrieking turmoil. The violent contrast plunged a doubt in my heart.

Yet there was one man who had not risked the contrast; had not sought the consolation of his hammock, the lighted mess-deck, a topsy-turvy nightmare though it was. The small, thin, sharp-featured signalman with the surprised expression had stayed on the upper deck, spent his off-duty hours in the lee of the funnel, trying to catch his courage from its slender warmth. It was too much for Swish, as he was called, to listen to the creaking and groaning of the ship inside at every swing, the crash of objects as they were flung down the slanting decks below as though they would puncture the ship's side.

His opposite number, opposite in both girth and weight, had had his apprehensions too. He had seen the behaviour of some of the others, those whose seasickness was not bad enough to make them want to die. He had seen fear in their faces, as they clung to solid structures while the ship rolled down, like people clinging to the overhanging edge of a precipice; their momentary horror as she hung, heeled over, perhaps never to come back again.

Signalman Burley tried to prevent his feelings being reflected in his face and actions like some of his shipmates. They had not been on the bridge as he had, watching the reactions of those in charge. Had he not found the navigator peeling an orange in his cabin when he had been sent down on a message? If an officer could do that, what was there for him to worry about?

The navigator was on watch now, but the sub-lieutenant had not gone down to his bunk at midnight; he was anxious as to the outcome of engines versus storm. I was certainly no less anxious than he.

I automatically looked to leeward trusting subconsciously that I would see nothing. My eyes were not adjusted to the darkness yet, anyhow. But I almost felt the gradual sliding of the vessel towards destruction, like an oarless boat dropping silently down a river current towards the crest of a waterfall.

"Wind's veering, sir,' said the navigator.

'Oh! Where is it now?' I asked, brightening for the first time.

'Sou'-sou'-west about. Decreasing a bit, I think.'

'Is it!' I exclaimed.

I checked the ship's head by compass. She was lying forty degrees to starboard of her previous direction, which meant that she had been turned by the wind. This was good – a veering wind was better than a backing wind. It would mean a north-westerly eventually, clear and dry. Collins read the barometer again. It had risen a little which was a further indication that the wind would veer more.

Sure enough, by 0200 it was south-west and its strength had dropped slightly below gale proportions. It was at this time that the chief sent word that he had the new bottom end bearing in place and was adjusting it to try to reduce the clearance. It would be an hour, however, before he would be ready. I conveyed the information to him that the weather conditions were improving and not to worry much now on that score.

When weather changes at sea, as it is more or less always doing in northern latitudes, it does so sometimes very quickly. I was not so surprised, therefore, to see presently the low clouds dispersing and a few high clouds become visible, between which stars began to shine. The wind dropped away and a great change came over the ship; the shrieking became a low murmur with an occasional moan and the moving parts of the ship and her creaking as she

30

rolled became much more audible. Then we felt the first cool wisp of air on our faces coming from the opposite bow – the north-west. The atmosphere began to clear and the waves, which were losing their whitecaps, were tumbling this way and that in an uncertain manner.

We searched the sea from north to west with the inadequate binoculars but could see nothing of the Island of Anticosti. It would still have been difficult to see land at a much greater distance than three miles. And since we had not struck the reef we could not be less than that distance from it.

No time was wasted hauling in the sea anchor and the cable although the men on deck seemed tired. But it was after 0400 when the chief engineer reported that he could work the engines. It was good to hear the engine-room telegraph ring again and to feel even the rather feeble throb of the engine once more.

3. Caribbean Interlude

The following afternoon we passed slowly under towering cliffs in brilliant sunshine and into the little harbour of Gaspé which was beginning to establish itself as one of the smaller naval bases. On the way we met one of the Gulf Patrol vessels, a converted yacht, which had been sent out to assist us. But we had been able to make enough way on our own, though slowly. The work done by the engineers the night before had been temporary, so I had decided to make for the nearest harbour where the troublesome bearing could be set up in quiet waters.

Gaspé was neither helpful nor entertaining. It was a dull little place. The top naval authority was mainly interested in the salmon streams and whenever I tried to present my problems I had to listen until this, or some other topic of local importance, had been discussed. The crew suffered from boredom, and at least one member tried drinking as a solution to the dreary state of affairs. He was a signalman, a blond, cheerful fellow, not very big but wiry and fairly strong. He was brought aboard early on the third evening by the naval shore patrol.

After some consultation between the duty petty officer on board and the leading hand of the shore patrol they approached the navigator, who had the deck that evening and who, at the moment, was leaning against the off-shore rail with a fishing line in his fingers, jigging.

'Signalman Fair, sir,' intoned the petty officer, 'was found drunk on shore at 1930, being apprehended by the shore patrol.'

The navigator looked from the petty officer to the leading hand standing beside him, a stranger.

'Are you the shore patrol?'

'Leading hand, sir. There's my patrol, sir.' He pointed to two men across the deck between whom stood the wretched signalman.

'That's the charge, sir,' the petty officer resumed. 'Where shall I put him?'

The navigator, whose left forearm still rested on the broad rail, jigged the line meditatively. 'In his hammock,' he said finally.

'In his hammock, sir. Very good, sir.' The petty officer saluted and carried on. The navigator went on with his fishing.

Ten minutes later the petty officer reported that the signalman had escaped. An hour later, he reported to the navigator, now gutting a fish, in more weighty terms.

'Signalman Fair, sir. Did improperly leave His Majesty's Canadian Ship at 2015 returning on board drunk at 2120, having been apprehended by the shore patrol at 2100, thereby remaining absent without leave one hour and five minutes.'

It was a long mouthful but he delivered it well.

The navigator scraped his knife on the rail and looked over at the culprit being held in a tight grip by the patrol.

'Pity we ain't got a cell down below, sir, or some such,' the petty officer said.

'Yes,' the navigator answered slowly. 'Just get a couple of hands and take him to his mess. Put a guard on him and don't let him go again.'

'Aye, aye, sir. Do my best.'

The navigator dropped his line over the side again.

A few moments later he made his last jig in that cool, peaceful evening, which was now becoming darker as the shadows of the cliffs across the harbour spread over the placid water. There was shouting and running. The navigator belayed his line and hauled round. He observed the prisoner heading aft at the double, followed hotly by the duty petty officer. The navigator studied the situation for a second or two then took up the chase.

The man lunged on past the guarded brow, around the quarter-deck and up the waist on the starboard side. Others joined in the pursuit. Signalman Fair was difficult to catch. He displayed such amazing agility that it was feared he would attempt to jump ashore from the rail. But instead he leapt into the rigging and, from aloft, hurled down the most unwarranted epithets at the navigator.

Then the chase seemed to reverse itself and prisoner Fair swung down and made after the navigator, who was by this time at the head of the party.

It came to the navigator vaguely as he passed back through the ranks of his followers, that he had heard there was something in

K.R. & A.I. about the seriousness of a man striking an officer or about a warning that officers should avoid altercations with excited or drunken men.

'Catch him, there,' he shouted over his shoulder. 'Don't let him get by the gun.'

They didn't. The prisoner fell into the arms of the men, struggled and was finally overpowered.

'Bring him down off o' the bloody fo'c'sle,' the navigator, having halted on the fore deck, bellowed between heavy breathing. 'Fetch a rope . . . an inch-and-a-half rope.'

Nervously they lowered him down the ladder to the upper deck.

'All aback, now! Lay him against the foremast there,' ordered the officer, adopting a stern Blighish attitude. 'Now,' – a man with the rope having appeared – 'lash him to the mast. Lash him up same as he was a hammock.'

And during the operation he walked around the mast inspecting the turns and hitches and issuing instructions.

There the signalman stayed, in a belligerent state at first, then in a drooping condition supported by his bonds for most of the night. He was no trouble when he was taken down.

There were no repercussions. The man did not complain – he probably only knew about it from hearsay – and the navigator felt he had done a good job. I could not agree with him formally.

During the four days we were in port our engineers worked hard, but it became increasingly evident that the trouble extended beyond the bearing. No matter how much it was adjusted, the propeller shaft would not turn satisfactorily. The best plan, I thought, would be to go to Quebec where we might refer the trouble to the builder of the ship. We were due there shortly, in any case, to join the trooper for her second voyage.

We felt rather uncertain as we crept cautiously out of the little harbour with four hundred miles before us, though we were soon working our way up-river at a somewhat better speed than we had hobbled into Gaspé. Nevertheless, it was with difficulty that the ship hammered against the strong tides which swept against her at the bends and traverses. A heavy and persistent knock in the engine accompanied us all the way.

The *Lady Rodney* returned from her first round trip and started off again on her second while we were lying in the shipyard. After

34

we had parted company in the Gulf ten days before, an old four-stacker destroyer had been dispatched from Pictou, where she had been exercising, and took over our job to St John's. Then another corvette had been assigned to escort the trooper until we were ready. It was with a feeling of defeat, annoyance and some embarrassment that I saw her pass down the river. In time, after many vicissitudes of this kind, I learned philosophy and patience.

The forward half of the crank shaft was taken out of the ship and sent off by road to its makers in Montreal. Keeping abreast of what was happening to it, I was told that they had put its thirteen feet of length on a lathe and were bringing it back to its proper proportions or, rather, grinding a bend out of it.

The job was certainly accomplished in record time. Within a week it was back in the yard again; and it was re-installed and connected up in the amazingly short time of two days.

I was impressed again by the efficiency and willing co-operation of this shipyard. Apart from its management, which was extremely helpful, it was perfectly symbolized by its two principle foremen, the walking boss and the little engineer, the latter's overalls permanently dyed by the marks of his profession. They seemed to work night and day, as French Canadians were willing to do, supervising all the ships in the yard at once, yet having time to give particular attention to us. I liked these men and admired them.

I experienced a little more than normal crew trouble at the yard; the men did not seem to be altogether happy among themselves nor did the senior hands enjoy the respect they should have received from their subordinates. I was aware, however, that this general state of affairs had not developed without some contribution from a higher level. The ship had had the misfortune, in her few months in commission, to have had three first lieutenants – the executive officer of the ship who was responsible for working the seamen, the co-ordination of departments and the general co-operation of individuals so that harmony would endure and discipline prevail. These changes had had a harmful effect. Unfortunately it seemed as though still another change would be necessary.

Perhaps some of the fault lay with myself. I may not have been ready enough to overlook weaknesses, I was perhaps too impatient or intolerant, or I may not have shown enough confidence in others, though heaven knows how could I ?

35

At this time another officer joined the ship. I now had four, one lieutenant, one chief skipper and two sub-lieutenants, and of these only the chief skipper – the navigator – had been in the ship from the beginning. But I was destined to keep the two sub-lieutenants, Collins and Neil, a long time, the former almost to my last days in the war. Collins was rather an unusual character, tall and blond with finely cut features and a very pleasant voice. I believe, in the years which followed when he became first lieutenant with me, he grew to know every thought which passed through my head, every action I planned to take. I never knew him like that. I doubt if anyone understood him well.

Sub-Lieutenant Neil, another fine looking chap though very different from the other, was making his first trip. It was soon evident that he possessed a quick mind and that he could learn the theory of the business quickly.

By the time the *Lady Rodney* reappeared in Quebec we had made some trial runs and, with the blessings of the shipyard, I was told all was like new below and we should have no further trouble.

'Hope I'll be of better service to you this time,' I told the captain of the transport before leaving.

And he laughed, 'Your troubles are over now, I'm sure. See you in Jamaica.'

He was an optimistic Irishman. I was optimistic, too.

We had left shortly after noon and were now going down the great St Lawrence in glorious sunshine, the green pasture land of the south shore shimmering in the heat and, in contrast, the Laurentian Mountains on the north bank seeming clear and cool. All was sounding well below and the crew appeared to be glad to be away again.

We passed through the Gulf in perfect weather this time and reached the Gut of Canso after dark.

It was a beautiful night as we went through the narrow, twisting strait before a strong, compressed tide, and we could see the dark form of the big ship behind us taking the bends with ease and grace. In the morning we were steaming south towards the West Indies in delightfully cool weather.

The situation for the moment was, for all practical purposes, perfect. But with an eye to travelling more slowly and not pushing our engines, I made the *Lady Rodney* zig-zag all day while we steered a straight course. We maintained our distance from her to a nicety.

The chief engineer had been reporting to me several times a day on the performance of the engines. It had been fairly encouraging but I had not regained my confidence altogether. He had not been too confident himself. But we had been doing our job for four days now – guarding a troop ship loaded with soldiers bound for an old West Indian garrison, supporting strategic moves of nations at war. We were fighting the Germans – in a way. Then the chief engineer came to my cabin!

He came after supper and I could see something was amiss.

'I'm afraid I'm running out of lube oil, sir,' he said in a distressing sort of way.

'Lube oil?' I queried, not expecting this one. 'Why, we took plenty before we left. There were four or five drums on deck and you must have had a hundred gallons in the tank.'

'I left with 350 gallons and that ought to have been enough but the engineers have been wasting it. Apart from that, I found the Mansel lubricators were feeding oil through at a very uneconomical rate. The yard opened them full out during the trials and they suggested leaving them pretty much that way. The day before yesterday I reduced them but the damage had been done. I've cut down on the supply for each watch, but I don't want to cut it down too much or we'll have more hot bearings.'

The chief's brows were raised, pressing lines across his forehead. He wiped his chest with a rag where the hair protruded above his shirt.

'We've got about four days to go,' I said. 'How much have you left?'

'About eighty gallons and that's not enough for four days.' He hesitated, then seemed to abandon any shilly-shallying. 'I'll have to run on soap and water part of the time and I can't go fast on that.'

'That won't work, will it, Chief?'

'It could at a pinch but I wouldn't guarantee what would happen. The bottom-ends keep none too cool as it is.'

Sitting upright on the settee I thought for a while.

'What sort of lube oil would our friend be using?'

'Oh! She's a turbine job, sir, and won't have the grade we would want, though she might carry some for her auxiliary machinery.'

37

'Well, let's hope she does. We'll try her anyway.' I wrote out a signal and sent it to the bridge.

Thank goodness she had oil, though not of the right viscosity, but by mixing it, it would be good enough. She could let us have a hundred odd gallons. So I arranged that we would pick it up in the morning.

The next day came in fine and clear, so I was anxious to obtain the oil before the weather possibly deteriorated. There was a light breeze and a moderate sea and that was good enough. I found we would have to go alongside twice because the *Lady Rodney* had no empty drums and we would have to provide them.

When I told the first lieutenant we were going alongside he said he would get the ropes up from below. 'I'll have two ready at either end. Will it be port side to, sir?'

'Well, in a way,' I answered. 'But we won't secure alongside. We couldn't do that.'

I explained why it would not work. 'It's not calm enough. It would have to be as flat as glass with no swell before you could tie up together and that's mighty rare out in the ocean.'

I elaborated a bit more because I wanted him to know. He accepted what I told him.

The trooper's captain headed his ship into the wind and slowed down. We came up on her quarter and edged in as we drew abreast until we were twenty feet off. The water in the narrow gap between us thrashed and spurted like the sea against rocks and the sound of the splitting waves was as deafening as Niagara. This was the cushion which must not be broken. Perhaps now the first lieutenant would appreciate the force which would be generated if the thousands of tons of steel came together.

A tackle hung down from the big ship's promenade deck and this was used to sway two of our empty drums across and into her open side-doors. Then we sheered off but in half an hour we were alongside again and this time it took much longer. Each forty-five-gallon drum had to be brought across singly and these were followed by a number of fifteen-gallon cans.

The navigator handled it well on the upper deck and had it been quiet I was sure I would have heard him demanding to know, of at least one man, whether he called himself a sailor. With the lubricating oil replenished we, the chief and I anyway, felt

38

better and we duly resumed our station once more, pushing along at fourteen and a half knots.

The weather became really hot that day, and so did the engines. The chief came along looking hotter than usual and, after expressing his appreciation again for the oil, glanced over the side and then down at the deck. When he raised his head, his brows were puckered.

'I'm playing the hose on three bearings, sir.'

'What's that, Chief?'

'Got the hose on three bearings.'

'Salt water!'

'Yes, sir. Not good, I know, but got to keep 'em cool.'

'Damn! Hot again. Three of them, eh?'

'Yes. Afraid so. Doing my best, sir.'

'Yes, of course.'

'But I can't guarantee anything.'

Why the hell did engineers always say that?

At about an hour before midnight, I was standing on the bridge talking to the officer-of-the-watch and enjoying the peace of the night. While things were not right below, they were still working. There was just enough coolness in the gentle breeze to make one feel comfortable and the stars shone brilliantly into the darkness. The ship rose and fell only a little and everything seemed silent except the bow wave as it broke and passed down the side. Then something occurred to make the night seem less beautiful. It was the figure of the chief coming round the corner of the asdic house. He was feeling his way carefully as though he were blind and as his outstretched hand touched the officer-of-the-watch, he said, 'Is the Captain up here, sir?'

'Yes, Chief. I'm here!' I said.

'Oh! Yes, sir. Sorry to bother you, sir, but I've got a bit of trouble below.'

'Oh!' I said. 'What is it? Bearings?'

'No, although those three are not right,' he replied. 'It's the water; I'm losing it.'

'Losing water! How do you mean, Chief?' This was a new one to me. I had never heard of losing water.

'Well, sir,' the Chief began. 'The evaporator has been going every day since we left and it's been making water all right but

39

where has it been going? I don't know. And now the stoker petty officer says there's only four inches in the feed water tank. He sounded it himself. The men have been using too much lately, doing all their dhobiing* I wish they'd learn to do it while they're in port instead of waiting until they get away to sea. I've had the evaporator connected straight through to the feed tank most of the day but she hasn't come up at all. In fact, she has four tons less in her now than she did at noon.'

'Well, search me, Chief! I'm sure I don't know.'

I did not see how I could have any knowledge as to where his water was going, but I must be sympathetic and not show impatience. 'Are you sure the evaporator is working properly?'

'Yes,' he replied, 'I'm making water all right, but it's not going into the tank. I've checked everything. She was priming but I stopped that. I've been underneath both boilers but can't find a thing.' Then he popped a nasty one. 'I'm afraid I'll have to shut down one boiler while I have another look.'

Shut down a boiler! I must have leaned back rather heavily against the after rail of the bridge, because the officer-of-the-watch turned round and the chief shifted his stance to another angle.

'I might find it quite quickly,' he said in a flat voice.

'That means,' I said slowly, 'that while you're carrying out a further investigation we must reduce speed.'

'I'm afraid so. I can give you ten and a half knots on one boiler.'

'Ten and a half! That's a loss of four knots.' I shuddered in spite of the warmth of the night. 'Do you think you would have any success in an hour, Chief?' I asked hopefully.

'Might have. I'll have another good look around and let you know if I find a leak in the pipes, and if I don't, I'll inform you by midnight.'

'Very well,' I said. 'Are you shutting down one now?'

'Yes, sir, number one boiler, as soon as I go down.'

'Thanks,' I said as the chief made off towards the bridge ladder.

I turned to Collins who had been listening to the conversation and was not very happy about it either if the grunt he gave was any guide. 'Where is the *Lady Rodney* now?'

* Naval term for laundry; from Hindu word for washerman.

'Well on the port quarter about two miles the last time I checked with the radar. I'll check again, sir.'

The ship was in that position. It was too dark to see a blacked-out vessel at such a distance. We could, of course, take up any station on her we chose but I had told her we would remain ahead during the night. However, if she did see us dropping back, she would think nothing of it.

We kept well out to starboard of her and soon realized by the radar that she was overtaking us. By midnight she was a couple of miles on the port bow.

I waited until nearly 0100 and, as the chief engineer had not reappeared, I called down the engine-room voicepipe to ask how things were going. The chief was a little more optimistic than before but wanted another half hour. At 0200 he was still no further ahead and came up to my cabin to tell me so. He said he would go on looking and examine things over again, but I could see the poor chap was getting worn out. It was very hot down below – the engine-room skylights had to be kept closed at night to prevent the light shining up.

Now I realized I had made a mistake. I had been too hopeful. When I found that we might not be able to re-establish sufficient speed to keep up with the troop ship, I should have sent a signal to her immediately by lamp, informing her of our condition. I knew this from the moment the speed had first been reduced, but the truth of the matter was I did not want to embarrass myself still further. I had hoped to have the second boiler in again in time to catch her up and be fairly close to her by daylight. She would not have known that we had had any trouble. But I had let the time slip by and now the ship would be over the horizon.

I wondered about submarines and how much danger the troops were in. Were there really any about? Who could be sure?

I was annoyed with myself. However, I sent a signal to the Commander-in-Chief at Halifax giving our position and explaining the situation and assumed that the *Lady Rodney* would be duly informed by radio. We could not communicate directly with her by radio – that was too risky. Any message we might have sent her, however short, would inevitably identify her and she would be obliged to acknowledge it. In doing so her position would be revealed if the enemy were to take directional bearings of her signals. But radio messages from a shore station were repeated several times on the assumption that the vessel would pick up one of the transmissions; and she would not be expected to acknowledge it. She could thus maintain radio silence. We, however, could transmit if we were alone and if it was important enough.

We proceeded on to Jamaica at little more than ten knots, drawing water out of number one boiler to feed number two – a most unusual procedure.

The men on deck worked hard, their bodies sweating but their heads protected from the scorching sun by their helmets – the gear which had proclaimed so clearly a month ago our ultimate destination. The men in the engine- and boiler-rooms perspired even more freely. But in the afternoons all hands rested except the duty watch. They made the most of the sun and the warmth and the blue, tranquil sea, out of which came the flying fish to interest and amuse, which was just as well since they would soon be shivering in bleak Icelandic waters.

The engines brought us to the Bahama Islands and on through the Windward Passage between Cuba and Haiti. It was evening when we watched the sun setting over Cuba. Then, from behind the hills, its rays of red and pink and mauve, gold, green and azure rose in fanlike shafts against the dark blue sky. There they stayed for several minutes. Slowly they diminished and were gone.

Next day we rounded the eastern end of Jamaica, where the beautiful Blue Mountains sloped down to the sea, and turned westwards towards Kingston.

We were met by the examination vessel off Port Royal in the heat of early afternoon and were given permission to enter. We steamed up the narrow channel towards the harbour mouth and between a small island at the entrance and a rock which forms a passage barely wide enough for a large ship to pass. It seemed incredible that one could pass so close to this rock, against which the translucent sea was washing, without its submerged jaggedness ripping a hole in the underside of the ship. A strong, hot wind, The Doctor, was blowing (it always does at this time of day, and as regularly dies down at four in the afternoon) but there was no tide. Presently we came opposite the wharves along Kingston's waterfront and, turning, came alongside a jetty immediately opposite the *Lady Rodney*. We came close to her stern as we entered the dock and I regret that some of her crew jeered as we passed – jeers, however, which our crew did not forebear to answer.

When I went to see the Naval-Officer-in-Charge, I learned that they had sent out an aircraft search party for us. Apparently the captain of the transport, when he came in, reported that we had disappeared and the authorities had reported this to Halifax who, becoming alarmed, had requested Kingston to look for us. Evidently my wireless message of several days before went astray. I inquired when I returned to Halifax where this signal had got to, but no one appeared to know, nor was anyone interested. It probably went the way of other mislaid and forgotten signals of those days.

Kingston, with its famous Port Royal of older days across the harbour, assumed a different aspect to that of my first visit a good many years before when I had come here while serving as a junior officer in a luxury liner which was starting out on a cruise to South America and Africa. The incident of which I was reminded occurred as a result of the officers' decision to purchase all their liquor for the four months' cruise in Jamaica where it was cheap.

Second Officer Davis, one of those grand characters who was always ready to organize things for the sake of group enjoyment or economy, duly ordered the consignment and its delivery was promised in ample time. But when the ship was made ready to sail, the liquor had not shown up.

We were all worried. 'Where is the stuff, Davis? You'd better nip ashore and 'phone the merchant again.'

'Can't, you idiot, the gangway's in.'

'Well, we can't afford to be without it.'

We held poor Davis responsible. We had paid him and he had paid the merchant.

A few minutes before sailing, when everyone but Davis had given up hope – he still had his binoculars trained on the dock gate – a donkey was suddenly seen ambling down the wharf drawing a cart. As it drew closer it was seen to contain many cases of liquor surmounted by a negro. All the passengers on the ship seemed to have congregated on the promenade decks and were leaning over the rails ready to watch anything there was to be seen.

As the cart came abreast of the ship the negro stopped his donkey and looked up the tall side and shouted for 'Mista Davis,

43

second officer'. The relieved Mr Davis, without embarrassment, wasted no time in having a cargo sling thrown over. The cases were hoisted inboard before the curious eyes of the passengers and the less curious but understanding eyes of the captain. We were saved!

If anything untoward had happened to the ship during the ensuing voyage it would have probably been because 'the officers had been drinking'.

But now I was here in different circumstances. And I wanted to do something quickly. I found a lieutenant-commander in the naval office – the Royal Navy controlled the port – whom I had known in Bermuda. He was called Trammy Fee – so named because he had been born in a tram. He took me to the engineers' office and the latter arranged to put the engine-room repairs in the hands of a contractor. The engineers, except one stalwart character, suffering from heat and thirst, took the opportunity of improving the shining hour with Fine Old Jamaica rum – or perhaps it was not such a fine old variety – and persuaded some of the seamen to join them, including the coxswain, who was the senior rating on board and, as master-at-arms, was responsible for the discipline of the ship. This left those not following the pursuits of the coxswain and his friends with a pretty free rein. Matters did not become seriously out of hand but they should have been very much better. One blithe hand on the lower deck discovered two senior ratings flaked out naked in their bunks after having been ashore in the early afternoon. He reported the phenomenon to his friends and went off to find a pot of paint. With this and his party he went aft to the P.O's flat and painted the middle of their bodies blue. It was unlikely that such dignity as the victims may have possessed would have been injured by rum, but it certainly was by the paint.

It seemed that either I had failed to implant a sound conception of the methods by which one maintains order in a ship in the officer upon whom this duty normally falls, or he himself would not or could not grasp it. He appeared to follow precisely the opposite course to the one I advised.

I had been given forty-eight hours to get the ship ready for sea again. We were to sail this time in advance of the *Lady Rodney* to make sure we kept ahead of her. What ignominy! The bottom ends were found to be in a bad condition; three had been taken down, and a main bearing was suspected. The fresh water made by the evaporator had not been leaking away, the evaporator was not functioning properly. This was put right and the bearings set up and I hoped the lubricators were conservatively adjusted. But we had no time even to run a dock trial, to turn the propeller for an hour or so while secured alongside. It was late in the afternoon now and I wanted to get out before dark. I asked the contractor what he thought about the job, and he said he did not think we would have to return, most of the ships he fixed did not, but that this engine-room certainly was in a mess.

With a supreme effort and considerable assistance from the junior officers, I managed to get the ship away from the jetty. The scene on deck as I did so, and the crescendo, was like the last street car leaving Sailortown on a Saturday night. I was not only uncertain whether the engines were mechanically sound enough to turn properly, I was not at all sure whether they would turn the propeller the right way when ordered. Would the legion below in the engine-room be like the Tuscan army before the Tiber bridge? Would

> *Those behind cry 'Forward!'*
> *And those before cry 'Back!'*

The coxswain, who was the man who normally steered the ship in and out of harbour, was not at the wheel. He had spent an hour at the wheel that afternoon in harbour, apparently under the impression that he was at sea. So I found a man who, I thought, would be a safer helmsman.

As we drew out into the harbour darkness descended. The Doctor had ceased to blow. We had come this far; we would go on, in spite of the tricky pilotage.

We got clear and out to sea, and although we stopped once or twice – to take a deep breath and try again – by midnight the engines were still turning over and we had worked up to ten knots. The next day all was comparatively peaceful, though there was a long line of defaulters on deck.

Our passage north was uneventful. We were relieved in the latitude of Bermuda and ordered into Halifax, since I had reported that further engine repairs were required.

4. Slow Convoy

It was the autumn of 1941. We did not stay long in Halifax but long enough to do two things, namely, to have fair repairs made to the engines and to dispose of several members of the ship's company. Not many, though, just enough to make sure that those who had been responsible for upsetting the equilibrium were no longer present; these were mainly sea lawyers among the senior hands. And a new chief engineer joined us. The first lieutenant changed for the fourth time.

It was rather a windy, early October day when we left, with the sun shining fitfully. There were several women, two or three together, some alone, standing on the jetty as the ship cast off her ropes, backed a bit and started to swing out into the stream. They seemed to take it in turns to wave. They looked bitterly forlorn. An officer on the fo'c'sle, a petty officer amidships, waved back. One or two others waved their caps to their wives.

There were few ratings, if their homes were far away, who could afford to bring their wives east. Fewer who had wives to bring. But one felt sorry for the solitary group as they grew smaller in the distance, and most of the crew must have been glad that their families did not have to go through all that.

We sailed to Sydney, Nova Scotia. There we spent the night, topped up with fuel and stood out of the harbour early the next morning, where we were to await the convoy we had been instructed to escort. Many ships were lying at anchor that morning in the fine land-locked harbour, ships of numerous different Allied and neutral nations, for this was the assembly port for the eastbound slow Atlantic convoys in these days. As we moved back and forth off the harbour mouth, I fell to examining the ships as they came out, one behind the other at intervals of three or four minutes, led by the Commodore's ship. It was always intensely interesting to me to gaze at ships. The more weatherbeaten and decrepit the ship, the more attractive she was to me; she had a story to tell and I could sometimes discern a part of it by just looking.

46

The newest might have been ten years old, the oldest perhaps forty or fifty. Some might even have been built of iron – the inch-thick plating of the 1880's before the days of steel. They were large and small, from about nine hundred tons to nine thousand. You could tell almost at a glance their nationality, or the country in which they were built, by the shape of their hulls and the construction of their upperworks. But as they came out they flew their ensigns, soon to be hauled down, so that you could not mistake their identity. They were all heavily laden, few that were not down to their Plimsoll marks and some with little freeboard, perhaps four feet between the water and the well deck.

The first ship moved slowly, marking time as it were, to allow the others to take their stations, so that the whole could form into three columns. Soon after noon the Commodore seemed to be satisfied that all were in their correct places for he ran up a flag hoist indicating that the speed of the convoy was to be seven knots. When every ship had signified that she understood his signal, the Commodore hauled his flags down and the engines of this heterogeneous collection of vessels simultaneously moved faster, although to the onlooker there was no perceptible change in speed.

For the protection of merchant shipping, the convoy system was not new. In the Middle Ages it was not uncommon for ships to sail in convoy. In those days there was little to distinguish an armed merchantman from a man-o'-war, so that a lone trader might be attacked and captured by a vessel which gave the appearance of pursuing a peaceful occupation. Thus the ships of Venice and those of the Hanseatic League had to be more or less armed and to sail in convoy so that they could afford each other some mutual protection. They may not, however, have been escorted. When England was at war with Spain, East Indiamen used to sail in convoys protected by British frigates and sloops. Towards the latter part of the eighteenth century, convoys of a hundred to a hundred and fifty ships used to sail from the West Indies to England. These were big convoys, but during the Napoleonic wars as many as five hundred ships would comprise a Baltic convoy.

Captains of slow cargo steamers in 1917 probably hated the idea of being herded together in vast bodies just as much as their sailing ancestors had in troubled times before. But convoys were

47

successful then. Thus, at the beginning of this war, the convoy system became operative at once.

It was by no means universal over all the oceans. The trade routes of the Allies were so like the threads of a cobweb that the transportation of freight would have been too seriously hindered had any attempt been made to assemble large groups of ships in more than a few of the world's ports and permit them to travel across more than one or two of the seven seas in convoy. But so far the risk of submarine attack on merchant shipping in oceans beyond the North Atlantic was not great, although it did exist. In these years the principal ocean convoys were the Trans-Atlantic and the United Kingdom – Gibraltar – West Africa convoys. But the Trans-Atlantic always remained the biggest and most important.

For nearly two days we steamed slowly across the Gulf and up the West Coast of Newfoundland. There were two corvettes, and between us it was our duty to escort this convoy out through the Belle Isle Straits and into the Atlantic where we would be reinforced by three more corvettes and a Town Class destroyer – one of those ancient ex-American four-funnel curiosities – whose captain would then take over the command of the escort force and the convoy. In the meantime I was in charge – not very happily, since I knew very little about the job.

What I did know was how to attack a submarine; but there would probably not be any around till we got further east. I also knew the coast and the Straits of Belle Isle; and I thought I knew where we would find the other escorts.

It was taking a chance to send me away so ill-instructed, but, being on passage to join a Trans-Atlantic Group, we were being used to take the ships around the coast and so release a coastal escort for other urgent work; and I was in charge by virtue of being senior to the captain of the other corvette, probably by a matter of only a few months. Responsibility always went by seniority. If the navy was escorting a convoy, the escort had to have overall jurisdiction; but the merchant ships took their orders from their Commodore.

In practice the Commodore formed his ships up and altered their disposition as he wished, took them along a predetermined track, deviated from the course if necessary after consultation with the senior officer of the escort, except in an emergency, and answered the complaints of the merchant captains. The senior officer of the escort could advise and direct the Commodore when he felt there was a need, and at all times was ready to help him.

Being almost devoid of practical knowledge I hoped no occasion would arise when I would have to display my ignorance before the Commodore.

No one could be blamed for this ignorance. Halifax did not, at that time, undertake to instruct a captain in how he should do any job assigned to him. There were no schools for this precise purpose any more than there were instructors to help him work up his ship on commissioning into a useful vehicle of war. Those ashore knew very little about convoying; those who did were mostly at sea doing it. It was the escort commander's job to acquaint his forces with the technique of shepherding the ships; but when he did not know, as in my case, he could only apply such common sense as he possessed.

We were favoured with good weather up the coast. It was crisp and clear with a hard, almost brittle horizon. The distant land occasionally separated itself from the water and became suspended in the sky. The mirage would sometimes lift the rear ships of the long columns eight miles behind us into the low white clouds, where they would float phantom-like. As we slowly advanced in ponderous fashion over the smooth, shining sea we held the weather and sighted The Labrador. Though it seemed very slow we at last entered the Straits of Belle Isle – and, as the Bluenose quartermaster wonderingly remarked, it was not 't'ick o' fog'.

Our ships were in, the leading ones anyway, and I held my breath in the clear night for fear the dense, dank shroud would descend, blotting out the course of the passage. Its width of ten to fifteen miles was ample in clear weather, but not if the fog came down. And the strong, treacherous tides could yaw and sway the tail of this crocodile of ships against the rugged Labrador rocks, or on to the sandy opposite shore of Newfoundland.

Before we were through the Straits, one ship fell out with engine trouble and our partner went to her assistance. She towed her into a little bay, Red Bay, where the bones of the British cruiser *Raleigh* had lain wedged in the rocks for nearly twenty years; it was the bleak haven she had once sought, probably to escape the fog or the icebergs. In this cove our casualty anchored and worked on her engine, which was to take two or three days to repair. She stayed there until the next convoy came by; then she came out and joined it.

Under the rugged precipices of snow-capped Belle Isle on a fine sunny morning, the Commodore slowed down to four knots to allow the convoy to change its formation from three columns, which stretched almost out of sight, to eleven columns with approximately five ships in each column. Ships flew a flag hoist indicating their number in the convoy while they laboriously took up their respective positions. In about two hours the convoy had assumed a broad front with the Commodore leading the centre column. Belle Isle was in the background now, tall, craggy, black and barren; the landfall Western Ocean mariners had sought for years, always with desire and fear in their hearts; the island which led the Newfoundlanders to the fishing grounds in summer and to their seals in winter.

Speed, seven and a half knots. Slow convoy! Course, east-north-east, the initial course of the great circle to the United Kingdom. Would all those who took their departure from Belle Isle that morning live to sight the green coast of Ireland?

That night the weather deteriorated, as was to be expected in October, and strong westerly winds with rough following seas prevailed for the next week. For two days we looked for our reinforcements.

'Nothing doing yet, sir, not a sign of anyone,' said the officer-of-the-watch, who acted as signal officer among other things. I had just had breakfast and was coming on to the bridge to see how things were, knowing really that there would be nothing new.

'We ought to see some of them today,' I said, hunching my shoulders as the strong breeze caught me in the back of the neck. 'But it's not very clear. Still, whatever part of the convoy they fetch up with they are sure to come up here in front. They wouldn't expect to find us anywhere else I imagine.'

I looked around. It was anything but a bright day, the usual grey dreariness with misty rain showers so that the visibility might be three miles now and a mile a few minutes later.

'Nothing new on the air, I suppose?' I asked.

Collins was standing with his chest against the rail, looking at where the backs of the dark waves beyond met the dun, fuzzy skyline. The canvas dodger was down and furled. No need for protection from ahead, the wind was astern or on the quarter according to the direction we happened to be heading while steaming back and forth across the wide face of the convoy.

'No,' he replied. 'We heard them again a little while ago altering course but by the strength of their signals only two of them are near us, the others seem to be quite a distance away.'

'Then we may meet only part of the group at first. I'd like to see them join up without delay. Two corvettes are no protection for fifty ships, although I've no information that submarines are this far west.'

The ship's stern heaved as a roller overtook her, rose bodily with a slow, lazy motion while the great westerly wave passed beneath her keel, its curling crest creaming just below the gunwale amidships. Then the stern settled and the bow lifted, swinging heavenwards as the great sloping back of the white-streaked comber swept forward in all its foaming majesty. As it went another came up behind it beyond the valley astern. In constant procession the waves rolled up and on – and so did we.

Sub-Lieutenant Collins was talking about the ship and the job. One of the things I came to appreciate very much was to be able to come on to the bridge at any time at sea and always have an officer to chat with. I do not suppose they appreciated it always; in fact, they must often have objected to my hanging around.

Presently I asked him how he found the ship now as regards harmony.

He was pretty well aware of the prevailing mood. Though the first lieutenant knew the important aspects, and had already encountered some of the men's problems, he had not been with us long. This young officer was used to the men and had the knack of bringing out the best in them.

'Everyone seems happy now, sir, and I really think you're through with crew trouble,' he answered.

I said I was pleased to hear it.

'It's never been like this before,' he announced emphatically.

'It looks a lot better to me,' I agreed, 'but then, I don't normally come in direct contact as you chaps do. The first lieutenant also seems well satisfied.'

51

Looking aft I saw the chief E.R.A. on deck. Not much of a day to come out for air, I thought. Engineers never seemed to be clothed properly. In spite of the drifting, misty showers Lloyd, the new chief, was taking a few paces back and forth on the small piece of clear deck, walking up hill one moment and down the next. I dropped down to the upper deck by way of the two steep ladders.

Walking aft beneath the boat deck and carley float skid I passed the two depth-charge throwers in the waist, keeping my eye on a curling beauty throwing itself forward along the side, and reached the wooden quarter-deck without getting wet.

''Morning, Chief,' I said.

He stopped. ''Morning, sir.'

'How're things today?'

The tall, thin chief sniffed. 'Could be better.' He spoke abruptly, then smiled.

'How much better?' I asked.

'A lot. Fact is, the main engine's not good at all. You hear it, sir?'

He looked at me intently to see if I was listening to the hammer blows that obviously hurt him.

'Yes, I do.' The knock, with every revolution of the shaft, was much louder here, above the engine-room, than in the forward part of the vessel.

'It really ain't fit to be taking us further away from the land. Wouldn't want to make too much speed.'

'How confident do you feel?'

Lloyd took off his cap and the wind caught his grey-flecked, brown hair. He put it on more securely, glanced at the sea astern as though scowling at the wind, and back at me.

'I'll get her across all right, sir. I'll get her across, though they ain't fit to go nowhere really.'

That was just about what he had told me before we started, though not so desperately perhaps. When he tried out the engines soon after joining the ship in Halifax, after the shore engineers had put the parts together again, the chief had said they were still in very poor shape. On the trip around to Sydney – which he described as the most extraordinary passage he had ever made – he said he wanted the bearings examined by the flotilla engineer when he arrived, to confirm his view. 'Never seen the likes of it in all

52

my twenty years at sea,' the chief had said. 'Halifax did their best but, if you ask me, sir, they were bloody glad to get rid of her. But I'll abide by what Sydney says. The engineer up there's good.'

Sydney's engineer said the bearings were not good at all but not so bad that he advised against sailing. I was told by the naval-officer-in-charge that if it became too dangerous I could put into St John's – which one would do in any case; there was no other place.

The old chief seemed almost glad to carry on. He appeared, although new on board, to be as anxious as the rest of us that the ship should not disgrace herself this time. I think his professional pride had something to do with his readiness to go. But it was he who was taking the biggest chance.

I liked this engineer very much already. I came to know Lloyd's funny little ways very well – and his qualities. With an up-and-down engine he was like a horse-and-buggy doctor. He knew what was wrong at the slightest faulty sound and how to correct it if it were adjustable. He knew his pumps and his boilers. He had oiled machinery and fired furnaces in Lakers and West Indiamen for a number of years. When it was more profitable to drive a taxi in Halifax than drive a ship's engines he had done so. He could improvise.

One day in Sydney, when he was chief of a mine-sweeping trawler, a shore engineer of the permanent force found him below fitting a bottom-end. He was scraping the metal of the bearing.

'What's that you're scraping it with?' asked the shore engineer incredulously, looking at the instrument.

'Knife,' answered the chief, eyeing it as though to see if there were anything the matter with it. 'Got it from the cook. Butcher knife, I guess. Someone swiped some tools the other day.'

He would never throw up his hands, like the proverbial plumber, and say he hadn't the tools.

I looked at him now. 'Come and tell me when any change takes place – for better or for worse. How do you find your men?'

'First rate, sir. I got a good gang. The E.R.As are okay. I haven't a worry in that respect.'

'That's good,' I answered and left him to resume his walk.

We were still working back and forth across the front of the

53

convoy, maintaining a distance of about two miles from it. The asdic was operating continuously; this device was the very heart of an anti-submarine vessel and without it she was almost completely impotent. From the time these vessels left harbour until they arrived at their destination, even though it took three weeks to get there, the asdic, like a clock, never ceased – unless it broke down, a habit which was common at the beginning.

How successful asdic was in the detection of submarines may be measured by the U-boat casualties. The device was the outcome of many years of research by several of the major powers, dating from the First World War. Its name was derived from a body known as the Allied Submarine Detection Investigating Committee. Each country represented undertook to explore certain aspects of the problem, but we may fairly safely assume that England and the United States chose to study the more vital potential components.

Asdic was something like an echo sounder. A sound wave was sent out horizontally – instead of vertically as from a sounder – from an oscillator housed in a steel streamlined box, called a dome, beneath the keel. The sound wave was confined to a narrow beam and could be trained in any direction. If it met an object in its path it would send back an echo which would be picked up by the oscillator and transmitted to the operator's headphones in the asdic house on the bridge. He had a little wheel, like a steering wheel, which he turned each time a sound wave went out through the water without a returning echo. Thus he swept a wide path ahead of the ship. If he heard an echo he shouted out and hung on to it. He could also switch off the sound wave and use the oscillator under the ship as a hydrophone. Through this the propeller noise of another ship would be heard quite a long way off.

Before I reached the 'midship house and my cabin, a hail came from the bridge.

'Ship ahead, sir!'

I leaped up.

Yes. It was a ship; about a mile off coming directly towards us out of the misty rain. What was she? She was turning, showing her broadside now, rolling in the trough of the sea and revealing her red under-paint down to her bilge. A corvette, and a lamp blinked from her bridge as she turned still more to assume an easterly course. She was one of our group, and she had a consort with her who now appeared through the grey haze following closely the movements of her leader.

'How many ships have you?' was her question.

'Forty-nine in eleven columns. *Castalia*, number sixty-one, Commodore.'

'We two became separated from the others. I will take over now. What is course and speed of convoy?'

'072 degrees five and a half knots.'

And with this brief exchange of signals a captain more senior than I took command. The proper group commander was still absent. The accidental separation of these two ships from the others was fortunate for us, though unfortunate for the group commander in the destroyer, and the other corvette. He was still endeavouring to find us.

It was difficult for him. With wireless silence at sea, except for very important messages and short range radio telephony between escorts, it was hard for him to meet us away out here in poor visibility. He knew our estimated position more or less all the time, but it did not necessarily follow that this was our actual position. Our speed had already dropped two knots since leaving Belle Isle because of heavy weather, and the convoy of nearly fifty ships had been yawing about in a high following sea for two days. We were probably quite far from the position we were supposed to have reached by this time. Sights for actual latitude and longitude had, of course, been out of the question for the destroyer as well as for us. He probably had not seen the sun or stars since leaving Newfoundland. Dead reckoning was the only thing. But that was not so accurate, as the old tramp skipper knew as he peered down at an old and dirty chart of the Western Ocean, water dripping from his sou-wester, with his stubby finger on a particularly dark spot. 'If that's a fly mark,' he said to the mate, 'we're all right. But if it's Sable Island, heaven help us!' In the Atlantic, dead reckoning was not an accurate form of navigation, but often it was the only kind.

More flashing had been going on between the senior officer and ourselves. The signalman came with a message.

'Close me for documents,' it read in the jolted pencilled scrawl of the leading-signalman.

As we came up to within about a ship's length astern of her,

55

hands were streaming a life-buoy over her stern. It drifted down on the end of a light line, disappearing between the waves, then rising, was tossed on a curling crest. The men on our fo'c'sle watched it, grapnels poised like harpoons, ready to throw. Up the life-buoy came almost abreast of the fo'c'sle head as the bow plunged down into the trough. From where I stood on the bridge it seemed as though our sharp stem below the bull ring would drive into the round stern of the ship we were almost boarding, as the bow swung up out of the chasm. With a rushing sound as the next wave broke, the stern rose clear, and above the roar I heard the first lieutenant shouting. The sea was thirty feet below the men now. One more dive and they hooked the buoy. The sea was churning at the flare of the bow, level with the fo'c'sle-deck, as they hauled it inboard.

From it was cut a canvas package, and the buoy returned to the sea. We sheered off and the other ship hauled in her buoy to attach to it another similar package to give to our old consort.

And so I received one of the war's most famous confidential books, as dry when it was unwrapped as when it was sewn up in its tarpaulin jacket.

'Wackies' it was called – Western Approaches Convoy Instructions, with the obvious short title, W.A.C.I. – a book from which I could obtain all the tactics employed by Atlantic escorts, the areas of command, signalling instructions; in fact everything I wanted to know. I was aware of the book's existence and had even looked through a copy in Halifax once when the captain of a British escort had shown it to me. Now I had it! I was all set. If a message came in talking glibly about 'Momp', I no longer had reason to question the signalman's reading ability. I knew it meant Mid-Ocean Meeting Point. Now I could fight anything! I had the gen!

As the days went by the weather gradually improved and by the time a week had elapsed since taking our departure from Belle Isle, it had become quite fine. The clouds sailed higher and were thinning, less like a vast canvas awning hanging from the sky. Their speed of travel overhead to the eastward had slowed down and every now and then the sun slid out – and with it my sextant. The breeze was still behind us but light enough to allow the blue smoke from the now black-rimmed funnel to rise straight up. The quietness on deck seemed peaceful, though the westerly swell still pitched the ship and sometimes gave her a corkscrew motion. But most of the men were becoming used to it and able to take a draw from a cigarette without feeling queasy.

The cook found he was becoming popular again. Lads would lean over the half-door of the galley and then work their way in and sniff around at the pots. They talked brightly. 'Anything good today, Cookie? What the hell's this stuff? Stoker's boots stewing?' The cook was a big fellow and could have thrown them out if he had wanted to, but he was good-humoured enough. He did not know, however, that some of his meat was used to torture a certain young, anaemic-looking seaman.

The rating in question had, at times, shared his nights and discomfort with the little signalman by the funnel. But he had worked himself down to his mess now and was often found sleeping in his hammock. He was eating, too, in this less boisterous weather. But his opposite number, who was opposite in every respect and a hungry character, found that he could have the young fellow's dinner as well as his own if he could find the opportunity of discussing the merits of the meal with him.

'Lovely piece of pork, that. Look at the hunk of fat attached to it. Colour matches the beans. But it's like rubber – fair bounces off your teeth. Eventually slides down your throat, though. Why don't you slosh the gravy . . .'

'I don't think I really want it,' the young chap would say. 'Had a sandwich half an hour ago.' And he would back towards the hatch and go up on deck for fresh air.

The coxswain and Lieutenant Black, the first lieutenant, seemed to get on very well. We had been lucky with the coxswain. He came aboard quietly in Jamaica and, in their revelry, the crew had hardly noticed him. He had been put ashore with appendix trouble in Kingston while coming round from the West Coast in a minesweeper. Duly repaired he joined us merely for passage to Halifax. He was quickly noticed by the officers, however, being a very clean-cut, sturdy young permanent service petty officer with a round, polished face as though he kept it rubbed down with sandstone. We earmarked him then and there, but being an R.C.N. rating the chances of keeping him looked slim. However, when the new first lieutenant came aboard I left it to him. Black was wise in the workings of the Halifax Manning Depot, and had him on the books as coxswain and master-at-arms in pretty short order.

This was one of our best breaks. And he had obviously come to regard the new first lieutenant with some esteem already, as we were all beginning to do. Black, who was almost as dark as his name, gave the impression of being a sort of Rock of Gibraltar, and his solid, rather staid exterior harboured unexpected succour within for the troops. Although he had had almost no experience of ships, this was not readily noticeable. He had the theory of the organizational structure of a warship, its domestic management and his responsibilities as executive officer clearly in his mind, and he applied them. But you would hardly notice him applying them. You would feel it later and then realize that he had been there all the time. And the men, cautious at first, were gradually beginning to find out that he considered their problems seriously. His cabin door was open to them from the day he came aboard.

Nothing out of the ordinary had occurred in these gradually improving days. The escorts, only four of us still, had been stationed around the convoy, we having spent most of our time on its starboard side where we had come to know the ships in the tenth and eleventh columns quite well. An old and large ship with exceptionally high masts, about 120 feet I thought they were, was leading the tenth column. She was deeply laden with iron ore and newsprint, so the documents I had been given at Sydney told me. Her maximum speed was eight knots, but there were slower ships in the convoy than the *Philip T. Dodge*.

Then there was the *Danae II*. She was the rear ship of the eleventh, the outside column, a little Scandinavian vessel, though possibly British owned now, loaded with lumber. She seemed small yet so self-possessed, against the great big dirty hull of the tanker beside her. This was the *W. C. Teagle*, carrying eight thousand tons of fuel oil to Belfast – a destination she never reached. I used often to watch her lumbering along with her decks partly awash when the weather was bad; great, wide, rust-streaked decks studded with brightly painted valves and small hatches. But she looked so steady and comfortable that she seemed very inviting. Often escorting convoys, we would look longingly at the slow, easy-moving stability of the large merchant ships and wish we could exchange places and get away from our ever-pitching, jolting, rolling corvette. But we all lived long enough to be thankful we were not obliged to transfer.

We had been having some trouble with the asdic gear lately. It had not been functioning perfectly, though through the ingenuity of the H.S.D., the senior rating who was responsible for its maintenance, it had not been out of order for anything more than short intervals. One of the reasons for the failure of this equipment was the lack of spare parts; it was essential to change certain constantly moving parts periodically. But on the evening of 14th October, when it took one of its turns, it did not seem to be just a matter of a spare part.

'The H.S.D. says he can't get it to work, sir,' Collins said, looking at the asdic rating as though in hope of perceiving in his expression some optimism.

'Do you know where the trouble is?' I asked the H.S.D.

'I haven't found it yet, sir, but I may.' He looked anxious. 'I've only been working on it for an hour, and although I've made all the routine tests I still have a good deal to check.'

'Well, keep at it. You'll probably find it before long. Take your time and do it carefully and systematically rather than rushing at it.'

'All right, sir.'

'What do you think?' I asked the signal officer.

'If something's broken he ought to find it before long, but these fellows don't know all there is to be known about the set.'

'No,' I agreed. 'But he has done fairly well so far.' I glanced up at my cabin scuttle. The deadlight had already been secured against the round glass to prevent the light escaping. 'It's too late now to report it to the senior officer. He should, strictly speaking, know all about it because he'll be counting on us to sweep out this side of the convoy. With no asdic we should really exchange places with the fellow who has the position astern of the convoy.'

'Yes, sir.'

It was about 2200 when I came back on to the bridge. I found the one thing there at least that was comforting – a mug of hot cocoa. I had reached the stage when nothing new in the way of troubles disturbed me very much. I lived in expectancy of them, like a man who has had rotten cards for weeks and would be surprised if he had anything else.

The engines were still the principal concern and they, as the chief said, 'were still turning, but none too good'. He did not like the sound of 'them bottom ends or the feel of the main bearings'.

Nor did I like the sound. The thump . . . thump . . . thump in the L.P. seemed to penetrate the whole ship. I could never get away from it. In my sleep it was a tomtom. When I awoke it was the blasted engine. To the engineers the sound of the knock must have been like hammer strokes on their tired nerves, and the hot bearings like the feel of a child's forehead in a fever. I lived with the uncomfortable feeling that one experiences when motoring with a weak tyre and expecting a blow-out at any moment.

'No luck on the asdic yet,' said the signal officer. Collins was on watch. 'But we've got the radar. That's still working.'

'Yes.'

'Might find a sub on the surface and steal up to him by radar and let him have it with the gun.' He punched at the woollen mitts which were plugging up the engine-room voicepipe to reduce the sound of the knock coming up from below. 'Or perhaps ram him,' he added, as an afterthought.

I took my nose out of my mug. 'Sounds good. It'll be a happy night for us if that ever happens – which it won't. You haven't noticed our being favoured with any luck to speak of yet, have you? I don't see much prospect of it changing. Why, the engines couldn't give us enough power to ram a submarine effectively, anyway. Or if they could they'd probably break down and stop in good time before the impact.'

I watched while Collins made another turn in the zig-zag, listening to the course he gave the quartermaster. She came round slowly.

When she had settled down on the outward leg, he said, 'I'll have a look in the asdic compartment below when I go off watch, sir, and see how the situation stands.'

'If you think the H.S.D. is too tired by that time to know what he's doing, turn him in until about six. He'll get at it again fresh then and maybe he'll think up something he's missed tonight. Let me know what you find.'

I took a look at the starboard side of the convoy through the glasses – they were not very good glasses for night-work but much better than the pair we used to have that made us squint. We had four pairs now, all new. We were zig-zagging at a mean distance of a mile and a half on the convoy's beam and I could just make out three of the ships, faint dark smudges in the horizon. Then I went below. I had intended turning in but when I came to do so I reconsidered it. I was gaining confidence in the sub-lieutenants, but not yet to a point where I could go to sleep with an easy mind.

The men too were uneasy, but not for the same reason. It was not the officers. They trusted them completely. It was the ship. The lack of harmony had disappeared, poor behaviour was gone. We seemed a happy and vigorous ship now, but . . . The ordinary seaman in the crows nest, the gunner's mate, the radio operator, could not fail to know our searching gear was not working all the time. They knew as well as the stoker in number two boiler-room that the engines were cranky and might fold up at any time. They knew we were short of speed – more or less always had been – and repairs had been a failure. Men had lost confidence in the ship, and in her ability to do her work.

Few admitted they were often frightened. They sometimes asked one another guarded questions, nonchalantly put but with vivid and desperate thoughts behind them. 'If the captain wanted to go fast he could really. He's only favouring the bloody engines because the chief wants him to, ain't he?' 'Ship rolls like hell but she can't turn over. They never turn over. Uh! T . . . turn over?' 'Corvette's too small to be torpedoed.' The answers were almost always reassuring, spoken lustily as a rule but sometimes flippantly. Confirmation was all that was asked for and this was given gladly by men in equal doubt. Only at night when two men were keeping watch together did they whisper their fears, admit that the precipitous plunge into the black depths between the billows scared them to death; only at night did they confess that they believed one day the ship would fail to climb the vertical face of the next huge oncoming wave.

A little before midnight I went out on deck again. The night was dark, which accentuated the luminous phosphorescence of the bow wave as it broke below me. The sound of its breaking was so familiar to my ears that it was not until I watched it that I heard its swish in rising and descending cadence as the ship gently rose and fell to the small sea. I heard the call of a gull but could not see it, and I heard the thump of the engines.

I returned to my cabin, took off my boots and lay down on my bunk. The navigator would be on watch in a few minutes.

61

5. The U-boats Attack

At 0100 I was awakened by the signal officer. He came to report that the asdic was still out of order. The H.S.D. had turned in but would be up first thing in the morning. After hours of frustrating effort he had finally put his head down.

When I awoke again it was to the sound, first dim and distant, of an insistent voice coming through the pipe above my pillow and becoming louder as I gained wakefulness. I sat up and said 'Yes' into the voicepipe.

'Explosion in the convoy, sir!' It was the first lieutenant.

With a word of reply I swung my legs over the bunk, slipped my feet into my boots and, grabbing my binoculars, was out in a moment and up the two ladders to the bridge.

'What do you see, Number One?' I was puffing as I arrived on the port side.

'There was quite a loud explosion in the convoy somewhere but we didn't see anything.'

'Where are we exactly now?' I peered into the darkness but could not see a thing except the straight foremast before the bridge.

'Five thousand yards on the beam of the convoy and steering in towards it at ten knots.' Black's words were clear and unhurried.

I looked out over the dark water and collected my thoughts. All we could do was search with the radar in the hope of picking up the submarine. Of course, we did not know it was a submarine. We had no definite information. But no alternative explanation suggested itself as the cause of the explosion. Ships did not just explode on their own, and after all it was submarines we were out here to catch. If a U-boat was on the surface and if we did encounter him, he would probably dive as soon as he saw us and we would lose him, except that we would know his approximate position and would be able to direct one of the other escorts into a likely position for picking him up with her asdic.

'Close up to action stations, Number One, and ring on 120 revs.' I said.

The first call to action stations! I, too, had wondered how I would react in the presence of the enemy.

My eyes were becoming accustomed to the darkness now and there was a brightness noticeable in the east. 'What time is it?' I asked the wheelhouse through the voicepipe.

'Five-fifteen,' came the quick reply. It was natural to say it this way. Most of us were running on an individual naval tradition which was only a matter of months old. It was just as well the young minds were not further confused with the dramatic and literary ship's bell system.

I began to hear noises all round me now – the men at the four-inch shouting their reports to the captain of the gun and the slam of the breach, the man at the bridge voicepipes receiving word that different parts of the ship were ready, lookouts relieving each other.

Down on deck the brawny captain of the port-after-thrower, who could lift a 300-pound depth-charge as a woman lifts a baby, checked the priming of his mortar and felt with his fingers the setting of the first charge.

The chill morning air made his crew shiver once or twice – or perhaps it was not chilliness alone. But on the other side of the engine-room casing where they were standing it was hot and noisy. Little jets of steam spat out as the great piston rods moved up and down in rotation, creating with their bottom ends a continuous sound of revolving machinery – and that perpetual heavy clank. An artificer watched the gauges, another had his hand in the engine, moving it with the crank shaft, feeling the hot bearings. A leading stoker moved into recesses with an oil can in one hand and a wad of waste in the other. A pump would sound easier as he emerged.

A steward and an able seaman sat together on a wooden batten they had fixed across the racks in the forward magazine. The muscular arms of the seaman were shaking as they rested on his knees. His knees shook. Everything shook and rattled from the vibration transmitted by the propeller through the hull. The wash of the sea sounded through the damp side-platings as the vessel forged ahead.

'Wish I was up top seeing what's going on,' the seaman remarked.

The steward looked at the iron ladder leading vertically up the hatch.

'You wouldn't see nothing. Too dark. Besides, you'd probably be squatting in the P.O.'s. heads keeping out of the wind – or relieving yourself. People worry up there at what they think they're going to see. You don't worry down here.'

'I don't know so much, sitting on a bunch of cordite.'

The steward was quick to answer.

'So what! We wouldn't be the only ones to get it up the back-side if the mag went off. We wouldn't be blown overboard, any-way, and have to swim. Nice and warm down here.'

The steward felt in his shirt pocket. It was automatic when he was doing nothing, waiting. But he had left his cigarettes and matches outside the magazine. He had heeded the warning and observed the rules. He needed a smoke too, in the worst way.

The first lieutenant on the bridge gave the navigator a short appraisal of the situation.

'Is the signal officer there?' I asked generally.

'Yes, sir,' came his voice.

'Caution the radar to watch very carefully and tell them that there's a U-boat about. Are there any signals in yet?'

'Nothing so far, sir.'

We worked the ship in and out, in to about 1500 yards from the convoy and out to 5000 yards. At 0540 an R/T signal from the senior officer was decoded which instructed us to cover the star-board quarter as well as the beam. That was all. No intelligence. As we ran in to the quarter the dawn was coming up and we were able to discern the corvette who had the rear position, well astern, apparently hunting or investigating something. She was a Free French ship.

As dawn advanced, a pale, tepid blush, we were able to make out the different ships in the convoy against the eastern sky. I was looking to see if I could tell which ship was missing, when I sud-denly perceived a small light blinking from what appeared to be the rear ship of the seventh column. The signalman beside me was already reaching for his lamp; he had seen it too. Soon he had the message. The leading signalman read it to me.

'Passed one boatload of men. Many in water on drifting wood. One capsized boat.'

Messages were now passing between escorts. The French corvette was detailed to pick up the survivors. The convoy steamed on slowly, turning more northward at 0730. The sky was overcast, but there was little wind or sea and the atmosphere was as clear as a bell.

Where was the U-boat now? How many times was I to ask myself this question in the years that followed!

We saw the two other escorts going first in this direction and then in that, like dogs with their noses to the ground trying to pick up a scent. But there was no point in our going hither and thither. We had nothing to sniff with. It was for this reason, after we had informed the senior officer that the asdic would not work, that we were sent back to relieve the French escort who was now over the horizon astern.

So we turned and proceeded back along the track the convoy had taken. I would like to have travelled faster, but the chief engineer had told me that we should on no account do more than twelve and a half knots.

In half an hour we sighted our ally and by 0900 we had reached the scene of the wreck. As the Frenchman left he told us that he believed he had picked up everyone. However, I thought we would make sure while we were here.

Wreckage was strewn over an area of about half a mile, floating in widely separated patches. It must have been a severe explosion which tore this ship apart. We passed slowly through it. Lumber there was, many small wooden hatch covers, gratings, doors, sides of deck houses ripped in jagged patterns, ladders and cargo – light stuff which would have floated up as the ship sank, which she probably did quickly. It was our first sight of the devastation of attack. It was not an attractive picture.

After an hour it seemed that we had examined practically all of it. The lifeboat from which the men had been taken was abandoned and we saw the one that had capsized. They were a forlorn sight, bobbing gently on the water. I looked down into the boat that had saved the crew. The brass linings of the rowlocks were bright where the oars had polished them. A grey blanket had been thrown on the bottom boards and a pair of mitts lay on the 'midship thwart where they had been dropped; their owner had not wanted his hands encumbered when boarding the rescue vessel.

All this mass of wreckage had to be scanned carefully, for one can so easily miss things unless the sea is glassy calm. In this weather – just a slight sea – a lifeboat could be overlooked and never seen at a distance of a quarter of a mile. Then we came upon a man alone in the water.

As we passed within twenty yards of him I saw that his final struggle to make himself more secure had brought about his end. He was wearing a large waistcoat type of life-belt but had evidently come across a life-buoy – a ring – and decided to get into it. He had ducked his head down into the water and at the same time passed one hand up through the buoy and grasped the opposite side to help pull himself up into the ring. But he had not fully taken into account the buoyancy of his life-belt. He had not been able to submerge it enough to get it under the ring and up through the centre. In his struggle and determination, his strength had obviously failed him and he had not even withdrawn his arm or taken his head from under the buoy.

On the buoy was painted *S.S. Silvercedar*.

The poor chap was clad only in a short shirt and I reckoned he had been in the water for five hours. The temperature of the water was around sixty degrees. With the movement of the buoy on the little waves the man's legs moved and made it appear as though he were feebly trying to swim.

We passed on, but in a few moments the depth charge officer, Sub-Lieutenant Neil, was at my side.

'He may not be drowned!' he exclaimed. 'He might be revived.'

'Surely not!' I answered, staring at him.

'It is possible. I'd like to try.'

This sub-lieutenant had just come out of Queen's University, where he had studied medicine for two years, and I had a high respect for his knowledge in these matters, a respect which he himself may have thought was excessive sometimes. But there were occasions when I had to catch hold of the slightest medical advice.

'Let him have a try, sir?' Black asked.

'Very well. Stand by in the starboard waist.'

I turned the ship round and came up to the buoy and stopped. I looked aft. They were hauling him in over the bulwark. Then

66

they cut off his life-belt and carried him forward and placed him on blankets under the break of the fo'c'sle.

We pushed on, covering what more we thought was still to be surveyed, and then at 1030 turned nor'-nor'-east, setting a course to overtake the convoy.

In order to catch the convoy, which was now nearly forty miles away, before dark, we could not, with the speed we were confined to, afford to zig-zag, which was really very important. Moreover, I knew that we should steer an indirect course to the convoy and then alter to intercept it when we were fairly close, as by steering a direct course – so the book of instructions I had recently received told me – a submarine might follow us with reasonable expectation of being led to a convoy. It was essential, however, that we should be there before dusk; U-boats did their work at night.

For three and a half hours our men applied artificial respiration to the sailor we had picked up, and although it had throughout most of this time looked very hopeful – his gums had been warm and his blood had not coagulated – he finally stiffened and it became obvious that further effort was useless. He was sewn up in canvas with a weight at his feet, and at 1410 the engines were stopped and his body consigned to the deep with appropriate prayers. He was rejoining the *Silvercedar* beneath him in fifteen hundred fathoms of water – a mile and a half below.

He had been a man between forty-five and fifty, a fireman I would have thought, who had probably been off watch sleeping in his underwear. He possessed no identification whatever.

It was my intention at this time to report the unhappy incident with a description of the man so that he could be accounted for. I decided against doing so later – I was only obliged really to report survivors – because I felt that the knowledge of his hours of mental anguish and physical suffering and then his near revival would be harder for his family to bear, if he had a family, than it would be for them to assume that he had probably been killed outright or drowned quickly.

Much as I tried to sleep that afternoon I could not. The picture of that forlorn body in the water simulating the power to swim disturbed me too much.

It troubled others. This was the first victim of enemy action we had seen – one of the tens of thousands of allied merchant seamen who were to be lost in the long, vicious conflict. We had seen the cold, lonely, miserable death of war. Probably some of us now were reminded that battles at sea, loss of life, maiming of men and ships, had been going on for two years – and we were only just in it.

By 1700 we had taken up a position astern of the convoy which was jogging along at the same slow speed but with a slightly bigger escort force by this time. We could see a fifth corvette and away ahead the low hull and four slender funnels of the escort commander's destroyer. This was most encouraging.

'The S.O. must have been out of St John's seven or eight days before he found us,' the first lieutenant observed, levelling his glasses up the ranks of heavy ships towards the dark grey needle-like object out beyond the leaders of the columns. She lay athwart the path of the advancing freighters, crossing and recrossing. Her thin little stacks, with a puff of blue smoke coming away from them every now and then, broke the straight, flush line of her slim hull.

'Ocean's big,' the navigator retorted. He looked rather like a pumpkin in his brown sheepskin coat.

'Obviously.' Black swung his binoculars on to the escort on the port beam.

'Not like Vancouver Harbour,' the navigator went on. He got no reply.

'You V.R's don't appreciate how big it is,' he tried again.

'No?'

'Can't use radio direction finding. Got to depend on seeing.'

But the first lieutenant did not rise to the bait.

An hour or so later, night stations were assumed which placed us away out ahead of the convoy and beyond the S.O. in his ancient little destroyer. The reason for our being here was because we could not detect anything beneath the surface, the asdic being still out of order and were of value only by our ability to detect objects on the surface by means of radar, something which all the escorts did not possess. Not that this equipment could have picked up so small an object as a surfaced submarine with any degree of certainty or at anything but a fairly short range, say a mile and a half. Our radar was a very worthy effort on the part of the National Research Council; but while it was very valuable, it was by no means the far-seeing and comparatively accurate counterpart which the Admiralty had developed and were installing in British corvettes.

Collins had told me that the H.S.D. was worried about not making the asdic work. 'He thinks it's a tube or a connection but he can't tell for certain. He'll go on working at it. You'd like the hydrophone watch continued, sir?'

I said I would.

The night was very dark and the sea had become rough with a fresh breeze from the nor'-west. The watch had just been changed round at 2100 when a burst of light was seen.

It went out as suddenly as it came but a dull glow took its place. It was four or five miles away and seemed to be somewhere to the rear of the convoy.

Then it died down like the fire of Stromboli.

Those coming on deck in response to the action alarm caught sight of it before it went out – perhaps smothered by the sea.

The night was black again.

The coder brought the R/T message up himself. It was from the senior officer.

'Ship torpedoed. Probably number 104.'

The coder, from the little office where he sat in jeans and a half-buttoned shirt deciphering messages as fast as they came from the radio room, had caught a glimpse of the reddish glow as he came out on deck. He had stood in the darkness below the bridge gripping the rail, his mouth half open. It had never occurred to him that battles would be fought in the black of night – he had only been in the navy ten weeks.

A few months ago he had been on the prairies, barely more than a boy. He had said to himself that if he were to go to war he would want to be in the thick of it – but he had not really wanted to go to war. Sense of duty perhaps, and a determination to face the danger he was secretly afraid of, persuaded him to join. Now he was close to it, in the midst of sea warfare at night.

He glanced at the dark shadows that peopled the bridge. They did not move much. He found he was shivering; and breathing fast, which was odd. He could put it down to the cold breeze in his face; but he knew so little of what was going on around him, only what had been in the signal he had brought up. He did not know in those dark moments that no one around him knew any more.

69

He suddenly turned and slid down the ladder, his sneakers making no sound on the rungs.

So the enemy was still with us. He had struck once more. Would this be a hit and run job like the early morning, or would it be an all-night affair by several U-boats, since it had begun early in the evening?

Number 104. Yes, I could place her now. Fourth ship in tenth column. The Norwegian *Erveken* carrying phosphate – if it really had been 104. She was one of the ships we had come to know during our sojourn on the convoy's starboard side.

Again I cursed my luck in being without asdic; we were as useless as a pack of fifty-one cards. But I was glad at least the radar was working. To make the most of it we went over to the starboard bow of the convoy, in case the submarine might have fired his torpedoes from that point and might now be trying to escape on the surface to the north-east, so that he would be ahead of the convoy and in a position to attack again as the ships advanced along the route.

Nothing detected, I turned back with the idea of covering the van from side to side. Our maximum of twelve knots was too much in the sea we now headed into to keep men forward at the four-inch gun, so they took cover under the break of the fo'c'sle and I eased down a bit. Even so, as the flared bow hit the waves, sheets of spray were flung up and thrummed against the lower bridge like hailstones.

After a while it appeared from radar reports and the courses we had made that the convoy was not proceeding in the same direction as it was when it had been attacked.

'What do you make of it?' I asked the navigator as we swept down to leeward quietly, the sea behind us now.

'Seems they're steering about east-sou'-east.' He was looking at the dimly lit compass card.

'I think so,' I agreed. 'Or due east. Must have turned.'

In my inexperience I had not expected this to take place without receiving due notification. Many months were to elapse before I could be reasonably certain that appropriate manœuvering signals would always be transmitted without delay, and that with equal certainty they would be received accurately.

Having convinced ourselves that the convoy had in fact made

an emergency turn of probably ninety degrees to starboard, we had then to endeavour to regain our relative position. In doing so we most unexpectedly encountered another corvette, *Gladiolus*. She said she was British! I had had no advice of her joining. She wanted to get her bearings. We gave her our idea of where the convoy was and what course it was making.

'Reinforcements!' someone said after the exchange of dim lamp signals at close quarters.

It was midnight by the time we were finally ahead of the ships once more. All was quiet, things seemed to have settled down again, the moon was coming up. All on board waited, as did the captains and crews of fifty or sixty other ships. Few knew anything of what had really happened, except that someone had probably been sunk. I wondered how many aboard this vast assembly of ships slept during the rest of the night. I did not, though I might just as well have done so, for there was no further attack.

Next day escort ships seemed to be appearing from everywhere and by the middle of the afternoon I counted fourteen.

'A proper blooming battle fleet,' Lloyd told the coxswain at the supper table in the P.O's mess. 'Reminds me of all the taxies that used to be on the rank back home when I was looking for a fare in a hurry.'

'That's no battle fleet,' the coxswain answered authoritatively. 'When we were over with the Home Fleet in '38 . . .'

'Enough of that, Johnny . . .'

Naval ships from other Atlantic convoys had been dispatched to augment our numbers because it was believed the Germans were gathering in force to attack us. They had been directed towards us by the submarine which had apparently held contact during the past two days. Americans were quite numerous. Some of their largest destroyers were present, and I watched one as she dropped astern and let go several depth charges. Six weeks had yet to elapse before Pearl Harbour.

As dusk closed in we shifted our position from astern, which was the only useful place we could be in daytime, doing a sort of sheep dog job, to our previous night station in the van. The weather was dull with an overcast sky and a light variable wind; the sea was quiet although the ship rose and fell to a moderate swell. In the tranquillity of the evening every creak and groan of

71

the vessel's beams and braces could be heard as she lifted, topped the swell and slid down the smooth declivity.

'We've got to make quite an alteration presently,' said the navigator, as he came on to the bridge from the asdic house where he had been looking over the signals pertaining to night movements. 'I see the convoy is to alter course by wheeling from 025° to 045° at 1920 and then to 090° at 1935.'

'So I notice,' I answered. 'Apparently the Commodore's idea is to endeavour to give the enemy the slip. By steering nor'-nor'-east all day and then altering to east well after dark he thinks that if the subs haven't closed in on us by then they may not notice our change of direction and go steaming on along our old course and lose touch. I hope it works, but our progress is so slow that I hardly think it will. However, it's going to be very dark before the moon rises. Perhaps we'll have a chance.'

'But the U-boats may not be with us now,' Neil, who was on watch, suggested. 'Surely one of all these ships would have seen something of them during the day.'

I said I had heard that they were hard to spot when they were following a convoy though if there were several in sight of us it would be reasonable to suppose that somebody would have seen one of them at least.

After looking carefully around I told Neil that he would have to take care in his zig-zag to avoid running foul of a nearby destroyer. 'We'll cross that Yankee's path every now and then I expect.'

'I'd noticed that, sir.' He was looking at an almost cruiser-sized, dark grey silhouette some distance from us. 'I'll watch out.'

As we had not been molested since the evening before and had passed through the greater part of the previous night without further incident, I thought there was some likelihood that our attacker might have then left the convoy altogether. But the reinforcing which had been done made it appear as though the Admiralty did not think so, and they probably had some intelligence to lead them to believe this.

I went down to the wardroom for supper, and soon after 1900 was up again to make sure that our courses were adjusted in good time so that we would remain ahead of the convoy as it wheeled to starboard. It would take about an hour for all the ships to alter their direction sixty-five degrees, and it would be a laborious process. The leading ships of columns had to turn first, and then successive ships would come round as they reached the point where their leader had turned. The Commodore's ship leading the sixth column would reduce speed one knot while those on the inside of the turn would reduce two knots to mark time as the outside column caught up. The manœuvre could not be completed quickly in pitch darkness.

In spite of the thump the engines made at every revolution I could hear now and then the dog-watch voices. Engine-room men, buttoned up, were taking the air on deck. But not smoking. All lights were doused. I thought of the Commodore. What a hell of a job!

The Commodore was probably a man of more than sixty. A retired admiral, as most of these Atlantic chaps were, used to the respect and comforts of the navy, and accustomed to manœuvering squadrons of large, sleek fighting ships, not a bunch of ugly, coal-burning, unevenly-matched tramps. He was not used either to the lack of response he often received to his orders, not because the merchantmen did not want to respond but because they so often could not. There were those who could not keep steam up when they were cleaning their furnaces – we had seen them dropping back, then struggling to catch up again. Others who lost the power to steer the required course in heavy weather, and could not keep in their columns. They were built to carry freight, as much as could be loaded into them, hence the bulky shape of their hulls, which offered so much resistance to the water that all the pushing in the world would not make them travel fast.

An unenviable job, the Commodore's, worrying and personally dangerous. He and the senior officer would have worked out this alteration of course during the day.

Sharp at 1920 we saw the first faint array of red and green lights at the invisible yard arm of the Commodore's ship a mile away. They remained for about a minute and were then extinguished. This was the executive signal to begin the turn.

The man in the crow's nest sang out, 'Object to port! Fifty degrees on the port bow.'

We saw a black, naked shape converging. Our American partner getting an edge on the turn.

73

At 2000 the last dog-watchmen of probably sixty ships, both merchantmen and men-o'-war, were being relieved by the hands of the first watch who would take over until midnight. No ship struck eight bells. It was prohibited; sound carried over the water too easily.

At 2005 the noise of an explosion met the ears of those on deck. Then a rocket – the thin, pink trail of a rocket – was seen shooting into the sky somewhere towards the starboard side of the convoy. A moment later another rocket.

High up, the first, then the second, burst, flinging their white stars out and down like an umbrella. Distress!

To some the sight and sound seemed distant, to others close at hand. The stars, fading, went out almost together.

So the dog-watchmen would not go below, but to action stations. And the turn had at least fifteen minutes to go.

What a time to be attacked! Yet the ships would methodically follow their almost invisible leaders and carry out the original plan – all except one.

We, probably like all the other escorts, went to action stations at once, and shortly afterwards fired a spread of star shells in a sector ahead of the convoy. As the shells burst high above the water 5000 yards away, the great yellow flares lit the ocean beneath, descended slowly and, with a great suddenness, went out as they fell into the sea. Eyes behind binoculars had anxiously scanned the lighted water; in less than a minute darkness even blacker than before enveloped us. Presently star shells appeared elsewhere around the convoy so that it seemed as though, had the the enemy been reasonably near when he fired his torpedoes and if he were still on the surface, he must surely be seen.

But no word came from any of the others; and we, after an hour and a half of searching to the limits of our station at a speed as fast as our miserable engines would push us, settled down once more to a small zig-zag at about eight knots, thus preserving what little energy seemed left in the ship. This was an unsafe speed for an escort. Twelve knots if the weather permitted was as slow as one should go, with a broad and irregular zig-zag, never remaining on one course for longer than four minutes. But now it did not seem prudent to follow this plan.

Action stations had been secured – broken off – and the men

had drifted below. The cook, with several willing helpers, had brewed some coffee as well as the usual cocoa.

'Wonder who got it?' the torpedoman in the galley questioned, stirring his favourite beverage rhythmically and looking at the others.

'What's the use of wondering if the tel don't know?' the cook argued, glancing at the telegraphist as though he ought to know anyway.

'If I got the signal,' the telegraphist answered, 'I wouldn't know what it meant. Comes through in Greek, you know. Coder fixes it up in English, nice and neat for the captain to see.'

There was one who did not exactly drift below. He arrived in the communications mess in a great hurry.

'What's up?' someone said.

The others looked up, because Signalman Burley was not one who showed anxiety, even if he felt it. This time it was very apparent.

'Gee! I'm for it!' he stuttered.

'For what?' the leading hand asked.

'Come on, out with it,' demanded Fair, the small, wiry signalman. 'You ain't bleeding as far as I can see.'

He collapsed on a settee. The others, seven of them, gathered round, insisting on knowing what it was all about.

'Kicked the coxswain in the pants, did you?' one of the coders speculated.

The victim leaned back, knees apart, hands thrust in his heavy duffle-coat pockets, though it was warm in the mess. 'Worse than that. It was this way. I was hanging round on the bridge waiting for Swish to relieve me when . . . I thought I saw you, Mac,' he said, looking pathetically at the leading signalman.

'You seeing ghosts? I been down here ten minutes.'

'All right. I know that now. I didn't then. But you're the only rating that's got a sheepskin coat like the officers.'

'Well, what about it?' Fair asked. 'Leading sig's entitled to one, ain't he?'

The unhappy fellow sat up, his face red now instead of white.

'Shut your blasted trap, will you!' He took a deep breath and looked at the leading signalman again as though wishing he were somewhere else. 'I thought it was you up there standing with the

75

jimmy, looking over the dodger. Both had sheepskins on with hoods up and they naturally had their backs to me.' He swallowed. 'I came up behind you, wound up and slapped you on the back – or on what I thought was your back – and said, "Secure, Chum! What the hell are you waiting for?" And then he turned round. And I saw it was the old man!' Someone whistled. 'I don't know whether I said "sorry" or not. I didn't stop to explain. I was so flabbergasted. I just slid down the ladder and darn near bowled Swish over as he was coming up.'

He fell back again. 'And that's it!'

'Did he say anything?' the leading hand asked, looking serious. 'The old man?'

'No.'

'Did he see who it was?'

'Don't know. I hope not. I shot off quick.'

There was silence. Then Fair broke it with a harsh command. 'Lash him to the mast!'

Above, quietness prevailed for two hours. I decided to lie down in the wheelhouse. I was very tired. And I could still feel the swat I had received from the big signalman's sturdy hand.

I closed my eyes and drifted off. As I did so I seemed to hear a distant shout, then another and another coming closer to me all the time until it was almost on the top of my head. At last I sprang up. I parted the blackout curtains at the door and went out and up the ladder.

As I felt my way to the fore part of the bridge I heard the officer-of-the-watch say, 'Convoy's attacked again, sir. You can see it if you look to the port quarter, about Red one-seven-oh.'

I looked aft along the edge of the funnel, over the lifeboat to where I knew the sky was meeting the water. I saw a light. Just a light. No particular kind of light. But it should not have been there. It was some distance away. Then it went out.

'Was that all you saw?' I asked.

'No, sir,' replied Sub-Lieutenant Neil. 'There was a big flash from that direction a moment ago then that light. I didn't hear anything so it couldn't have been gun fire.'

'How's your head now?' I asked.

'Oh-five-oh at the moment, sir.'

'What's the time?'

'Quarter to twelve.'

'Then I hardly slept at all.'

'You weren't down fifteen minutes,' said Neil.

'Ring action stations,' I told him.

As he did so I heard a heavy rumble. Another ship!

'When you take your thumb off that button,' I said to the sub-lieutenant, 'tell the W/T office that another attack has been made and to waste no time in decoding and reporting signals.'

'Aye, aye, sir.'

I heard him talking to the telegraphist through the voicepipe.

We increased speed a little to cover more ground and I told the radar operator through the pipe at my elbow to keep a particularly sharp eye on his scan. There was the usual racket of men closing up to action stations, the first lieutenant was shouting through the megaphone beside me at the four-inch gun's crew, the signalmen were jabbering and the navigator was questioning the officer-of-the-watch on the immediate events.

I turned to the first lieutenant when he had stopped shouting orders. 'Two of them have been torpedoed, apparently. We're still out in front and we'll be going to starboard in a minute or so. I wish somebody would fetch up with a U-boat instead of allowing them to have it all their own way.'

'It wouldn't be much use our doing so,' was the response.

No, it wouldn't. We were pretty much of a white elephant. Damn our limitations!

We plodded on while I tried to persuade myself that we might at least use the gun to advantage. But this prospect diminished after the first lieutenant had put up some star shells and revealed nothing.

6. Flotsam

In fifteen minutes a message was received confirming our belief
that two ships had been torpedoed. We were not told who, though
it said one had been in the centre of the convoy and the other in one
of the starboard columns.

Shortly after this, one of the signalmen came hurrying to the
bridge again.

'Signal from the S.O., sir.'

The small white circle of illumination from his masked flashlight shone on his signal board. 'Says, "Proceed to rear of convoy
and pick up survivors"'.

'All right, thanks,' I acknowledged. 'Port fifteen.'

The ship was swinging round. No sign of the Yankee.

'Pilot,' I shouted. 'You there?'

'Aye, aye, sir,' came his voice from the other side of the bridge.
He came over.

'We're going to the rear. We'll go down the port side. We're
ahead of the fourth column now, I think. Mark the chart, will you?
And make a careful note of the courses after we get clear.'

We steered about north-east to clear the columns. We did not
encounter the Yankee, whose path I expected to cross. But
this did not surprise me because it was pretty black and she
might have been anywhere. I had not been told by the senior
officer the disposition of all these reinforcing ships – there were
too many of them for him to describe the whole protecting force
probably.

When I felt we were beyond the first column we turned and
faced the pathway we had travelled over.

'Keep a good look-out for ships and escorts,' I shouted, warning
those responsible for watching. 'We might be taken for the
enemy.'

I trusted we were outside the convoy – not running down into
the midst of it. The radar seemed to indicate we were all right.
But with the conglomeration of marks on the scan the operator

found it muddling. The arc of the radar beam, or its possible degree of inaccuracy, was no better than forty degrees.

'Ship ahead to starboard!' came a strident shout.

'Lights!'

A black form slid out of the darkness. Two coloured lights, green over red, flashed high above her, hung as though in unattached suspension for an instant, and were gone.

'Challenge!'

The signalman repeated my command as he pressed the key of his lamp. No response! Then the black ship swung by. It was an American destroyer.

We passed on.

'Must be some fancy fighting lights,' the leading signalman was saying.

Yes. We could only guess what they meant. We had never heard of them before. He would probably not have known our recognition signal either since he was a neutral. Anyway, we had identified one another for ships, not U-boats.

Another cry. 'Red four-oh – an object!' this time from the masthead.

The bridge lookouts confirmed it as the dim outline of a small vessel appeared to port.

Now suspicion struck sharply.

'Hard aport! Guns!'

As our ship swung round the first lieutenant gave the captain of the four-inch the bearing and the layer kept the gun trained on the vessel. It appeared to be going with the convoy. The distance closed rapidly as we turned about. Then I saw a funnel . . . a hull . . . growing longer.

'Corvette!' the first lieutenant shouted.

Several others echoed the report as the craft appeared sharply before our eyes. No fancy lights this time! Not a glimmer! She was so dark and silent that she might have been gliding alone crewless. But I knew many eyes would have seen and recognized us.

We swung round and resumed our course, and I had the feeling of satisfaction that the look-out men had learned their job.

When I thought that we had cleared the port quarter, we turned and felt our way across the rear with the object of reaching the centre column and setting a reciprocal course from there so that we

79

might pass over the spot where at least one ship might have been when hit.

Suddenly, like lightning, a colossal flash leapt from the convoy. In a moment it resolved itself into a tremendous flame which shot upwards from the water, accompanied by a roar like the passing of an express train. The great column of fire, whose diameter might have been equal to the length of the ship from whose tanks it sprang, seemed almost to reach the cloud base. The whole convoy was lit up by its brilliance: I caught a murmur around me, as of the letting out of breath from many throats.

Then, with equal suddeness, the light went out as though consumed by some fire-eating monster, leaving utter blackness.

But as our eyes became once more accustomed to the darkness, we saw a great black cloud of smoke, like a dense thunderhead, rolling across the sky to leeward – all that was left of a cargo which had until now been destined for the machinery of war on land or in the air. Nor was there probably anything left of the tanker who had stood on across the ocean despite the enemy, knowing that if she were hit this would be the way she would end her life.

There remained in my mind's eye a picture of the greater part of the convoy as it had presented itself for the brief moment of the illumination; some ships in clear profile, some in silhouette, poised as though, while in the act of forging their way through the water, they had paused to watch the destruction of a friend.

No one aboard could have survived.

I turned away to the westward with a sickening feeling which must have been shared by all who witnessed the attack, except the U-boat commander who fired the torpedoes.

It was soon evident that we were not the only ship looking for survivors; three or four others were doing so. Lights were seen now and then which presumably came from lifeboats but it was difficult to tell how far away they were. On a dark night, if you did not know what the light was attached to, you could not easily determine whether it was near the horizon or close at hand, and its brightness might not give any indication. We made for two of these but lost them and then steered for a flare which burned only for a short while and which we knew could only be a distress signal. After continuing in its direction for a while, a small light became visible, towards which we altered course, but it did not stay on long enough for us to gauge how near we were to it. Men were posted on deck with grapnels and boat ropes and all were staring into the darkness. The scramble net in the waist had been dropped over the side – the net which the leading seaman from Newfoundland had been teased for making by some of the crew on leaving port not two weeks before. None who laughed had been across the Atlantic.

Then the light came on again and by its bobbing movement it was obvious that it was quite close. But it went out. The ship moved along slowly. Ten minutes elapsed.

'Boat abeam, sir!' came a voice from below. It was the first lieutenant.

'Don't lose sight of it!' I shouted. I could not see it myself. None of us could on the bridge.

Black and his men could make out something from the low level of the upper deck as it moved up the undulating swell against the faintly paler background of the sky.

The engines were going astern to take the way off the ship. They clanked more than ever.

'Come ahead now, sir!' the first lieutenant called as he watched the luminous foam swirling from the propeller up along the ship's side.

I manœuvred according to directions until I gathered we were in a position to drift down on to the object.

Below they saw a square, box-shaped craft. Rocking gently, it bumped against the side.

In about five minutes the first lieutenant shouted up that he had recovered the occupants and all was clear. We pushed off to continue the search. Further explosions had been taking place in the direction of the convoy, and following one distant boom a fire had been visible.

The moon came up before 0330. It could not penetrate the clouds, but it lessened the darkness greatly. Wreckage became visible; odd bits and lumps and bobbing spars, scattered across the moving water. Then congested wreckage as if regurgitated from a gastric eruption below. We went through it slowly, examining as much of it as the moonlight would allow. We passed boats and rafts but all were empty, though small, almost tiny lights attached to some of them still flickered intermittently. Several other escorts

F

were in the neighbourhood and I took it that they had attended to much of the rescue work.

After some time the first lieutenant came to the bridge.

'Who was on the raft?' I asked.

'Two Norwegians,' he replied, taking off his cap and rubbing his forehead. 'The chief officer and chief engineer of a tanker called the *Barfonn*. The chief officer is in the wardroom but we took the chief engineer along to the seamen's mess deck on Neil's advice. He seems to have a broken leg. Neil is along with him now; said he shouldn't be taken down a ladder and thought a flat bench in the upper mess deck would be the best thing.'

We all had great confidence in our half-fledged doctor. 'Is he going to set the leg?' I inquired hopefully.

'I don't think he's going to go that far, sir. It's the upper part of the leg or the thigh. He's lashing him down tight and giving him drugs.'

'Did the chief officer say there were any more of their men near them?'

'No.' The first lieutenant looked over the water where it was brightest. He had talked to his first victim of war, hauled two of them to comparative safety. 'He said the others got away earlier and he didn't think anyone else was around. The ship was torpedoed twice, apparently.'

'I'd like to see the chap as soon as I get a chance.'

Black was silent. His heavy sheepskin with the hood hanging down from the collar made him look round-shouldered in the faint shadows of the moonlight. I knew that he was deep in thought. We had all seen much lately; and he seemed to be weary.

'What are you going to do now, sir? Rejoin the convoy soon?'

I was leaning with my elbows on the rail, looking ahead. 'No. We'll never catch up with them now. We'll search until daylight and then have a good look round in the forenoon and as soon as we can we'll make for Iceland. I've already sent a signal to the senior officer requesting his permission to go there because of fuel shortage and engine trouble and he has concurred.'

Accordingly we carried on the search, not moving far from the area we had originally come into, because I at least knew there had been casualties here, whereas I could not depend on striking the exact location of an earlier casualty if we went further back while it was still dark.

Down below the chief engineer threw his cap on the bench and moved under the ventilator. Professional disgust was marked on his lined face as he gazed at the big rods moving up and down. He felt he needed the cool night air which was being sucked down the shaft. The E.R.A.-of-the-watch came round from the condenser and stood beside him.

'Running better than she sounds.' He had to put his mouth close to the chief's ear.

'Umph!'

'Well oiled.'

Lloyd did not seem to hear at first. Then his scowl deepened. His lips moved as if he were gearing up to say something.

'Not too much, now. Give 'em just enough. Don't pour it away.'

'I won't.'

'Bloody damn thing!'

'Yes,' agreed the E.R.A. and took a step or two and bent over the guard-rail. His hand went into the engine. After a minute he straightened up.

'Not too bad,' he said in the customary raised voice.

'Bad, I say.' Lloyd's tall frame was more stooped. He shot a penetrating glance at the E.R.A. 'Haven't been over ninety-five revs, have you?'

'No.'

'Mind you don't. Ninety-five's our half-speed and full-speed, both. Nothing more. I told the old man ninety-five was all he would get – I told him ninety-five.'

'That's plenty. What's he up to now?' The E.R.A. nodded his head upwards.

'Looking around. Making miles.' He glared over the canvas apron into the crank pit. 'Don't know where this is going to end. It'll stretch me out in a six-by-two if we ever get there.' He sniffed and grasped the front of his shirt and rubbed his sweating chest.

Then he went from bearing to bearing feeling with the hand of a doctor. Finally he picked up his cap but did not put it on. Instead he held the top of his head with his free hand and drew in with his nose. As he moved towards the ladder he beckoned the E.R.A.

83

'Watch 'em. Send word if there's any change.'

When he reached the deck daylight was beginning.

It was a typical Western Ocean dawn as we steered off to the westward; slow to come, hardly perceptible. Then you noticed things you had not seen all night. The mast was grey, no longer a black pole. The rust on the windlass showed reddish-brown. The leaden sea wandered, meandering out to the grey sky, moving only slightly. The clean, white seagulls could be seen now instead of only heard, moving their heads as they glided by, watching the ship for what might not be wanted by the humans who lived in her. Further over they might have alighted unknowingly on oil-covered waters never to rise again, like the ships beneath.

No other escorts were left now. They had all gone on before dawn, probably in haste to rejoin the convoy. I figured that if we steamed back along the track the convoy had taken since turning on to its new course the night before, we would see anything there was to be seen. We had not far to go to find ample evidence of destruction.

The sea being almost calm with only a slight to moderate swell, wreckage could be seen at a considerable distance, if there was much of it. There was. We saw it ahead strewn across our path. First we entered a large patch of oil, fuel oil, covering an area of about half a mile. The heavy brown liquid flattened the dancing water breaking away from the stem of the ship and turned the crystal bow waves into slimy unbroken mounds. Then we came to a sea of flotsam.

The signal officer leaned over the wing of the bridge. 'This is more than came out of one ship!' he exclaimed. 'Must be half a dozen.'

Hundreds of bales of cotton, most of them split open, floating high on the water; lumber, flat boards and square logs of many different lengths; case goods, much of it food, some broken with their contents washed out, cans drifting away. There was that commodity which became so scarce, paper, fresh from the pulp mills of Canada, and barrels. Amongst it all was a varied assortment of lifesaving appliances, boats and rafts of different designs, circular life-buoys, cork belts here and there. And there were, of course, wooden parts belonging to the upperworks of ships.

Collins spoke over his shoulder. 'It'd be nice to have some of that gear, sir. A lifeboat. Those are better than ours. Could I take some hands and try to pick one up? Swing it up on one of the mine-sweeping derricks.'

Like a true Canadian Scotsman he hated waste. But he was also a master purloiner for the benefit of the ship, a distinct asset in one who was to become a first lieutenant. I had no doubt he could do what he was suggesting, but we were not here for that. Nor did I like stopping.

I looked at my list of ships. '*Bold Venture*, Panamanian, iron and cotton.' Mostly a deadweight cargo, she would have gone down within one or two minutes of being torpedoed. '*Ila*, Norwegian, steel and general cargo.' She would sink rapidly. '*W.C. Teagle*, fuel oil.' Beside her we had travelled two thousand miles. Now the remnants of her cargo streaked our sides.

We worked through all this mass of debris, this way and that, but could find no life, which made me hope that all who escaped had been picked up during the night. All hands who did not have to be below were on deck voluntarily searching.

We pushed on. Within an hour more wreckage was encountered; not much but enough to indicate that a ship had foundered. Those who had gone below when nothing was discernible were called up by their messmates. They would not miss the opportunity of looking however tired they were.

Near the motley bits of what had once been parts of a ship were two boats, one a motor lifeboat, the other a large whaler which it appeared, by the rope from its bow, had been made fast at one time to the motor boat. Coming close alongside we saw that the occupants had been rescued.

During the war I saw many empty lifeboats, and never did they fail to give me an unhappy feeling, a conviction that the shadow of disaster floated close alongside or was hidden beneath, that its mysterious passengers had known fear, tragedy. The boats we saw now revealed something of these things, though they were also mute evidence of rescue. The whaler's sail lay rumpled across the thwarts, yet the mast had never been stepped. In the sternsheets was an open watertight container painted white with a red cross. Someone in the boat had been hurt, had needed covering and care. Over the gunwale of the motor boat, a fine, solid craft, lay a

85

boathook. Attached to the galvanized hook was a garment, perhaps a shirt, I could not see exactly.

We went on to the westward. Soon a wisp of smoke was sighted ahead. From beneath the dull, hard horizon came a mast, then a ship. It turned out to be a lone corvette. Her lamp winked.

'Have you seen Convoy S.C. 48?'

'Yes. To the eastward.'

'Where is it now?'

'Wait.' In a few moments we had worked out on the chart where we thought it was. We flashed our estimation of its position.

He said he and another ship somewhere out of sight astern of him had orders to reinforce the convoy and remain with it to England.

'Has it been beaten up?' came the question.

'Yes. You will see the wreckage on your way.'

I wished him luck as he passed; a strong, upright, self-possessed little vessel; the rust streaks marring her white and pale blue camouflaged hull made her look all the more hardy. As she went by, sliding easily over the small swell I did not know that her captain, to whom I had been speaking by light, had once been a friend of mine, a school chum. We had neither seen nor heard of one another for twenty-five years – since the day he had left the classroom in England and had gone off to sea. I had soon followed him, but our tracks had never crossed until now, on this bleak, sad morning in mid-Atlantic. A year later I berthed alongside this ship in Londonderry. Then I saw and recognized him, in spite of his beard, though only after he had told me his name. We celebrated.

After a while we met the corvette to which he had referred and gave him directions also. Then he informed me that he had taken off the crew of the torpedoed ship *Rym* an hour before and said that the captain had reported her a total loss but still afloat.

At 1000 we came up to the little Norwegian *Rym*, now lying inert with a great hole in her starboard side abreast the main hatch. She was kept afloat by her full cargo of lumber – probably the safest cargo to carry in wartime. She was low in the water with a list of about fifteen degrees to starboard, so that the deck on that side was awash. She had carried her cargo on deck as well as below in the holds. The lumber in the fore hold was gradually drifting out

86

through the hole in her side and pieces on the upper deck were being washed off, since the steel deck had been pushed up and split open and the steel wire ropes holding the deck cargo down had been parted and the stowage broken. She was a dead, forlorn-looking derelict lying there alone in the vast ocean. So recently she had been full of life and personality, the only home her sailors had had since their native Norway had been invaded. Now the same enemy had reached out still further and wrecked their little ship.

The thud of the torpedo at midnight; its explosion in the timber; the sudden awareness of master and crew that their turn had come. The inspection, the appraisal, and the tricky business of dropping out of the convoy without being run down by the ships coming on astern. Then being left behind, a ship by herself, heeling over lifeless. They would have heard and seen the rest of the one-sided night battle from a distance; and then, in the morning, nothing but themselves. Until the heartening moment when a naval vessel came in sight.

No use trying to sink her by shelling now. The sea-cocks had undoubtedly been opened. She would sink in her own time.

We went on another ten miles but, finding nothing more, turned back to the eastward to cover the ground once again. No sign of human life was seen along the path which those forty-seven ships had taken the night before, leaving seven, perhaps more, beneath the oily swell.

Emerging from the wreck-strewn sea, I suddenly became aware of another searcher, one which I had never expected to see. Coming directly towards us was a flying boat, no more than two hundred feet above the water, travelling very slowly. It seemed as strange a sight and as unnatural as if an albatross had come up from its native haunts in the Southern Ocean and suddenly appeared over a northern sea.

As she drew nearer, a light flashed on and off, a signal was being passed. She was one of those slow giants, a Catalina. She circled around us, leaning over laboriously yet gracefully as she turned, sometimes showing her broad belly, until she had received our message. Then, straightening out, she flew off to the west. It was the first time I had ever seen an aircraft so far out at sea, six hundred miles from Ireland.

We left the scene at 1300 in position latitude 57° north and longitude 23° 15' west, and steered due north at eleven knots, the best speed the engines could now make. We had enough fuel to take us to Iceland, a matter of 450 miles, if we did not zig-zag and if we met no severe contrary weather; otherwise we would not reach it. I had continued with the convoy beyond what was called the prudent limit of endurance. But when weather is fair, you are rather inclined to let optimism influence your judgment.

No need to eat now before lying down; I had had something to eat on the bridge at noon. But I was terribly tired. Counting up the sleep I had had since the first ship had been torpedoed fifty-six hours ago, the various snatches amounted to a total of about three and a half hours. Perhaps it was not surprising then, as we straightened away on our last course with the job over, that I could not give the navigator my final instructions before leaving the bridge, without falling asleep. We stood together. He was leaning against the window of the asdic house and I against the bridge rail. I could speak, coherently only about half a sentence and then my words would dwindle off into nonsense. I knew it and struggled against it and by standing erect and moving about a little I thought I eventually conveyed to him what my wishes were. Then I went below and collapsed into my bunk.

Nearly two years later I met the navigator when he was in command of an examination vessel in the Gut of Canso. We were talking of the past.

'Do you remember,' I asked, pouring out his third rum, 'when we turned north for Reykjavik from the scene of the action against S.C. 48? It was a bit after lunch and I was going down to turn in.'

'Yes,' he answered. 'I remember turning north and taking over.'

'Do you know,' I went on, 'I was so tired that I was falling asleep as I was speaking to you. I felt quite embarrassed in case you noticed it. Did you?'

'Did I?' There was a broad grin on his chubby face. 'No, sir. I was too sleepy to know what you were talking about.'

The convoy, as almost all convoys did, got through, but with a loss of nine ships in the final count. A British force escorted it on its last lap. It never zig-zagged, of course, it was too slow for that. Evasive steering was tried as directed by the Admiralty, with a view to bypassing the supposed main concentration of submarines.

Also tactics were adopted by the Commodore which were calculated to elude the shadower.

No one to my knowledge saw a U-boat close to the convoy either before or after any of the attacks, although two corvettes had independent encounters with them while they were on their way in to support us.

As for ourselves, I was disgusted with the incapacity of our ship. But we had learned a great deal. We had received our initiation into submarine warfare and knew the kind of things that happened. We also knew how we ourselves had reacted and how we might expect to react in the future.

After supper that first evening tottering north I asked the chief E.R.A. to come to my cabin.

'Can you make it, Lloyd?' I asked. But I knew what his answer would be.

'Yes, sir.'

He threw his head back perceptibly and sniffed.

'Fuel?'

'How long, exactly?' He looked at me earnestly.

'Day and a half at this speed. Say thirty-eight hours from now.'

He fixed his gaze on the oilskin on the peg, swaying slightly. His mind was darting through the tanks, calculating the dregs.

'Yes, sir. We've enough.'

As usual, in answering a direct question, he spoke with positive conviction. This was not to say, however, that tomorrow he would not reverse his opinion. But that was an engineer's privilege, especially when talking to someone like myself who hardly knew a thrust block from a stuffing box.

This was encouraging but his next remark was not.

'Them bottom-ends! And the main bearings! Bad shape, sir. Mighty bad. Could you stop for a while?'

'Do I have to?'

'Well . . . I shouldn't ask you to, sir. No. I'll manage. I'll get along.'

'Good.'

He looked down as though to see if his oily shoes were blackening the uncarpeted deck. Then I saw his forehead wrinkling again. 'Will you have a look below?' he suddenly asked.

'Yes. I'd like to. Haven't been down for a while, have I, Chief?'

I called up the pipe to the bridge and said I was going to the engine-room and would call again when I was back.

The chief held the collar of his reefer jacket close to his neck. It was chilly but the decks were dry – not a drop coming aboard.

It was not as bad below as standing alongside a steam hammer, but it was bad enough. I wondered how some casting did not crack under the slam of the worst bottom-end.

I looked at the leading stoker going his rounds, the E.R.A. on duty standing on the plates watching the machinery. I saw the tele-graph with the pointer at half speed, the revolution indicator, the brass gauges with their trembling fingers. As I stood beside the chief gazing into the main engines and up at the cylinders above I was reminded of M'Andrew's Hymn:

From coupler-flange to spindle-guide I see Thy Hand, O God,
Predestination in the stride o' yon connectin'-rod.

The chief turned his head towards my ear.

'I might take her up a bit, you see, if we stopped.'

'Yes. But I don't want to. We're a bad enough risk now not zig-zagging. I don't want to make it worse by sitting still like a duck.'

'No . . . You're right, sir.'

'Nothing'll snap, will it, Chief?' I asked.

'No, probably not. But it's the burning out of the bearings. It means constant watching and care. If they get hotter I'd have to ask you to slow down.' He sniffed. 'Had salt water on 'em one time, day or so ago. I never liked that. Bad practice. But I had to when you pushed her up for a while.'

'Sorry, Chief.'

'It's okay now, sir.'

I slid a bit on the oily plates as the ship lurched. I was not used to the slipperiness. The chief grasped my arm. 'Thanks,' I said. Then I told him the engines sounded ghastly to me. 'Do you think they could ever be put right?'

'I can't say as she'll ever run proper. Never heard the likes of 'em in my life. What have they got in Iceland in the way of a machine shop?'

He'd asked me this before.

'I've no idea. Never been there. But it's a naval base so there ought to be a good one. Several, I expect.'

The chief's fortress of moving steel was like a battle ground. It was a fight to keep the propeller turning. The engineers would hear the knocks and feel the shudders in nightmares for years to come.

'You'll be all right soon, Lloyd,' I tried to say encouragingly. 'You've brought her this far; its only a short leg now.'

He came up with me and we talked for a few minutes at the door above. The air, as I came forward along the deck, smelt very sweet after the stagnant stink of oil and steam.

Casualties on the voyage had not been confined exclusively to merchantmen. When we reached Iceland I was questioned as to when I had last seen H.M.S. *Gladiolus*. I told them the evening of the worst night. No signal from her had been heard for three days, she was not with her group. She appeared to be missing. She did not come into harbour and soon it became obvious that she never would. The Admiralty posted her as lost with all hands, due probably to enemy action. This little corvette had risen to fame in her short life, for she had sunk one submarine and had helped to kill a second. Her destiny impressed itself on me.

The big U.S. destroyer *Kearney* made Iceland. But she came in holed in her forward boiler-room from keel to upper deck. She was the Yankee who had shared the van with us. She, too, had benefitted from the fine weather on the run north. If it had been otherwise, she would surely have broken in half. It was surprising she had held together even under the smooth conditions. Two months were yet to go before the States would be at war with the nation whose navy had torpedoed the first American man-o'-war since 1918.

The episode was publicly deplored. Roosevelt said on the radio it was an unprovoked attack on a United States vessel, a neutral. Who was I to dispute that? I suppose it was a matter of definition.

The morning following our departure from the most lonely graveyard I had ever looked upon, I went down to the wardroom to meet the Norwegian officer we had picked up. He was a well built, blond, healthy-looking man of over forty. He spoke good English in a kind of shy, slow way which I had noticed before in Scandinavians.

'I'm glad to meet you at last,' I said, after shaking him by the hand. 'I hope you'll excuse me for not having welcomed you aboard earlier. Have you been made quite comfortable?'

'Indeed, yes,' he replied. 'Everyone has been very kind to me, and to the chief engineer. I'm ashamed to say that I have been a little seasick though. I'm not used to small vessels like this.'

We sat and talked for a while as to how the chief was getting along. He was an elderly man apparently, over sixty. He was in pain but bearing it stoically.

It was comfortable in the wardroom. The Norwegian was occupying the arm-chair, which I had great difficulty in making him retain when I came in, and I lay back on the settee. Coffee was being brewed for us in the galley and the rattle of the cups being made ready in the pantry could be heard through the serving hatch.

Presently I asked: 'How was the *Barfonn* lost and why were you the only ones we found?'

'The ship was torpedoed aft,' he began. 'It was a little while before I could be sure on which side we had been hit but I think it was the starboard side. It was about midnight. The engines were damaged and some after tanks were opened up. She didn't list at all; the oil that came out of the tanks was replaced by water. On examination, it looked as though the ship would not sink immediately but she would not move. The captain gave orders to abandon ship, and rightly so I think, and nearly everyone left, mostly in the boats. One was a motor boat.'

'But I didn't want to go much,' he went on. 'So I stayed behind with the chief and five men. We thought the navy might consider us worth towing. She was a fine big ship. How do you think the torpedo found us? We were in the middle of the convoy.'

'I don't know,' I said thoughtfully. 'You had five columns of ships on either side of you. Perhaps the sub fired into the centre from ahead.'

The steward brought the coffee in.

'Why did you eventually leave her?' I asked.

'We left about an hour later when the ship was torpedoed again. That was what the captain thought might happen.

'When all the others had left,' he continued, 'the seven of us went aft to the poop and cleared away a raft. It was a good raft with

92

ample capacity. We intended to leave it lying there on the poop-deck and if the ship went down we would float off with it as she sank.

'We sat there for a while and then I decided to go up to the bridge to collect a few things from the chart house. I got what I wanted and, as I stepped out on to the lower bridge, the ship was hit again. Being stopped I felt this explosion more than the first. The ship shuddered violently. I ran aft but found only the chief there; he was lying down and in some pain. I lifted him into the raft and soon got in myself as the ship began to settle. The chief told me that the explosion lifted them from the deck and all but he were thrown overboard. He had come in contact with a ventilator which had apparently prevented him from following the others but had broken his leg and generally shaken him up. The ship went down fairly quickly and we floated clear.'

That was all. Raising himself from the depths of his chair he drank some coffee. Then he slid back, crossed his legs and relit his pipe.

'You saw nothing of the others?' I asked.

'No, nothing.'

I thought of the subsequent events.

'We had great difficulty in finding you in the dark,' I said. 'We saw your flare easily, of course, but you were some distance away then and you didn't burn it long. Why didn't you use your flashlight more?'

The chief officer took his pipe out of his mouth with a large hand.

'I didn't want to betray your presence,' he answered simply. 'I thought the U-boat might still be around. I doused the flare soon after I lit it, and I thought by occasionally showing the flashlight you would find me all right. I could see you quite a way off against the night sky.'

'That was extremely considerate of you. I appreciate it.'

He drained his cup. He seemed to have enjoyed the coffee.

'Did you think you would be picked up so soon?' I asked.

'I thought it might be the next morning, but I was quite content to stay there for a week myself. It would not have been good for the chief engineer though.'

The casual sort of bravery of this man was something I had

93

never met before, nor did I ever recognize it as clearly in anyone else since, although it may have been present. He had purposely protected our ship at the very possible expense of himself. He was quite prepared to drift about the Atlantic in mid October in an open wooden raft supported by steel drums, with an old man with a broken leg as his only companion. His raft would not have been seen in the daytime unless a ship came pretty close to it. And his flares would not have been much use to him because he would not have known if ships were in the neighbourhood unless they were almost on top of him, because they showed no lights.

He had, however, been wearing a rubber suit which covered him from his toes to his neck and which kept him warm and dry. It resembled a rubber overall suit attached to a pair of sea-boots, and had elastic at the neck and a yellow hood so that only the face appeared. Worn with a life-belt, it enabled a man to float in the water upright without getting wet. Our friend told me that the Norwegian government issued them to all their sailors, and that his men mostly lived in them, cumbersome as they were. No other Allied nation provided their seamen with such protective clothing, to my knowledge.

A wonderful race comes from Norway! That country provided and manned a vast amount of tonnage, mostly in small ships, for the carriage of food and war supplies to the European battlefields at a time when losses were the most severe and when bottoms were almost more vital and valuable than the materials they carried. Their ships were often slow, but they were manned by the finest seamen in the world.

I finished this voyage with the sober realization that it was the merchant seamen who took the real onslaught of the enemy at sea. Their ships could hardly fight back against the elusive submarine and, due to their ponderous bulk, could not manœuver quickly to avoid their attacker. They always presented the best targets.

The men who lived in these ships could not have been unaware of their vulnerability. They pushed their ships along, never knowing when they would be singled out for extinction. In convoy they had little knowledge of how the enemy was deployed, and not much more when travelling alone. They lived, as it were, on the edge of a volcano. The constant suspense must have been awful.

These men may have tramped from Cape Town to Rio alone

and unprotected save for an old heavy gun, crossing an ocean where powerful German surface raiders roamed. Up the Brazilian coast and through the Indies, still alone, to North America, where soon there was to be such devastation that upwards of a hundred ships (half a million tons) a month would be lost. Then in convoy across their familiar Western Ocean where their lives were in constant jeopardy, not only from the enemy but from the perils of the sea. On the coasts of the United Kingdom they would be haunted by torpedo-firing E-boats and hidden mines, and hunted by the bombers of the *Luftwaffe* who might well bring to an abrupt end, under the very lee of their home port, their ten thousand mile voyage.

In the semi-silence of war few people knew of the colossal tasks these unsung, un-uniformed and unnoticed heroes achieved. If any became known, too often they were overshadowed by the epics of the fighting men who had done no more and probably less. None but their families really knew how dangerous were their missions. If they came home – which 30,000 British merchant sailors failed to do – they soon had to turn again and face the same onerous conditions.

We who served under the White Ensign did not go through the torments they went through, nor did the other fighting services. A merchant seaman could fortify himself with nothing but hope and courage. Most of them must have been very afraid, not for days and nights but for months and years. Who is the greater hero, the man who performs great deeds by swift action against odds which he hardly has time to recognize or greatly fear, or the man who lives for long periods in constant, nagging fear of death, yet has the fortitude and endurance to face it indefinitely and carry on?

There was a motto in my old boyhood training ship: 'Quit ye like men, be strong.' It may have helped those who had been weaned to the sea by this foster mother and who could still remember it.

95

7. The Queen

We spent two months tied up alongside the depot ship at Hvalfjord on the west coast of Iceland, but although the Engineer-Commander there did his utmost to repair the engines – he even took the shaft out again and turned it on a lathe – they were not working properly when we went down the fjord on our final trials. It was astonishing that we accomplished the voyage home. But nobody was sorry to leave Hvalfjord, with its sudden gales which disrupted shipping even at the head of the haven. It was not the most comfortable place to stay in, particularly in winter.

A further month went by while the ship lay idly against number two jetty in Halifax Dockyard. The engineers were beginning to say they did not know when the new shaft that we needed would arrive, and I did not want to wait for it. Moreover the *Baddeck* was a knave of the deepest die. My confidence in the future of the engines was shaken and I frankly did not want to sail in her again. But I could not very well apply for another ship myself and leave the others holding the baby. This was not to say that I was the soul of loyalty to the crew; it was partly selfishness. I did not think I could hope to find another group of officers and men the equal of the ones I had. It was not sound reasoning, of course, because generally there was much the same percentage of good and bad in every ship. However, I was not prepared to take the chance.

I debated what I should do. I had spoken to Captain (D)* about it, the same officer who, as the Commander in the dockyard six months before, had arranged for my Caribbean 'expedition', and while commiserating with me he knew of no way by which I could join a new ship and keep my old crew.

But wonder of wonders! He called me to his office one morning.

'Well,' he said, greeting me, 'I have another ship for you.'

'Really, sir?' I answered, anxiously.

'The Corvette, *Sackville*, which is lying alongside you is to be decommissioned tomorrow.' He puffed at a cigarette. 'I have

* Senior officer in charge of escort vessels: literally 'Captain of Destroyers'.

arranged that you shall take her over. You are to decommission your ship tomorrow and then recommission this one with your own officers and men. How will that suit you?' he added, with a wide grin and the sparkle in his eye which I had always liked.

I hardly knew what to say. To be so suddenly freed of the bane of my recent life and to gain everything I had wanted!

'Splendidly, sir,' I got out. 'It's very good of you to have arranged this. I appreciate it very much.'

I left him pleased and happy once more, and when I gave them the news in the wardroom half an hour later the officers were also delighted. Then we all went up on deck and had a really close look at the ship that was to be ours. We had not paid more than casual attention to her before.

She had been built in New Brunswick and had first sailed from Saint John only three months before. The reason for her being decommissioned now was something of a mystery, a mystery into which I did not go deeply. Something had gone wrong with the conduct of affairs. The officers and men had been discharged from the ship and scattered throughout the fleet with the exception of one rating, the leading signalman.

Next day we wasted no time in completing the formalities and duly shifted things over. As a matter of fact, we shifted rather a lot. Much of our time in harbour had been devoted to fitting our old ship out with all the devices and improvements we could think of. These things could not be left behind to rust.

A few days later I was sitting at my desk in my cabin when a visitor I had not expected knocked at my door and stepped in. He was a heavily set chap, almost ugly until you got to know his face, who had been the senior officer of the escort group to which we had belonged when we had taken that ill-fated convoy to the eastward in the Fall. He was a permanent force lieutenant-commander of the 'Temporary' variety, having come back for the war after being retired from the R.N. He shook my hand vigorously.

'So you've got a new ship, eh!' he said, seating himself on the settee. 'I'm glad to see you're out of that other wreck.' He was a hearty sort of fellow and full of energy. He told me he had just come into Halifax after being refitted down the coast, and expected

G 97

soon to return to Newfoundland to resume operations in the Mid-Ocean Escort Force. 'When will you be ready?' he asked.

'In a week or so, sir,' I said, getting out the gin and glasses. 'I believe we are to have a few days exercising at sea before going on operations. It's a new scheme.'

'Yes, I believe we're all having it now; a damn good idea.' He lifted his glass. 'What I wanted to ask you was whether you'd like to join me in the Mid-Ocean job. We got on pretty well together before, although your ship wasn't all she might have been. If you'd like to come I'll ask the chief-of-staff if he'll assign you to my group. I don't know whether he will, of course, but there's a chance. I'm going to see him today.'

This suited me admirably.

'Yes, by all means, sir,' I said emphatically. 'I was hoping to get back on that run. Indeed, I'd be delighted to join you.'

A week later we went out for exercises. This was the first organized attempt to carry out a programme of 'working up' ships after they had been newly commissioned or were starting out from a refitting yard with a high proportion of new men in their crews.

This over, we ammunitioned in Halifax and cast off.

As we passed down the harbour we could not help glancing at our old ship. She was lying quietly against the same jetty, no smoke rising from her funnel, no one visible on her decks. Perhaps I should have had some affection for her, but I felt little. She had her back towards us and looked as if she were pretending not to look. Just as well. She had had her own way.

Outside we picked up a medium-sized passenger ship as arranged and steamed north-east. Two days later we stood off the famous port on the extreme edge of the continent while the pilot boarded the passenger ship. We pitched gently to the even swell as the green water passed under us and rolled in on the high, precipitous cliffs of Newfoundland. Then we followed the bigger ship in through the Narrows whose gorge-like formation was further constricted by Chain Rock and the boom.

On arrival at St John's I paid the customary visit to Captain (D) and to the Commodore. I was pleased when they both welcomed me back to the Newfoundland Command, though I felt very guilty about my recent uselessness to them. They would in

98

truth have welcomed anybody. They were hard up for ships; but I was very pleased when they told me that we were after all to have the same group commander. However, not all the ships were ready yet, so it had been decided that we should occupy our waiting time in training.

The opportunity to carry out training at sea from this base was provided by an old time naval commander, captaining a corvette. He did very well I thought, though he had a tendency to forget sometimes that a corvette was not a battle cruiser.

There was one incident in this brief programme which nearly cost the tax-payer a million and me a nasty inquiry if I had survived.

Four of us, all corvettes, had steamed out to the Grand Banks to practice manœuvres and hoped at the same time to encounter a U-boat in the convoy lanes. Fog settled down, of course, we were in the area where fog shrouds the ocean for eighty of the hundred summer days. Early one afternoon the asdic operator on watch picked up an under-water contact and we went to stations. Being on the Banks, I thought it was as likely that we were in contact with a school of cod as with a U-boat. However, we did not work on assumptions; and, moreover, it was an opportunity for a bit of practice, if nothing else.

To attack a submarine I had to station myself in the asdic house, watch the compass and direct the steering of the ship from this position, since there was no compass outside on the bridge. This was a bad arrangement and was subsequently altered.

To begin with it was a bit of a squash inside the asdic house, and there always seemed to be wires leading from the compass in every direction, some attached to headphones; there was a drop-leaf table on one side and a folding stool which seemed to open up when trodden on; and there was my collapsible bunk which I had had fitted against the other side of the little compartment. Once wedged in alongside the compass it was a job to get yourself out. And to be able to make an exit was important. It was almost better to crane your neck in from outside through an open window. But that would have given you a distorted view of the compass card, and you would have needed the sight of a seagull to read the degrees. So for action stations I had posted an officer on the bridge for the express purpose of taking independent action to avoid collision should he find we were likely to run into something, and to report anything untoward.

Our asdic contact was reported to the Commander, who replied that he would detach himself from the other two ships and assist us. We attacked once, dropping a pattern of depth charges, and after losing contact could not pick it up again. We commenced to search, and while doing so I reported our courses. Messages were going between us by radio telephony, and presently we received a signal that he was coming on an opposite course to ours at fourteen knots, which was about the speed we were making. The visibility in the fog was about five hundred yards.

The asdic rating reported contact again. I had headphones on myself, and heard it, and was intent on listening and watching the compass, when the officer out on the bridge turned to an open window of the asdic house and shouted in to me, 'Ship ahead, sir.'

I heard him and pulled off the phones, disengaged myself somehow from my confined position beside the binnacle, trod on the wretched stool and tumbled out the door to the back of the bridge. In a matter of three more seconds I was at the fore part of the bridge and was instantly met by the sight of a corvette almost dead ahead about two hundred yards away, bearing down on us. Our combined rate of closing was twenty-eight knots.

I saw that she was a little on the starboard bow – her starboard side was very slightly open. I instantly ducked my head to the wheelhouse voicepipe which my hand was gripping and shouted 'Hard aport'.

I repeated it, although the quartermaster could not have failed to have heard me. Then I stood glued to the deck waiting to see if the bow would turn to port soon enough.

The distance between us closed. If we were both to keep on straight we might just skim past starboard to starboard. But we might not! The slightest deviation towards one another would bring a head-on crash.

In a ship so responsive to her helm I could not see how it could take so long for our bow to swing away from that ugly direction. I saw only the bull ring in our stem, and beyond it the rapidly increasing size of the blue-white hull of the oncoming ship.

Then, at last, there was movement. The swing began. Our ship had felt her rudder. Now she was turning. Now picking up – turning fast. It was as though she had thrown up her head and decided to swivel on her heel.

But the other ship did not let go. She was coming too! To my dismay I suddenly saw her turning in the same direction, following us like a charmed snake. We were both turning into one another! And the relentless bow of the other vessel seemed to have a diabolical accuracy about it.

The facts were obvious. The other captain had given the order to alter course to avoid collision at precisely the same moment as I had. But he had put his wheel to starboard. This was in accordance with the rules of the road. I had put mine to port. This was in accordance with the rule of avoiding an obvious collision.

The other ship had been fine on my starboard bow. If I had turned to starboard and she had failed to turn, in that split second I would have been cutting across her course. It was a matter of determining, in no more than one second, the less dangerous direction to take and at very close quarters. It was not unlike the almost automatic decisions you make to avoid people coming at you on a crowded sidewalk.

At less than a hundred yards I was certain the other ship's bow would strike us beneath the bridge. I held my breath and leaned to the left pulling at the bridge rail in an attempt to help the ship round. I ordered the depth charges to be unprimed, not that there was a hope of unpriming them in time.

My heart sank. To lose my new ship, with engines which ran properly – everything I had wanted! Or even to damage her. It would at least mean being out of action for a long time; perhaps for ever.

The other captain must have had similar fears. We would appear to him as he appeared to us.

Then I saw the possible escape. Like birds that converge and fly together yet never collide, both ships were in full turn, their deep rudders hauling their hulls around.

The bows of neither ship would cut into the other! The flares of the two fo'c'sles might crash together, perhaps come together with glancing blows. That was all.

Then suddenly a new danger appeared. The ships' sterns were swinging so fast that if the fore part of the ships did not touch, the two quarters would hit with tremendous force if their movement could not be countered. And it was aft that the depth charges were carried! I passed the word, 'Hard astarboard.'

Would we escape this? The ships were drawing parallel and their hulls had not touched. There was ten feet between us. Our swing was almost arrested. Strangely, the other's was also. Her captain had done the same as I.

'Helm amidships.'

Looking aft the two ships' sterns closed. But I felt no bump or even shudder from where I stood.

With steadying helms we opened the distance between us. The two sterns had come within two feet of one another.

As we drew away the Commander waved a red woollen mitt at me and shouted above the din between us that we would continue the course we had now assumed. We were so close that I imagined I could see beads of perspiration on his forehead.

There is a Deity who sometimes protects ships in fog.

8. The Barber Pole

'We are all agreed, then, on the details of my standing orders,' said the senior officer. 'They will be amended from time to time in all probability, to take in new or alternative screening diagrams or defensive measures which we may have to adopt to counter any changes in present U-boat tactics.' The senior officer of the Third Canadian Escort Group of the Mid-Ocean Force was terminating the discussion at the pre-sailing conference in the offices of Captain (D), Newfoundland. His five captains were present as well as several staff specialist officers and Captain (D) himself.

The senior officer was a clear-spoken man with a pleasant voice, though I knew it could be sharp and his words could be terse. He sat now in his square fashion at the head of the long, rather old table in the back room, his quick eyes glancing from one face to the next. He was confident enough of what he was saying and did not need to look at Captain (D), seated beside him, for confirmation.

Except for one, he saw around him men of his own age, about forty. Next senior was one of the two destroyer captains, a regular reserve lieutenant-commander, until two years ago master of a passenger liner in the West Indies trade, a broad shouldered, sea-wary mariner whose voice had the soft tones of Nova Scotia.

The other destroyer captain was the youngest of all; half his twenty-six years had been spent in the navy. He had done well in his chosen career, though his unassuming, even shy disposition would not encourage a stranger to expect it.

The other three in the group had all been in the Merchant Service at one time. Immediately before the war their activities had been diverse; tugboat operations, stevedoring, and in my case an unpretentious business career. All three were certified master mariners.

In this group there was a high degree of sea-going experience for the senior officer to rely upon, but pure naval experience was limited. He went on with what he was saying.

'I would like to emphasize again the need for maintaining wireless silence as much as possible unless we're attacked or you have a message of sufficient importance to transmit. Make sure you have every ton of fuel you can get into your ships before sailing and your armament is working properly.'

'We are of necessity a defensive force and must operate as a cohesive team, but if any of our number finds the opportunity of taking the offensive without unduly exposing the convoy, he has my blessing to take it. To borrow a quotation from an illustrious admiral of older days: "No captain can do very wrong if he places his ship over or alongside that of the enemy." I hope we shall have a modicum of success.'

He was fond of the dramatic touch. But then these were often dramatic days.

'Thank you, sir,' concluded the senior officer, turning to Captain (D), who nodded his head, looked at us and seemed to collect his thoughts. He was a big, handsome man with brown curly hair and particularly bright eyes; affable, yet never seeming to speak unnecessarily, and when he did it was always to the point and usually ended in a smile.

'You have heard your senior officer and I concur in his organization and arrangements,' he said, addressing us in an easy manner which had a natural charm about it.

'I must reiterate his statement that you are normally to follow defensive tactics rather than offensive, however distasteful it may be to you, unless you come upon the enemy; then you must do your utmost to destroy him. We are not constituted for the offensive, because escort groups are not large enough. We must adhere to the policy which has been laid down by the Admiralty for North Atlantic convoys and to which this command subscribes: "To insure the safe and timely arrival of the convoy at its destination". This can only be achieved by constant watchfulness during the long monotonous voyages in front of you, and by keeping your ships and men, and particularly your officers, in a high state of efficiency so that submarines may be intercepted and dealt with before they can close the range sufficiently to fire at the convoy.

'Remember that my engineering and electrical staff, shipwrights and the rest, are here to see that you do not sail from this port in an unseaworthy condition or lacking in fighting material or effectiveness. Use them. But give them every possible assistance yourselves during the time you are in harbour. See that you receive proper attention at the British bases. You have, I hope, a year's operations in front of you; I trust none of you will come to grief, I know none will falter. I shall look forward to seeing you every month or so. The very best of luck to each of you.'

He inspired confidence and made you feel he was behind you with his own personal strength as well as the resources of his base. And that, indeed, was as it should have been. But Captain (D) had all the sturdy background of a naval career, much of it served abroad, some of it with the R.N. He had commanded a destroyer flotilla not so long ago and knew the narrow sea lanes the troop-ships followed as thoroughly as we were to come to know the broad cargo highways.

The conference was ended. Captain (D) shook hands with us and we filed out through his staff office.

Glancing out the window and down the hill over the ugly tops of buildings towards the narrow harbour, the view was like a grey pool beneath the overcast afternoon sky, dun-coloured slopes rising from the other side dotted with a few small black houses. But the scene was brightened by the little vessels lying against one another at the wharves at the foot of the cliff, most of them a camouflage of white and green and blue. Moored to the buoys were merchant vessels in tiers of two and three, a powerful sea-going tug with a bow wave painted on her stem; a long, heavy tanker, once a German U-boat supply ship and now serving as a fleet oiler; and, of all incongruous companions, a sealing vessel, very old, with a clipper bow and high masts and a tall stove-pipe funnel. But, belonging to her era, there was a picturesque wooden river boat lying opposite her towards the upper end of the harbour, her super-structure bulging with decks. She was the base ship substituting for an office building. Down the harbour towards the entrance were other merchant ships at anchor.

This was Newfoundland's greatest port, in and out of which had sailed the numerous local fishing fleets and fishermen from the outports to pledge their season's catch to outfit their voyages; the biggest sealing port in North America; the foreign refuge from hurricanes of the Portuguese schooners. This was the haven which had so often lent protection to traders broken by storms or raped by icebergs. Now it was our base.

We went to the Naval Operations room on the fifth floor of the big hotel to check the latest disposition of submarines and intelligence; and then returned to our ships across the little harbour.

That evening, 26th May 1942, we sailed out of the harbour one behind the other in order of seniority, the newly formed Third Canadian Escort Group, or C.3, six ships strong, two lean River Class destroyers and four corvettes. Spreading out in line abreast, a course was set to the east-south-east towards a point a hundred miles away where we were to rendezvous with an eastbound convoy and take it from a Western Local Escort Group which had brought it out from Halifax.

It was good to see the ships spreading out over the sea on either side of you again; to stand on the bridge and watch the bow dip into the now slow Atlantic swell, throwing the green water of the fishing grounds out on either side. After months of delay and the constant feeling of the war going on and you not there, you were, at last steaming towards it – or actually in it. I believe everybody was glad, though some momentarily less than others – those who were unused to a heaving ship and felt its discomfort.

That night fog enveloped us, a fog that for days blotted out all else but the little circle of sea around us. We should have intercepted the convoy soon after dawn, but it was late afternoon before the group fell in with it. We came down on the mass of ships almost silently – by radar. As we dispersed, unseen, to our pre-arranged stations around the convoy, our senior officer, in a single coded message, took the convoy from the Commander of the Western Local Escort. The local gathered itself together and headed back to the westward.

Our ship's station was on the port quarter. We felt our way in to the first column, closing on the convoy course; we wanted at least to know by sight the rear ship of the column who would be our nearest neighbour. More suddenly than expected the fog darkened to starboard. Almost at once a ship, five times our size, was close aboard. We sheered off to keep our distance, yet remained near enough for a while to verify her identity and let her appearance imprint itself on our minds.

She was black all over, heavy and ponderous, laden right down to her Plimsoll marks. Her upper deck was crowded with army vehicles and tanks. As she rose slowly to the swell, the water ran from her clean sides like a wave spilling from an ebony rock. Great posts for masts with crosstrees and light topmasts above. The bridge had a wheelhouse made of concrete – it seemed very thick and heavy. A signal lamp flashed with a misty blur from an opening in the wall telling us her pennant number. By this we knew she was the rear ship.

We opened out and left her in the fog. Except for two or three glimpses of her, that was all we saw of the convoy for four days. We kept in touch with the ships we were guarding by radar.

On the fifth night the weather cleared, and in the morning there stood the ships, column on column as far as the eye could see, mostly large ships and not such a motley collection as we had accompanied before – this was a fast convoy, nine knots instead of the slow seven. It seemed almost unbelievable that we had been close alongside this great company of vessels and travelled with them over the ocean for seven hundred miles and seen no more than one.

They were in good station, too, in spite of the fog. And all they had had to keep them properly abreast of one another was the occasional use of their whistles, and in line their fog-buoys, which they streamed astern as a guide or warning to the vessels behind. On the outskirts of the convoy, ahead, astern and on the port side we could see our escorts, small against the great, heavily laden merchantmen. Those on the starboard side we could not see, they would be nine or ten miles away.

The passage was a comparatively quiet one. It took us nine days altogether, which was rather quick even for a so-called fast convoy. After emerging from the fog we had two glorious days, one of those infrequent spells when the great expanse of blue Atlantic water undulates very gently, as though unhurried, and casts brilliant flashes of the sun's reflection into your eyes, and the sea's almost still surface ripples here and there into cats-paws stirred by some light air from the north-west.

Then, in the night, as usual, a wind came up and the weather turned nasty – rough and blowing, wet and chill. Perhaps this helped us to negotiate the region, considered to be the more thickly populated submarine area, unharmed and apparently unsighted. Aircraft were patrolling quite a long way out now and perhaps this may have had the effect of impeding the U-boats' progress or keeping them submerged longer than usual.

And so we arrived in the Western Approaches, a name which became familiar and famous to all who came and went across the North Atlantic. It represented the waters of the United Kingdom seaboard through which ships passed when sailing to ports in Great Britain from the west. It was presided over by the Commander-in-Chief of the Western Approaches who flew the flag of a full admiral over his headquarters at Liverpool.

At ten o'clock on a clear morning we sighted the blue ridge of a mountain appearing as a low dark cloud just above the horizon. As we neared it I recognized Bloody Foreland, the beginning of the Mountains of Donegal.

A little later on we parted company with the convoy, being relieved by a single trawler – all the protection that was needed to take the ships to the Clyde, Belfast and Liverpool. But some ships were bound for the east coast of England. They were taken by another trawler to Loch Ewe where they would join a coastal convoy and make their way around the north of Scotland.

At mid-afternoon our six ships entered Loch Foyle and the sight which met our eyes was almost breath-taking. No wonder this land was called the Emerald Isle! Its greenness seemed greener than any other grassland I had ever seen, even though I had been born here. The fields came down almost to the rocks at the water's edge and cultivation stretched back up the slopes to where the peat hills began. An old ruin stood close to the water, its broken walls covered with ivy and creeper; its name, Greencastle, was apt.

We went to the tankers at Moville and fuelled, then took pilots and proceeded up the Loch. After forty minutes we rounded a bend at the upper end where the shores on either side came almost together and found ourselves in a river, the Foyle River. After a few more minutes we turned another bend and there before us stretched one of the most beautiful river reaches I had ever seen. It was straight for three miles and its width was about two hundred yards but the ship channel no more than a hundred and it hugged the right bank. All along this high bank, which sloped steeply away from the edge of the stream, was a wood, broken only here and there by old walled gardens. The trees, in the full leaf of early June, spread their branches out over the water, forming a canopy to

108

shade the fishermen who, now and then, were to be seen casting their flies into the placid water. There were brilliant clumps of rhododendrons in the wood and bordering the gardens, pink, red, lilac and purple; and many wild flowers and ferns growing beneath the trees. The birds' songs, many different kinds of birds, and the scent which came out of the wood added such charm to the picture that I felt as though I was at peace with the world and all the world must also be at peace. I think others felt it too.

The ship was still cutting the quiet water with a pleasant sound when I came back to more material reality. Although the pilot was competently guiding the ship along, her safety was still my responsibility. We were approaching the bend at the end of the reach and as we took it, a sharp right angled turn to starboard, the river broadened out and the wood was left behind; and there stood a city not a mile away.

The Maiden City, it was called – besieged but never conquered. Londonderry, or just 'Derry, whose ancient wall had withstood the siege of James II, was now the great outport of the Western Approaches. In peace-time its harbour used to accommodate only a few ocean-going ships; mostly coasters used its facilities. But since it had been established as a naval base, jetties had been built along the river bank below the commercial wharves to accommodate the little ships. Against these in 1942 constantly lay destroyers and corvettes in threes and fours just in from the sea or ready to sail out; they did not stay long.

It had been a peaceful trip, in which the routine of a ship at sea had gone on unhampered. On the mess decks tempers had occasionally become frayed, which is only to be expected when men of different temperaments are thrown together at close quarters – for Atlantic convoy work was not all fighting U-boats; much of it was boring.

The morning after our arrival a conference was held in one of the destroyers which was attended by the captains of the six ships. Policies and tactics were discussed and training while in harbour was arranged with the shore staff. Before we adjourned the younger of the two destroyer captains submitted a design for a group insignia which he said his first lieutenant had conceived.

It consisted of a band of red and white diagonal stripes on the funnel, or the foremost of two funnels. Since there were no other suggestions forthcoming, the design was adopted there and then. I told the first lieutenant when I returned from the conference and he said he thought it would stand out clearly. The funnel was camouflaged pale green and blue.

A week later, just before sailing, I was standing on the jetty talking to an officer belonging to the shore base.

'You'll be sailing this evening I suppose,' he said, looking across at my ship. 'I see you belong to the Barber Pole Group, they are leaving at 1900 I understand.'

I too looked at the ship. The band on the funnel did rather remind one of a barber's pole. We must have been the only ones not to have noticed it; everyone else seemed to and we became known generally as the Barber Pole Group. This was perhaps the most famous of all group insignia for, although I felt that it never should have continued after the original group dispersed, it lasted until the end of the war, having subsequently been adopted by a number of other ships who became connected in one way or another with one of the originals. In fact, a song was written about it.

9. Westward Again

One's movements were never certain during the war and I could not be quite sure that I would return to the United Kingdom again, so I took this opportunity of making a hurried trip to England to see my mother, my sister and brothers for the first time since 1934.

My mother's house was in the little village of St Feock a few miles from Falmouth. It stood overlooking the estuary of the River Fal and the garden, which was one of the loveliest in a land of lovely gardens, sloped gently down to the sea wall. One could sit by the old sundial on the lawn and look out, beyond the palm trees at the foot of the garden, upon one of the most pleasing views on the Cornish coast.

We made one or two little jaunts around the countryside. It was beautiful, and now I realized, or perhaps remembered, for I had spent most of my childhood in this corner of the world, that I was in a flower country. Here rhododendrons grew along the roads in profusion and stretched back into the fields; honeysuckle and roses bloomed together in the hedgerows.

It was very wonderful; but, of course, it could not last. I returned to my ship and shortly sailed again, westward.

The passage was much like the trip eastward; no action but hour after hour of tension, wariness, vigilance. After that another voyage from St John's to Londonderry. This, too, was uneventful as far as enemy engagements were concerned though life on board was not altogether dull. Crossings had not become monotonous yet. The sick-berth attendant, a conscientious, loyal little fellow devoted to his calling, was serving his first punishment, the only punishment he ever had in the navy. He had inadvertently missed the Irish boat train from London coming back from leave. He was seven hours late and was given fourteen days stoppage of leave. This appealed to him since the homeward passage took two weeks.

He had reached the age of twenty-seven during the last eastbound trip. He was quite an age, many thought. 'But he's a real doctor type,' they said. 'Got a pill for everything.' The same ruddy pill, some thought.

The communications mess decided to celebrate his birthday by giving him a drink. Two tots of rum were surreptitiously saved and he was duly given the four ounces neat before midday dinner.

'Swalla' it down in two gulps,' said Signalman Burley as they coaxed the sandy-haired, wiry man to drink to the anniversary of his birth. Grinning, he held the glass up in one hand and with the other fingered, somewhat nervously, the small bandage roll he always kept in his shirt pocket for emergencies. He had never taken a drink of any kind before.

'Down the hatch, Tiffy,' said one of the wireless operators, 'like you make us down your medicine.'

As they all stood around, the deck beneath them heaving and now and then swaying sideways unexpectedly, Tiffy lowered the stuff down the hatch and lost his breath. But they patted him on the back and it returned. Nothing seemed untoward. He knew the swinging lamp was as it should be.

After a big dinner they sent him to the signal officer, their divisional advisor.

'Come in, Tiffy. What is it?' said Collins.

'Don't exactly know, shir.'

'Well, why don't you? Anybody sick?'

'Can't 'member any, shir.'

Tiffy, neat as ever, stood holding on to the edge of the desk which seemed to him unusually unsteady, his blue eyes tending to close. He struggled with them, arching his blond eyebrows.The signal officer leaned back against his bunk and surveyed the sick-berth attendant.

'Stand up, man! We've got to keep erect in the navy.'

'Yeshir.' He let go the desk and grasped the chair which teetered, but he managed to get it back on its four legs again.

'Everything in order?' Collins questioned.

'They tell me, shir . . . they tell me . . . tell me . . . its my birthday, shir. Today, shir. Birthday, shir . . . they tell me.'

Tiffy's head was moving from side to side. He was looking for the signal officer. He heard his voice in the distance.

'Good. I presume then that you're having a happy day – no need to add my wishes, I'm sure. Take the afternoon off, Tiffy.'

'Yeshir. 'ank you, shir.'

He had not far to go alone. A few paces from the door two of his friends happened to be handy and led him to safety.

It was 25th July 1942 when we set out on our fourth voyage. After two strenuous days and nights of exercises off the coast we refuelled at Moville and sailed out of Loch Foyle in the early morning to rendezvous with a westbound convoy off the Mull of Oa, a promontory on the southernmost island of the Hebrides, across from the Irish coast.

Command of the group had changed by reason of promotions. One of the destroyer captains, the stocky Nova Scotian who had come from Canada's Caribbean merchant fleet, was now raised to the rank of Commander. Our original senior officer was to remain with us in his corvette until he, himself, was promoted to Commander's rank to take charge of another group.

Of the two I had no particular preference. I had had a high regard for the leadership of the first and I came to respect the direction and conduct of our second just as much. There was an advantage in our new S.O. being in a destroyer because these ships were equipped with better radar, radio and plotting facilities.

Leaving Inishowan Head behind us and swinging along in line ahead over the strip of sea towards the Mull as a low, bronze sun, breaking through the summer morning dampness, cast a copper pathway to Kintyre, our little force soon sighted wisps of smoke rising from vessels still hull-under. Pressing on, the distant ships came up quickly, thin masts, then funnels, upperworks and high sides.

The array of ships looked impressive against the far headland and being light they stood tall and bulky, seeming larger than those of the laden eastbound convoy we had recently brought in. Not so the tankers which occupied the centre columns; they were low, their many oil tanks filled with water ballast.

First sight of the new convoy attracted the usual attention and as we closed on the forty-one slow-moving vessels, all hands but the few at the fires and engines were on deck examining the nearer ones critically, trying to assess their age and speed. As we steamed up, broke and separated as the destroyer's flags came down, steering off to our respective stations, waved greetings were exchanged between merchant and naval sailors. Then we settled down to escort O.N.115 across the Western Ocean.

Neil, the torpedo officer, did not know whether it was customary in the escorts to have prayers on Sunday mornings but as this and our previous ships were the only ones he had been in and prayers had been held in both when conditions allowed, he presumed it was the usual thing. Sometimes Divisions preceded prayers and sometimes Captain's Rounds were conducted afterwards. Now, on this first Sunday, the day following departure, all hands not on duty were mustered on the quarterdeck awaiting prayers. Some of the duty watch had been released to attend.

Neil – now a lieutenant – standing with the navigator and P.O's against the winch at the fore-part of the tiny, wooden-decked space, could not see his depth charges for people. He had become known as the torpedo officer, or just 'Torps'. His duties now embraced everything that came within the scope of the torpedo department and this included all electrical equipment, wiring, fans and demolition gear. One might normally think of the torpedo department as dealing solely with torpedoes. Actually the missile itself engaged comparatively little of the department's time and there might be a dozen torpedomen carried in a ship which carried no torpedoes; they were really electricians.

The bodies of the sixty men whom Torps faced now swayed rhythmically as the ship rolled easily to the slight sea. He knew them all, some well, some not as well as he would have liked. But he was convinced of their dependability, their readiness to go as far as their knowledge would carry them. With only one or two exceptions they were keen, spirited and physically strong, smart despite their rough appearance in their sea-going clothes. He glanced at the coxswain, neat as usual, an exception in appearance, standing at the ship's side looking along the waist, watching the first lieutenant on his way forward to report 'Lower decks cleared'.

The torpedo officer admired the young coxswain. He had experienced some benefits from having him on watch with him at night. The coxswain and the chief bosun's mate, both permanent service men, still in their early twenties, were serving as second-officers-of-the-watch during the dark hours. It strengthened the bridge forces. The coxswain's round, cheery face belied his sharpness. He was much respected by all, especially for his knowledge of

114

naval law in his capacity of master-at-arms and, perhaps equally, for his superior acquaintance, gained in peacetime service, with those important naval factors, routine and protocol.

Neil felt the cool northerly breeze on his face, a clean-scented breeze with none of the dust and pollution of shore breezes. It was a brisk morning with a diffused circle of brightness in the sky where the sun shone behind a thin layer of high cloud.

He glanced sideways and saw that Lloyd, the old chief engineer, had his new false teeth in position for Sunday morning payers. Next to him was the senior E.R.A. an ex-Great Lakes engineer, and next again the second senior, a man with rather a high, husky voice, unmistakably from the North of England, who was by trade a printing engineer. Neil presumed he had been a good man with printing machinery. He was a good marine engineer, he understood; all three E.R.A's were. He supposed both these engineers were happy. The engines were running 'beautiful', he had heard the chief say; but kept so by the tender and constant care of the engineers and stoker ratings in the engine-room.

As Neil's eyes passed over the men waiting to be drawn to attention – as best they could in the confined and cluttered space – he recognized some of them by incidents in which they had been involved, others only by their appearance. The little, sharp-featured leading steward with the rather long chin and the Liverpool accent. He knew him not only as one who was always in and out of the wardroom but also who, when often taken to task for being absent, usually seemed to have just been ashore on behalf of the very person scolding him, such as for his laundry.

A little beyond him was Signalman Fair of 'masted' renown who, during a kit inspection recently, was asked why he had most of his clothes marked with the initials I.O.D.E.

There was the gun-layer, a young man with a quiet, almost sleepy appearance. At gun drills his heavily lashed eyes did not seem to impede his vision as he looked through his telescope.

The torpedo officer was surprised to see in the rear the bland face of a coder who was normally expected to be missing. He had always claimed to be too seasick to do very much, except when within some fifty miles of base – on the homeward, not the outward journey. They said he could, being a Bluenose, smell the proximity of land. Yet why should a Nova Scotian suffer so?

The ship's company was supposed to be mustered by divisions –
seamen, stokers, communications – but they abutted one another
so closely that they were inclined to get mixed and tangled up with
the mine-sweeping derricks, the patent log, drums of oil and the
inevitable charges of high explosive with their brass handles pro-
truding from one end attached to hydrostatic pistols. Thus it was
not odd to see the tall, serious-looking cook from Southern
Ontario standing next to a heavy, red-headed seaman, the man who
could lift a depth charge alone. On the other side of the cook was a
French-Canadian boy, humour flickering over his ever-smiling
face, who appeared always to wallow in untidiness – unusual in
people from the Province of Quebec. He, like most other French-
speaking Canadians in the navy, was energetic, anxious to learn
and into everything, especially if it were wet work.

The coxswain took a pace to one side and gave a nod to the
officers. The torpedo officer called, 'Ship's company', and all
hands stiffened from the stand easy. Heels could be heard on the
iron deck coming down the starboard waist. The bulwark dipped
to show an approaching wave then lifted, leaving only the sky
visible beyond the rail. Gulls called from above.

The first lieutenant called the ship's company to attention as
he arrived on the scene. The order was executed by shuffling noises
rather than the snap of the barracks parade-ground. Then 'off
caps' and 'stand at ease'.

I opened my prayer book, which I had carefully marked with
paper clips – slips of paper always blew away – and started with a
short opening prayer and then turned to the prayer I liked best.

O Eternal Lord God, who alone spreadest out the heavens, and
rulest the raging of the sea: who hast compassed the waters with
bounds until day and night come to an end: Be pleased to receive into
thy Almighty and most gracious protection the persons of us thy
servants and the Fleet in which we serve. Preserve us from the
dangers of the sea, and from the violence of the enemy; that we may
be a safeguard unto our most gracious Sovereign Lord, King George,
and his Dominions, and a security for such as pass on the seas upon
their lawful occasions; that the inhabitants of our Empire may in
peace and quietness serve thee our God; and that we may return in
safety to enjoy the blessings of the land, with the fruits of our labours;
and with a thankful remembrance of thy mercies to praise and glorify
thy holy Name; through Jesus Christ our Lord. Amen.

A short prayer followed for the protection of our loved ones and then the Lord's Prayer and the Blessing. As I closed my book and turned to reach for my cap which I had hung on a hose nozzle on the after bulkhead, I heard the first lieutenant giving sharp orders including the putting on of caps. Then I turned and faced aft again.

As an added attraction – or perhaps just an attraction – I invariably followed prayers by a statement of our position and what seemed to be ahead and any information which might be of interest to all members of the crew. This time it did not differ much from the usual in most respects.

I spoke of the value of the convoy, particularly of the fourteen tankers. This was a fast convoy, officially nine knots but according to my list of ships the slowest among them was recorded as ten. If all went well we could count on being in St John's next Tuesday week.

The submarine situation was not good. They appeared to be well deployed across the convoy tracks from two days steaming from Ireland – that would be tomorrow – to half-way over. Intelligence indicated that they were mostly operating in packs; that there were believed to be about eighty at sea at the moment – a greater number than had been reported before though some were in the Caribbean rather than up here – and that they were emerging from the yards much faster than we could destroy them.

I went on to say that, from reports, there seemed to be very little decline in the skill and daring with which U-boat commanders were pressing home their attacks, or the capacity of the crews, despite the great expansion of the submarine fleet. 'And to date it is believed that Germany has had no difficulty in finding the men. They still have time to give their submariners the most intensive training, both ashore and afloat. They are taught the theory in special schools and undergo quite a long period of sea training in the Baltic, during which they are put through every evolution in the most rigorous manner. So severe is their training at sea, I am told, that several U-boats have been lost during exercises. Their men are well cared for ashore, too, and well fed, both on food and propaganda. Don't think, therefore, that the efficiency of the U-boat is on the decline. They are still hard to catch and sink. They are, as you know, sturdy and very manœuvrable.'

I exhorted watchkeepers on deck to keep a good lookout and everyone to consider carefully whether they were certain they knew everything they could about their particular job in action and, finally, the necessity for wearing life-belts always, whether working, eating or in their hammocks. Too often 'Mae Wests' were taken off. This would have to be a punishable offence in future.

The service and my remarks over, the men were dismissed.

For the next two days things went along normally. The weather became unpleasant when the wind veered to the east but it did not remain in that quarter long; it hauled around to the south and with it the air became warmer though the sun did not shine.

At 2200 on the third night of the voyage the radar operator in the corvette on the port bow of the convoy ahead of us saw a small spot appear on a bearing directly away from the convoy. It became a little larger and soon after this I read the captain's signal, 'Radar contact bearing 220°. Chasing'. It came in pretty close to him but he saw nothing with his eyes. He pursued it but the range opened and the spot faded from the scan.

So a U-boat had come on the convoy! He had seen an escort from his almost water-level height and had turned away. Having the greater surface speed he had escaped easily. We had been sighted!

We had felt that the freedom we had enjoyed could not last; other convoys near us had been attacked frequently during our voyages, yet we had escaped.

Nothing further was done that night; all escorts kept their stations. The senior officer did not think it wise to detach an escort at this stage to try the usually futile task of searching for the raider, even if he was the sighter and would hang on for all he was worth.

Early in the morning a local radio transmission was heard which was identified as German. Thereafter a number of these broadcasts were picked up, on which some of the escorts were able to obtain bearings. Transmitting on medium frequency was rather unusual but apparently this U-boat intended telling his friends, who obviously could not be far away, and to do some organizing on his own. With some disregard for his own safety, which he must have known he was jeopardizing, he continued to bleat away intermittently for the next two days.

In view of this, the two destroyers made several sweeps to a depth of thirty or forty miles from the convoy in an effort to track down the informer. At noon on the second day, away out on the starboard quarter of the convoy, one of them suddenly caught sight of a U-boat. The destroyer's twin screws churned faster as she turned, leaning over. Then she gathered speed and made off towards the small black object resembling, through the young captain's binoculars, little more than a conical buoy surrounded by foaming shoal water. But the eyes of those in the U-boat's conning tower evidently saw the manœuvre clearly. She slid beneath the surface while the destroyer was still several miles away and could not be found below.

Late that night the same destroyer was sent out by the senior officer who had arrived at the decision that at night, too, he could no longer follow a policy of strict defence. By this time the destroyer had pinned down the U-boat's transmissions to a fairly fine degree of accuracy, for she had taken many bearings during the last thirty-six hours and now had the measure of the tap which the German operator applied to his key. She reached a position twenty miles on the convoy's starboard beam, then knew that she was hot on the enemy's trail. The atmosphere had become very clear and in the bright moonlight the sinuous smoke rising above the convoy could be seen through binoculars by the trained eyes in the destroyer without much difficulty. So our tricky opponent could shadow comfortably at this apparently safe distance.

How much emphasis had been laid on smoke! I heard it again and again, 'Smoke' and 'Smokers'. Try as they would the old coal burners could not control it perfectly. How could they with often inexperienced firemen in their stokeholds and draft systems that were not constructed with a view to smokelessness? And coal-burners were not the only guilty ones either, oil-burning ships often smoked. I waged a ceaseless war with the chief engineer of each of the ships I was in on this one aggravating point and they, in turn, carried the war to their boiler rooms.

It was more than likely that the U-boat saw the destroyer. He might even have seen her a number of times, but continued to send out his signals at frequent intervals. In between he made broad zig-zag runs at high speed, perhaps seventeen knots, back and forth along the convoy's course never allowing the smoke of the ships to disappear from his view for very long. Consequently the destroyer never knew which direction the submarine was going to take after he had made a transmission. Had she possessed a modern radar she would most likely have been able to intercept him, but the young captain had to depend on a visual sighting which he could not make despite the moonlight and the white wake which the fast-moving craft would be creating.

At dawn the submarine made one more transmission – her last – and started rapidly towards the convoy. Then the destroyer saw her, six miles away under the dawn side of the sky, a small silhouette, moving.

The captain of the submarine saw his opponent too, but this time he could not remain on the surface, he dived at once. The destroyer raced towards the spot. On approaching the diving position she slowed down and commenced to search by asdic. Within ten minutes an echo came back from the long ping which travelled under the water. She attacked. The depth charges exploded and the sea erupted, and the surface vessel passed on. Turning, she came back, her search gear on a broad arc. Then her officers and look-outmen saw a sullen patch of sea, a circle of stagnant water – oil! An unusual feat for a first hurried attack.

She delivered two more ten-charge attacks with deliberate care and stealth but it became evident in the listening gear that the U-boat had now gone very deep. This had become a two-ship job.

Presently the corvette who had detected the approach of the submarine two nights before joined the destroyer to assist her in the hunt. Her captain was our previous senior officer and now he was at what he had been itching for. I envied him indeed when I saw him draw away to starboard and out of sight but I was glad he had been assigned to the task. The S.O. must have had a great struggle to fight down the temptation to delegate himself to join the intriguing contest, but he was a man who held tenaciously to his duty. I observed, from the incoming signals, the drama that ensued. The officers followed it as the intercepted messages came to the bridge. And the wireless men followed it, and its progress was intermittently broadcast to the men throughout the ship.

CORVETTE: 'Have you anything?'
DESTROYER: 'No.'

CORVETTE: 'Contact bearing 224, 2200 yards.'

DESTROYER: 'Hold it. Am moving eastward.'

DESTROYER: 'Contact bearing 350. Make attack slowly and watch my flag.'

CORVETTE: 'Contact bearing 228, 1700 yards.'

(Several messages passed between them, each giving bearings and ranges).

CORVETTE: 'Attacking.'

CORVETTE: 'Lost contact at 400 yards.'

DESTROYER: 'Opening doppler.'

DESTROYER: 'You are over target.'

CORVETTE: 'Your "over" coincided with my timing. That ought to fix him but he is very deep.'

DESTROYER: 'Think shot was good. When you regain contact stand off and direct me.'

By mid-morning five more depth charge patterns had been dropped by the two ships. But the U-boat still seemed to be underway and manœuvring normally. As one ship conned and the other attacked, yet another pattern went down. Three minutes later two heavy underwater explosions were heard which were louder by far than the almost inaudible rumble of the bursting depth charges six hundred feet below. Did that mean success?

But the ships jockeyed for position again, tried to regain contact. Ten minutes passed while the asdic beams of both ships swept and probed. Twenty minutes elapsed but still no echo returned, no whisper from the depths.

What followed was told to me afterwards by the destroyer captain. About twenty-five minutes after the two heavy explosions – a phenomenon which was found to be not uncommon in the death-throes of German submarines, though what caused it we did not know – his yeoman remarked that seagulls were bunching and diving to the water at a spot midway between the two ships. The captain had noticed it himself but had paid no particular attention to it. Suddenly he realized what this might mean. In several minutes he had covered the intervening distance, had called away his whaler's crew and was taking the way off the ship. The whaler was dropped and the men pulled as the sea birds continued to swoop down and land on the water in the manner of gulls when they see food. Unlike their almost tame coastal cousins, these ocean gulls scattered as the boat approached but they were seen to be squabbling among themselves, as they flew upwards, for the morsels they had found.

The boat returned to the ship with the horrible evidence of the shattering eruption which must have occurred within the submarine, violence which had burst the bodies of its human occupants and wrought internal destruction even against the tremendous pressure of the sea.

Thus ended the career of one of Admiral Doenitz' dreaded U-boat fleet. Who she was none of us knew. How much damage she had inflicted on our shipping could not be known either, but by the behaviour of her Commander one would be led to assume that he was the victim of over-confidence, bred perhaps of a surfeit of success.

Yes, the U-boat fleet was dreaded. It was loudly proclaimed by Hitler through his propagandist Goebbels that it was the instrument with which the vital lifeline of the Allies was to be broken, and the heads of the Allied states knew that their own chances were less than even. Already in 1942 five hundred merchant ships of two and a half million tons had been sunk.

Why had the U-boats not attacked during the past few days? Perhaps we had kept them out of range, perhaps they had not wanted to attack yet. It looked to us as though the real strategy of pack attack was being applied: the original sighter would hold on to the convoy and summon the others and as they gathered round they would shadow the ships until the full force of their combined strength could be mustered. They would learn the strength of the escort and their disposition around the convoy. Some would perhaps play the part of decoys and try to wheedle one or more of us away when the appointed hour for striking approached. Then the attackers, receiving their final orders from Control Headquarters in Germany or France, would find the gap and strike.

It was possible that the Commodore's action during the past two nights had something to do with preventing an attack, though in view of the very good visibility this was doubtful. Our course had been west-sou'-west the day before yesterday but that night he had swung his ships round to south-by-east and back to the original course at daybreak. Soon after dark the next night, while the destroyer was out hunting, he again altered course to south and at dawn altered back to south-west. These were very wide alterations but the convoy was comparatively fast. No great divergence from the mean line of advance had been made, though such deviation did mean that the convoy would remain longer in dangerous waters.

After dark on the evening following the group's first success against the enemy, the destroyer which had been engaged in it left for St John's. Because of the long sweeps she had made at fairly high speeds she was running low in fuel and had calculated that if she left now and travelled at an economical rate direct for St John's, a distance of five hundred miles, she could get there without running out. This was the great curse of naval ships, the fuel problem. Destroyers were particularly susceptible to it but then they were not built with the idea of making the long passage of the Atlantic on continual operational duty.

The prospects now were not bright. We were not likely to have air cover for a day or two yet, and then very little, even if the airfields in Newfoundland were not shrouded in fog.

The Admiralty was still informing us that we were being shadowed; that 'You may expect to be attacked tonight'. They knew this from the many bearings they would have taken of the radio sighting reports the U-boats would have made to their Control Headquarters. Wireless direction-finding stations on both sides of the Atlantic and to the north enabled them to fix the position of most of the submarines.

But we were not attacked. That night and the next day and the night that followed were quiet and surprisingly peaceful. But the other destroyer had left; she was in the same predicament – down in fuel. The senior officer had left as the second night started. We did not see him go. It was like knowing that a friend was stealing away not wishing to disturb us.

So the convoy stood on with only four corvettes to guard it, and our old senior officer took the helm again in the absence of the Commander.

We watched and waited, quiet though the night was. We could not search beyond the convoy, as we were too small a force. The moon was just past the full and thus shone nearly all night which was dangerous.

The second day of August dawned fine and clear, the kind of

morning and time of year, I thought, when in peacetime I would be making ready to leave the big city and drive down to the sea for a holiday – I did not think I would ever take a holiday by the sea again, a little stream or a small lake in the mountains would be enough water for me. The sea was perfect now – rather unusual. Its dark blue surface under the paler blue sky was ruffled by a light breeze and the ship rose and fell gently to a slight westerly swell. Despite the danger it foreshadowed, it made me feel young and confident.

I had spent much time on the bridge with my glasses to my eyes and now, in the late morning, I was still searching the horizon feeling that if there were a submarine who had the convoy under observation on this side, surely I could see him in this clear atmosphere. The first lieutenant came on to the bridge and stood beside me, he had finished his work on deck and the men had gone to lunch. Lieutenant Black's mornings were always occupied in seeing that the ship was cleaned up properly inside and washed down on deck, if the sea was not already doing it for him, watching for fraying ropes and the chafing of gear which was subject to so much wear with the movement of the lively ship.

'When do you expect to see the other group?' he said at length.

'I don't know exactly. Anytime between now and late this afternoon, I suppose. They can't be so far away now.'

The C-in-C. Newfoundland, had notified us that the Western Local assigned to take the convoy over from us was being sent out earlier than usual. This had been cheering news.

The first lieutenant stretched his shoulders back and took a deep breath, enjoying the good air and the warmth of the sun. Presently he remarked that he had seen a signal in the log that we were to remain to the limit of our endurance. 'How long do you figure that's going to be, sir?'

'Roughly a couple of days; longer if we can make it.' I continued my sweep of the horizon. 'The S.O. told me just now that he intended pushing off as soon as the Local arrives, his fuel's down, too, owing to his running about the other day. And he always has claimed his fuel consumption is much greater than anyone else's, as you know. I sometimes wonder if he mixes his drinks with it; or is it that he allows about twenty per cent reserve.'

'He'd stay as long as he could.'

Black had picked up a pair of glasses and was looking while we talked.

'Yes, I know he would really, but I'm annoyed because the S.O. of the Local will take over. We who are left don't know this particular organization and, although it can't differ much from our own, the slightest variation might hinder complete co-ordination.'

He was silent for a minute, then agreed. He was a good chap to have beside you. We had been together nine months now – since I had returned from Jamaica. I admired his extreme conscientiousness. He did his job thoroughly and only came to me on matters of policy or when he was definitely uncertain of what should be done. What I particularly liked about Black was his absolute fairness to the men, though he was often stern and insisted on hard work and no lead-swinging. He would sometimes disagree with me about their employment; their hours of work, perhaps, when I wanted to accomplish a job quickly – painting the ship maybe, or carrying out a training programme. But the logic of his reasoning and the guardian-like spirit with which he upheld his men's cause made me nearly always accede to his wishes. It was known by all hands and came to be expected, that on arrival in port he was the first executive officer of any of the ships to be ashore to arrange for their pay and leave.

I lowered the glasses to my chest. 'You know, Number One,' I said, glancing aloft, 'I think I'll just go up to the crow's nest and have a look around from there. I could see a mile or two farther.'

As there was hardly room in the nest for two I sent the seaman down. This was the first time I had been in the crow's nest of a corvette, the little barrel-shaped affair high above the ship. It was interesting.

You certainly had a good view of the ship beneath you – the sharp-pointed fo'c'sle deck, the big gun on its circular platform immediately below. And looking back, the bridge, the blackening funnel and the stubby, duck-like stern beyond the engine-room skylights.

After about fifteen minutes I was ready to go down. I was getting hungry and it was lunch time, but before doing so I had a last look round. Suddenly an object came into the field of my binoculars . . . a small vessel!

125

My heart gave a leap. I held the glasses as steadily as I could and examined it carefully. It was almost on the horizon and not easy to make out at that distance. It looked rather like a destroyer coming more or less towards us but it had no mast. 'Yes, I think it is a submarine,' I thought aloud, 'coming towards us – or going away.' I dropped my glasses keeping my head still and my eyes fixed in the same direction and measured the horizontal angle between the forestay, which I could see out of the corner of my eye, and the submarine. It lay roughly ten degrees on the starboard bow. Then I turned round and shouted down to the bridge, 'Are you on a steady course now?'

'Yes, sir,' the officer-of-the-watch replied.

'Then, alter ten degrees to starboard and ring on a hundred and eighty-five revolutions – there's a submarine ahead.'

I looked again and after a moment found it. I studied it, a clearly defined, small thing which split the sharp horizon line as a distant farm house breaks the edge of a western prairie, and confirmed my earlier opinion. Then I could not keep my binoculars still, they began to shake and I lost sight of the vessel. The increased speed of the propeller had set the mast vibrating like a pneumatic drill. It was impossible for me to keep my binoculars steady. I jumped out of the nest and swung down the mast ladder and up on to the bridge.

'Shall I ring action stations, sir?' asked the officer-of-the-watch.

'Not yet. Have you seen it yourself?'

'No. Haven't seen a thing.'

'Should be dead ahead.'

The others could not see it, nor could I now. It would barely be visible from the bridge, anyhow; its distance I reckoned was seven miles.

I reported the sighting to the senior officer and went on.

The submarine did not come into view again. This was disappointing. The bridge was also shaking violently, almost enough to throw the compass off its gimbals.

It was soon evident that the U-boat had either dived or turned away and sped off. So we continued for twenty-five minutes and then commenced a systematic search of the area where we estimated he would be, dropping one or two charges in different spots.

After nearly an hour we had not gained asdic contact so concluded that we had missed our quarry; with the start he had, the chances were in his favour. So we reluctantly gave it up and returned to the convoy which we reached soon after 1300.

Collins, now a lieutenant, who doubled as asdic control as well as signal officer, came out of the asdic house viciously jamming his cap on. He turned to me.

'Hell! Where the devil did he go! Gear's all right, sir. We'd have picked him up like a shot if he'd been within range.'

'I'm sure,' I agreed.

'He just beat it, I'll bet. Don't you think so, sir?' He glanced at me and then back along our wake.

'Must have, I suppose.'

'That's the first time we've ever seen a U-boat and then he eludes us. I've been waiting for this opportunity for heaven knows how long and we don't even get a ping. We'll probably never have another opportunity like that and we couldn't have missed him by much.'

I knew how he felt, and I knew he thought that I might have stayed longer.

'If we'd had more escorts we could have stayed with it,' I said, 'but in these circumstances we couldn't in spite of his being ahead of the convoy.' I suggested that he ought not to be so pessimistic. He would have another chance.

'I hope so,' he said laconically. The asdic job was a most aggravating one.

At 1600 the relief group hove in sight, two tiny vessels at first, coming over the horizon from the westward, then another and presently two more. They had been spread out in line abreast at intervals of about three miles but the far ships were now converging on their leader as the convoy came within their view. Soon three of them took up positions on the convoy. The other two, one of which was the leader, a British destroyer of First War vintage, passed down the side of the convoy close to us and continued on in the opposite direction. They evidently intended making a sweep astern for lurking submarines but it seemed a little odd, unbecoming almost, for the senior officer himself to go.

We were now six around the convoy, our own acting senior officer having departed as the others joined because of his fuel shortage. The two who had gone off astern should be back before dark though, and that would give us a very fair force.

I had had over an hour's sleep on my settee after lunch so felt pretty fresh, though I was somewhat dispirited over past events when I went down to the wardroom for supper. But apparently the officers were more so. All but the first lieutenant were there and the three were throwing words around which were half in fun, half in earnest. The asdic officer's ears were under review and were considered insensitive. Neil, the torpedo officer, was accused of dropping charges for the sheer delight of witnessing their eruption and shaking the bed of the engines. The navigator was helping himself to macaroni as though he were bailing out the bilges of a small boat.

'Too many ships are allowed to go sculling about looking for subs,' he said, shaking the spoon over his plate with feeling, 'when they haven't any justification for leaving. We had justification! We saw one, didn't we? And that was the first time we moved away from the convoy the whole trip. But these fresh eggs,' jerking his fork and thumb in the direction of the stern, 'no sooner arrive but they bugger off and trawl around out-of-sight with less sense than a doryman.'

Well, there may have been room for argument.

The meal ended on a brighter note. Neil stated that he had balanced the wardroom wine books and, by using what he called 'a reasonable tolerance factor', had accounted for the missing bottles. But nobody was interested. A worn out tune came over the loudspeaker and the steward brought in some prune-like oranges which he said had just been discovered in the storeroom.

At 1945 an asdic contact was obtained about four miles from the convoy and we immediately carried out an attack dropping five charges. It was not a good contact but not uncertain enough to be disregarded. Twenty minutes later we let another ten charges go. Then it disappeared. We spent an hour away altogether but we felt as we returned that it was probably not the real thing; we had not been thoroughly convinced of it, yet I could not afford to ignore it. And we were approaching the edge of the Grand Bank of Newfoundland, the great submerged continental shelf with its steep cliff-like side where the water shallows abruptly from a thousand fathoms to a hundred. Fish were usually found in great quantities here and fish were the bugbear of asdic operators; many a depth charge had been dropped among them. This was annoying because conditions from now on would be much less favourable for the detection of U-boats.

It was almost dark when we rejoined. The senior officer was evidently back because I asked him what night station we were to take up as we had probably been absent when he had signalled his night orders, and he replied that we were to remain on the port beam. Unfortunately we could not see where the other ships were stationed and the radar could not distinguish them. There was no moon yet but we presumed there was a corvette on the port bow of the convoy and one on the quarter. We were soon to learn where our escorts were but not by the light of the moon.

10. Close Quarters

The sea itself filled my thoughts as I gazed down at the dark water from the lee wing of the bridge. I marvelled at its phosphorescence and at the strange fascination a phosphorescent sea always held for me. Brilliant like boiling silver on ebony, a million drops of shining metal falling from the bow wave. The sea could be beautiful. It was tonight.

The sea fascinated sometimes. But I hated it. How long had I hated the sea? Why did I? Was it fear? God! I would hate to drown! Yes, that was one fear which had been with me constantly. The prelude to drowning must be terribly lonely. One storm stood out in my memory, one in the Roaring Forties. It came into my mind automatically with the thought of drowning.

I took my hands out of the pockets of my sheepskin and rested my elbows on the rail. No breeze touched me, sheltered there behind the dodger. The ship lifted and leaned imperceptibly, settled quietly and leaned the other way. The noise of water rushing alongside as she forged ahead would have been noticeable only if it had ceased.

There was a time when I had loved being at sea – when I was a boy, a young officer. Those had been carefree days. I had delighted in the rugged life and had wanted to see new places, new things. There was excitement in saying to myself, 'Now I'm in Australia.' 'Is this really China?' 'So this is the Land of the Rising Sun on the edge of the Far East.' Those had been wonderful times. The Pacific! How lovely that ocean could be. How peaceful the water and verdant the earth; great islands with palms, brilliant flowers, gay birds and natives with their hair dyed blue and yellow and red. But I was not there now. I was on the Atlantic; nor would I wish to be any further from home. The desire to travel had worn thin. Home! That was the only place to travel to now; the one place in the world.

How the Atlantic's grim personality, its wartime personality, brought into sharp focus those who were waiting ashore. How much dearer, more vital, they seemed to become when one was in danger. And this was not selfishness altogether. It would not be easy for them if I were lost, and I pictured with physical distress their shock at getting the news. Yes, this was what made me dislike it. I wanted to be with my family and clear of risks.

Yet there were other reasons too. Maturity had brought a hatred of discomfort. How I loathed being wet; sticky all over with salt. The dreadful jolting and tumbling when you could not take a step without holding on. It had been fun in earlier years, but I had been softened by my years of comfort ashore. I was not really old – barely forty – but old for this job.

Why think of these things? Maybe I did not like the sea; there was no denying I hated the Atlantic, the ugliness of it, the grey dreariness, the eternal whine of the wind in the rigging. But it would not last for ever. One day the war would be over. One day, if I survived, I would be free again. Meanwhile I knew the sea better than I did the land almost and I was at home in a ship. Home! Damn that word!

Then the porpoises came. Three at first, in echelon, speeding just beneath the surface of the water towards the ship. They turned in perfect formation, like a naval squadron, and cut outward towards the curling bow wave. Then more came, fifty, a hundred, silver streaks woven in the clear black ocean. They fell in with the ship's track but at twice the speed, the young ones following their parents. They veined the water with bubbling phosphorescent pathways. They did not leap. Perhaps they would if I watched them for a while. I wondered how . . .

I came up straight . . . stood still, straining eyes and ears.

Two points abaft the beam I calculated.

'Captain, sir,' came an urgent voice.

I wanted to wait a moment, to assess. Would it be in the third column, the centre column?

'Captain, sir.'

'Yes, I heard it. How's your head now?'

I listened while the officer-of-the-watch asked the quarter-master.

'Two-five-six degrees, sir.'

'Ring action stations.'

131

I heard the alarm gongs ringing below and then the sound of running feet. I turned the ship towards the convoy.

'Signal from the S.O. sir, "Operation Blueberry".' I recognized the leading signalman's voice; he was always on his toes.

Then it was as though a hundred moons were shining on the convoy. Flare after flare burst into light high up in the sky, wavered and descended slowly, suspended by their invisible parachutes. All the water between ourselves and the ships was brilliantly lit, no submarine would escape being seen if he was under that umbrella of light.

After an interval of several minutes we turned back and stood away as we knew the others would be doing.

'*Now,*' I said to the first lieutenant who was standing beside me, megaphone in hand. 'Green four-oh to red four-oh, star shell, sweep.'

He leaned far over the forepart of the bridge and bellowed the order to the four-inch gun's crew. There was a shrill whistle then the deep bark of the gun, then another and another between which could be heard the slam of the breech. There were the lights, like the lamps of a sloping street, spread in a neat row away ahead, each a little higher than its predecessor as they fell gently to the water. We saw our neighbouring escort coming away from the convoy's bow and we searched with glasses the water lit by her stars as well as our own. There was no submarine, no object on the sea beneath those glaring yellow orbs.

We continued for a while turning more easterly and firing star shells at intervals. Then, our distance run, we altered course to the north-west to overtake the convoy. This, we estimated, would be the best direction to take because the convoy had by now turned ninety degrees to starboard and all ships, excluding possibly those which may have been damaged, should, according to the Commodore's signals, be steering nor'-nor'-west.

We were receiving signals! This was different from the fiasco we were involved in last year when convoy movement signals never reached us.

But still we did not know what had taken place, even whether a ship had actually been torpedoed and, if one had, whereabouts in the convoy and from which direction the torpedoes had come.

132

'Should have word by telephone at any moment now, sir,' the signal officer suggested optimistically.

'Yes,' I agreed. I was glad to hear Collins say that. 'But no one may know,' I added, more soberly.

I had been thinking in the last few minutes what I would do. It did not take much debating because I knew at the beginning where I meant to go and only wanted to review the cons. I had been convinced for some time that in such a situation, if the U-boat was forced to dive to avoid illumination, the likely place he would go would be to the rear of the convoy. And we were in the delightful position of having steered towards the spot where the rear of the convoy had been when it was attacked.

'Not quite so dark now, is it?' Black remarked, taking his binoculars down from his eyes and looking out over the sea.

I tried to gauge it. 'Perhaps not'.

We were standing together on the port side of the bridge, the navigator was on the starboard side and between us were three signalmen and two lookout men. It was a small bridge to accommodate so many if we all wanted to look towards the way we were going at once, but two of the signalmen were aft a bit so there was enough room to move about a little. Collins had been coming and going between the coding office on the lower bridge and the asdic house where his second duty lay.

'The convoy'll advance a bit yet before the moon rises,' I suggested.

We were endeavouring to penetrate the darkness both with our eyes and with the radar. Presently I saw something.

'Surely the convoy can't be that slow!' I exclaimed. 'That's a ship I see and smoking like hell.'

'Ship ahead,' cried the starboard lookout.

'Yes it is, sir. A ship.'

I called for a signalman to stand by with a small lamp. Half a minute passed.

'Can you see which way she's going, Pilot?' I asked. I had moved over to the starboard side to clear the foremast from my view and was now beside the navigator.

'Looks like she's crossing ahead.' He spoke slowly. He was trying to define the silhouette.

'I think you're right but if she is she's not on the convoy's course.'

The dim outline of a big hull beneath the thick column of black smoke pouring from her funnel, gradually became more distinct as we approached, and it soon became apparent that she was not going to cross ahead of us.

'She's stopped, Pilot, or has very little way on her.'

'Signal, sir.' It was West, the leading signalman.

'Yes, what is it?'

'From K129 to S.O. Believe two ships torpedoed. Am close to one still afloat. No U-boat in sight.'

'Umph! I might have known he'd be there,' I said, partly to the navigator and partly to myself. I knew his love for salvage work.

'He'd have been the rear escort,' the navigator figured, 'so would have come across any disabled ship first.'

By this time we were close enough to the smoking merchantman to signal. I told the leading signalman to ask 'What ship', and warned him not to use his light long in calling her up.

From where I stood I could not see any beam of light coming from the small lamp the signalman was using, so was satisfied it could not be seen far.

She lay like a black ghost as we came up and passed her a little distance off. Our eyes were used enough to the dark but, even so, we could make out little more than her shape and size and trim. No details were visible. Nor was there any sign of a corvette in the neighbourhood.

We could see she was on an even keel and had no marked list. As to damage, that was obviously hidden from us, but the huge column of inky smoke rising into the starlit sky told us of something severe below. A stopped ship at sea was always a pathetic sight to me, like a hurt and frightened animal crouching down, resigned to its fate.

Then we saw a glimmer of light from her darkened bridge and heard the signalman spelling out her name as he received the dots and dashes.

'*Loch Katrine*', the leading signalman announced.

'Make to him, "Are you in danger of sinking".' The message went out and before we had drawn away far the reply came back: 'Think not.'

We went on but not in the direction of the convoy. We would

look around first; a ship torpedoed but not sunk might be attacked again. The enemy might be close by.

'Radar says he has two ships now, the one astern we've just passed and another bearing green five-five, one mile, both about the same size.' The navigator had obtained the report through the voicepipe.

So neither of the two reported casualties were sunk! Unless this one was a straggler.

'Ask the radar if he can detect an escort,' I said.

After a brief interval the navigator said yes, the radar operator could see something which resembled an escort near the ship on the starboard bow. This looked as though our salvage expert was investigating the condition of this other ship. I reported the name of the first we had met to the senior officer and that she was apparently not in imminent danger of sinking. I thought we would go back to her presently.

Soon matters made our course of action more definite. A further signal from the corvette K129 came in indicating that she was alongside a torpedoed ship and that another escort was in the neighbourhood picking up survivors and would render assistance, if necessary, to the ship nearby. This was the first intimation we had that another escort was in the vicinity. She was evidently the one we had recently noticed in the radar; K129 would not have been noticeable, her form would have blended into the ship alongside which she seemed to be lying.

I sent another R/T message, this time to the two ships engaged in the rescue work, 'Shall screen your operations.' This was plainly our duty though I would have liked, later on, to have broken off to help the cripple we had passed.

We had been warned time after time not to undertake salvage work or even rescue work without having the protection of another escort. This advice admittedly was not adhered to very closely and, in fact, it was often difficult to do so, yet it was sound advice, for escort vessels were all too few and could not be spared. Not that merchant ships could be sacrificed more readily, but corvettes, if torpedoed, were almost as good as lost at once.

The injunction had obviously been disregarded by the first corvette coming on the scene and the second escort appeared to have adopted the same attitude. Placed as we were, therefore, the situation obviously demanded that we should act as their protector. So the two merchantmen were duly plotted on the chart and we commenced to circle them, passing each at about a mile distant.

The ship forged ahead at fifteen knots, faster than I would have preferred to go because of the high consumption of fuel at that speed, but we could not go slower than a quarter of a mile a minute if we were to attempt adequately to screen the ships. I sent a message to the senior officer informing him of what we were doing. I thought he would not welcome the absence of three escorts from his group but hoped he would not recall us before our partners had completed their work.

As I stood searching the sea ahead and on either side with my glasses, I wondered how the convoy was getting on, whether it had been attacked again – we had neither seen nor heard anything. I was vaguely concerned as to whether it had turned back on to its original course yet. We had had no signal that it had. It could not continue long in that formation, advancing in a long line on a narrow front. It was just past 2300 now and only an hour since the attack, so the convoy could not be more than ten miles from us. It would not be hard to overtake now but if we remained here long, we might have difficulty in finding it and quite a job to catch it, for every hour delayed would take two hours to make good. I supposed that these escorts would be finished in half an hour or so, then we would all go on. But I was not concerned really, except that I would have liked to have seen if there was any salvaging to be done. I had always had a hankering for a towing job, though likely enough these ships were past towing.

The first lieutenant went below to see that everything was in order and I asked him to inform the stations at the same time how the situation stood. He returned in about fifteen minutes to report that all was well.

'No light showing anywhere?' I asked.

'No,' he said, tucking his muffler tighter into his duffle coat. Then, nodding in the direction of the ships, 'Any word from these fellows yet?'

'No.'

'Won't talk more than they can help, I guess.'

'No.'

'They have a calm enough sea for the job.'

'Yes, they have.'

'Damn persistent, these U-boats.' Black was looking through his glasses.

'Yes, damn persistent, but what a night to wait for!'

'It amazes me how they get away with it.'

'Sickening, isn't it?' I agreed.

Presently I asked Black if he had looked in the galley when he was down. He had.

'The fire was drawn, I suppose?'

'Yes, sir.'

In a little while we saw on the starboard beam the black column of smoke again and the plot indicated that the derelict had not moved since we had first come upon her. The radar bearing of it was checked with the visual bearing and it coincided – the antennae was not out of alignment. We worked round it keeping a mile or so off.

I looked at the sky. Light cirro-cumulus clouds were moving slowly from the west, sometimes covering the stars and then revealing them. The night was clear, as good a night as it had been a day. I calculated the time of moonrise, it would be a little before 0100.

After some minutes the other ship came into view; she also seemed to be still. We could not see any escorts but that was hardly to be expected because they were small and their camouflage would make them less visible. But the radar could not pick them up either. They must be right in close to one or other of the merchantmen which would obliterate them from the radar. As we pressed on, the stricken ship came abeam to starboard, standing out more clearly than the first, but began to fade as we dropped her back on the quarter.

I heard the navigator acknowledge a report from the radar operator.

'Radar contact red four-oh, mile and a quarter, sir.'

His voice came with a note of urgency in it.

A few paces took me to the port side. The first lieutenant followed.

'Tell him to hold it and we'll put it ahead,' I called over my shoulder to the navigator, and to the rating at the wheelhouse voicepipe, 'How's her head?'

I had my glasses on the smooth, dark water beyond the port bow. Almost immediately the answer came back:

'Oh seven five, sir.'

'Port fifteen. . . . Steady on oh three five.'

I turned my head subconsciously to the right to compensate for the quick swing of the ship to port so that I could keep my eye on the compass bearing of the reported object. Once or twice I looked over the top of my binoculars to glance at the bow of the ship to make sure I was directing my gaze ahead.

'Red one-oh, one mile' came the report from the radar. Ten degrees on the port bow.

'Steer oh-two-five.'

'Object's small but getting larger,' called the navigator repeating the radar operator's report.

'Can you see anything, Number One?' I asked.

'Not yet, sir.'

'Ought to be showing soon. Stand by for star shell.'

He passed the order and had his binoculars back to his eyes in seconds.

'Radar says about ahead now, sir, three quarters of a mile. Going into the ground wave.'

Curse these glasses, I thought, why can't I see through them? But it was like looking for a black spider on a dark wall.

'There it is! A bit to starboard!'

I took a quick glance at the first lieutenant to see exactly which way his glasses were pointing. Then I looked again and this time I saw it.

'Submarine, I think, sir,' Black said slowly, quite steadily.

I looked hard.

'Looks more like a fishing trawler to me.'

Surely, I thought, that's a trawler. High in the bow and high aft. We're on the edge of the Banks, too. No. That's not her stern, she's high amidships. It's her bridge, her conning tower! Now I can see her stern. It's low. It's a submarine! Beam on.

'Full ahead.'

The order was instantly passed. Tenseness reigned. The engine-room would be tense, too. Full speed meant an emergency.

'Fire, Number One.'

A shrill whistle sounded and I shut my eyes. Then the gun went off and I opened them again. After what seemed like a long wait the star shell burst. There she was! A U-boat silhouetted against the falling ball of light.

I had no need of my binoculars now. The U-boat lay broadside on, about fifteen degrees on the starboard bow, less than four hundred yards away. Her bow was pointing directly across our course and I saw a short boiling wake at her stern – she had obviously just got under-way and was working her propellers at full speed.

I altered course five degrees to starboard. Was that enough? Was it too much? Was she diving? Yes.

'Fire again.'

I gripped the rail and watched the U-boat. Then a blinding flash came before my eyes. I had failed to obey my own orders. When the gunlayer blew his whistle before he pressed the trigger all eyes were to be shut. So intent had I been that I did not hear the whistle and the gunflash momentarily blinded me. I had to give up temporarily and hope that my vision would be restored quickly.

'Take over, Pilot, I can't see. She needs to come a little more to starboard, I think.'

I felt for him with my left hand and touched his sleeve. He made a small alteration of course to starboard. I stared and blinked alternately and felt desperate.

'Is she going down?' I asked the navigator.

'Yes,' he replied.

Then came Burley's voice close by me.

'Shall I fire a snowflake now, sir?'

'Yes,' I answered.

God bless that man, I thought; he never forgets!

A moment later there was a swoosh and up went the rocket. Five seconds elapsed, then it was as though a great arc lamp had been switched on. The rocket had exploded ejecting it's brilliant flare a thousand feet above.

I saw again. The U-boat was still before us, fine on the starboard bow, barely a ship's length away. But the upper part of her conning tower only was showing now.

'Stand by to ram!'

Then, hardly dropping my voice, 'Set pattern A.'

The asdic officer heard and passed the order on.

Would we make it? Would we reach her in time? We were desperately close.

In the pool of light shed by the flare we saw the U-boat's conning tower disappear. Our bow was almost on her, almost in the luminous whirlpool where her conning tower had been, the great white wake showing the short straight course she had steered – she had had no time to turn before she dived and she could not dive and turn as well.

In three seconds the bow cut the disturbed water. I waited for the crash. Another thirty feet . . . it did not come. The streak of foaming, whirling water was beneath the gun deck now. I heard no grind of steel nor felt the keel touch. Now it was beneath the foremast.

'Fire.'

Collins caught my shouted word. 'Fire one – Fire two – Fire three' – he intoned as he pressed the buzzzers. Neil and his men aft would respond instantly to the ringing bells.

I looked over the port side. The disturbed water did not extend beyond the ship on that side. The flare fell into the water astern and all was blackness.

I jumped to the starboard wing of the bridge. The streak was abreast of the after gun platform, its phosphorescence making it as clear as a white line on a highway. Then there were simultaneous explosions.

Four seconds later there were two more. The ship shook violently.

I turned and looked ahead but I would not have seen anything if there had been something there. I was shaking badly and I felt rather weak and my mouth was dry. I wanted a smoke of my pipe. I had failed to ram him – even to hit him. If we had touched him we would surely have felt it; and to scrape him would have done more damage to us than to the vessel below. The only way was to hit him squarely with the stem, and that I did not do. I felt disappointed. But mostly I felt relief.

'How far have we gone since firing?' I asked the plotting rating, speaking through the asdic house window.

'A thousand yards,' he replied after a moment.

'I'll turn now and see if you can pick him up,' I said to Collins. We turned and steamed back on a more or less reciprocal course but allowing for the movement of the submarine in the direction we had last seen him going. In a minute or so the asdic officer reported he had contact. He and the operator held it and we ran in and fired five charges. We thought it was a pretty accurate attack.

But something else was more intriguing. A strong smell of diesel oil came to us. We all remarked about it at once and looked over the side to see if any oil was visible on the water. It was too dark to see anything and we soon ran out of it. This immediately started conjecture on the bridge. Obviously it was from the U-boat.

Presently we came back again and regained underwater contact. Although it was fading and uncertain we let go ten charges set to explode deep. The sweet odour of diesel oil was heavy in the air on this run in, and by the length of time we took to pass through it, it was evident that it had spread over a much wider area.

A few minutes later Neil, the torpedo officer, appeared on the bridge. He was breathing fast.

'What are you doing here?' I asked, wondering why he had left his post when we were using depth charges.

'It was the finest thing I ever saw, sir! Think we are wasting ammunition now.'

'What do you mean?'

'Why! Didn't you see it?'

'See what?'

'Didn't you see what happened on the first attack?' he queried incredulously.

Then he told the story.

The depth charge from the starboard thrower sank fifty feet and then exploded, as did the others. It must have touched the U-boat's after deck as it went off, for a moment later the bow of the U-boat broke surface a few feet astern. She rose up out of the water to an angle of about forty degrees exposing one-third of her long slender hull. Her momentum was still carrying her forward at right angles to our course. As she hung for an instant poised in this precarious position, a depth charge which had been dropped over the stern rail exploded immediately beneath her and she disappeared in the huge column of water.

'She'll never surface again, sir,' Neil concluded.

I was dumbfounded. What I had tried to do as a secondary action had succeeded.

We resumed the patrol.

An hour later the moon came up behind light clouds and the ships at once became clearly visible and at a much greater distance. This was not good if other submarines were about but we did not know whether the ships were abandoned or not, we had had no further word from the two escorts. If we did not hear, the only thing we could do was to continue to screen them until the morning when we would see what had been done or what there was left to do. I did not care to break silence with a signal now asking how the situation stood.

The moon made it light enough now to recognize people on the bridge and it was at this time that I saw the chief engineer emerging from the shadow of the asdic house. He had neither coat nor cap on, which was unusual for him when he came to the bridge.

'Captain, sir?' he said in his inquiring sort of way.

'Yes, Chief.'

'Can you reduce speed yet, sir?'

'Why? Anything wrong?'

'I've got a hot bearing down below, sir, and it's good and hot. I've been running the fire hose on it for the last hour but that ain't good for it.'

'Why, no it isn't,' I said.

Lloyd was a great chap. He would keep the engines going fast if he thought I really needed it and adopt any measure within reason before admitting defeat. But I knew it was against his principles and very distasteful to him to run salt water on bearings. The bearing must be very hot! I had put half speed on the telegraph again after the emergency was over but I had kept a speed of nearly sixteen knots by ordering it on the revolution indicator.

'I'm sorry, Chief. If I'd known you had trouble I'd have gone slower. To what speed do you want me to reduce?'

'A hundred and thirty revs would do it, I think, if you don't mind,' said the chief, hating to ask for it.

'Why, yes, that'll be all right. Let me know soon if it's cooling down.'

I asked the navigator to decrease the revolutions accordingly.

'She'll cool down, sir. If she don't I'll tell you.'

Then he burst out, 'Sir, I could've touched it with me hand.

142

That submarine, I mean. She came up that close to the stern I could've stretched out me hand and touched her. Could've spat aboard of her. Black all over she seemed to be – bottom and all.'

'Close as all that? You were on deck?'

'Why, sir, I just came up from the engine-room to see what was doing and then . . . it was just happening. I thought she might've taken our rudder off as she came up. It was wonderful! Just wonderful, sir!'

He hesitated, seeming to feel that he might have expressed himself rather exuberantly.

'Well, I must get along below. Thank you, sir,' and off he went.

Twice we passed through the patch of diesel oil but could see no wreckage. It could hardly be expected that we should, because small objects on the water would most likely escape the keenest eye, however bright the night.

At 0130 it became foggy and before long the visibility was no more than three hundred yards. The air grew chilly and wet and the moon, as it rose higher, spread a gloom over the ship as its light partially penetrated the vaporous ceiling. We went to the second degree of readiness which released one or two men from the various stations to fetch coats or oilskins for the others and make cocoa or soup, and it permitted the cook to light the galley fire for a short while and the gunlayer to send for his trousers – he had just finished washing down his lower half when the alarm had sounded and in his hurry could not find them. I passed word to slow down to six knots, because there would be practically no danger now to the disabled ships – fog was our greatest protector. We would jog along until daylight if the fog remained, which it probably would, and if nothing untoward developed I would perhaps send half the men below to stand by in less discomfort. It was always a question to know when it was safe to belay action-stations. This lesser speed, too, would give the hot bearing a further chance.

The slow speed was a relief to the men in the boiler rooms. Four hours at stations, most of it at high speed requiring full pressure, was trying. The stokers had sweated copiously as they tended the burners behind the blazing furnaces, changing them as they carbonned up.

There was the feed pump to watch too, and the fan. But there were still moments when a stoker could stand back from the face of the furnace and have a word with the P.O.

The stoker P.O. in Number 2 boiler room was a steady type and he knew the value of public relations. They were down in a steel compartment, a cofferdam from upper deck to keel, sealed off from the rest of the ship. They could see nothing of what was going on. But they could feel the sea in the small pendulum motion of the boiler room, and they could feel the sudden violence of exploding depth charges, as though they were just beneath the steel plates they were standing on. The stoker P.O., however, had his small means of communication.

This was a voicepipe connecting the engine-room with both boiler-rooms, and the engineers posted a man to pass any information which could be gleaned during an action through to the stokers, as long as a man could be spared. Thus when an attack was about to be made the bridge told the engine-room and they told the P.O. in the boiler-room. But the bridge sometimes forgot and then it seemed to those below that they were being torpedoed, until the multiple detonations convinced them that they were not.

We had come into the oil again and the smell of it was as strong as ever. We were supposed, according to instructions, to obtain a sample of any oil which had been expelled from a submarine and I had been speaking about it to the first lieutenant earlier. But it was not easy to pick up samples of diesel oil. However, now that we were going slowly Black thought he could get it.

'Where are you going to try it, Number One?' I asked.

'On the port side of the upper deck, I think, beneath the bridge. So if you want me I'll be right handy.'

He sent for the chief bosun's mate and went below.

The navigator and I stood in the port wing of the bridge, coats buttoned up, hands in our pockets. We were talking in a desultory sort of way. He was hungry. So was I. I said that Burley usually had a sandwich for me when I was up, and a cup of cocoa.

'I don't think he will tonight,' the navigator remarked. 'He's hurt his hand.'

'Not when he fired that snowflake?'

'No, before that. When he was coming up after the alarm went.'

'Bad?'

144

'Broken or sprained perhaps.' The navigator tucked his muffler tighter into his sheepskin. 'He stayed up here just the same and passed your wheel orders and fired the rocket but he was pretty uncomfortable, I guess. Said one of the lads going down from the bridge to his station knocked him down the ladder as he was coming up – it was dark, you know – and he landed across the small-arms hatch. Lucky he didn't break his back.'

'Yes. Tough luck. Hope it doesn't put him out.'

It was very quiet. The breeze had died out with the fog and the small bow wave could hardly be heard – an occasional lap, that was all. Heavy drops of moisture fell now and then from the rigging and made little sounds as they hit the deck. We could faintly hear the turn of the asdic wheel.

The sick-berth attendant crept on to the bridge on the other side and whispered to Leading Signalman West that he had strapped up Burley's hand. He had had a casualty!

'That's good, Tiffy. Any bones broken?'

'I don't think so but he won't be able to use the signal lamp for a while.'

West looked at his friend with envy in his eyes. 'Gee! I'd like to get below for a smoke.'

The S.B.A. looked across the bridge and then behind him. 'I've got one here,' he whispered, moving a hand in his coat pocket.

'Alight? Hell! You fool! What did you come on deck for with that?'

The S.B.A. suddenly felt sensitive.

'All right. Come here,' said the leading signalman in an undertone.

Behind the asdic house the S.B.A. took his hand carefully out of his pocket. West cupped the prohibited light in both hands and drew in, sucking its balm down his windpipe. He looked up at the misty vault overhead as he slowly let the thin smoke out of his lungs. Then he pushed the half-burned thing back into his friend's hand.

'Best I ever had, chum! Now you better bugger off down, quick.'

The leading signalman resumed his stand. He was smiling. Tension had dropped away.

The radar operator called again. I could hear quite distinctly what he was saying to the navigator through the voice pipe from where I stood.

'I've just started up again, sir,' came the voice, 'and I think there's something in the ground wave. It's too close to get the direction.'

I stood up against the dodger and looked ahead.

'Keep a sharp look-out there,' I sang out to the look-outs and signalmen on the bridge. 'Radar reports something close.'

'You're not sure?' I heard the navigator say down the pipe. Then he said to me, 'He's not certain at all, he just thinks.' The radar was either right or wrong to the navigator.

'Tell the wheelhouse to stand by the telegraph,' I said.

I peered into the fog, glasses were no use, they only magnified the vapour. I naturally looked in the direction in which we were going because that was where our greatest risk of collision lay.

Two minutes passed. I remained still, looking, listening. Then I heard a shout from the deck below.

'Submarine on the port beam.'

It was Black's voice.

I turned instantly and saw it; a U-boat, fully surfaced, lying motionless, no more than a hundred and thirty yards away. She was a little before the beam and her bow was pointing almost towards us showing the fore part of her starboard side at a fine angle. A backdrop of fog hung behind her grey, shadowy conning tower.

'Full ahead! Hard aport! Port beam – submarine – open fire!' The gun was already loaded.

Then the first lieutenant was up. He was yelling at the gun's crew.

'Train her fast. Red eight-oh. Shoot when you're on.'

He looked along the bridge rail then down at the gun again.

'Red nine-oh. Swing her round!' he shouted.

'Come on! Get her on!' I called back to Black as I glanced down at the gun barrel and back at the high, blunt-nosed bow of the still, silent craft. The guntrainer was coming around but ninety degrees was a long way to wind a four-inch quickly.

The ship glided slowly on. She could not pick up headway

146

swiftly like a destroyer. And she was too sluggish on the helm at this speed to turn fast – there was little point in it, anyway; the enemy was inside our turning circle.

The U-boat was end-on now, wraiths of mist passing over her fore deck and before her superstructure farther back. Her hawse-pipes resembled great eyes staring at us.

The navigator muttered what I was thinking, 'Hope she doesn't let loose.'

She was drawing abaft the beam but either the gunlayer or trainer, or both, could not find her. The dimness of the foggy night made it difficulty for them. Then the submarine drew just abaft the safety bearing and the gun could not reach any farther. Perhaps three quarters of a minute had gone by since she had first been seen.

Then there was a colossal sound of escaping air, as though the top of a high pressure chamber had been blown off, and the U-boat went down like a stone.

She had made no forward movement, had obviously vented all her ballast tanks at once. One moment she was there, fully buoyant, the next she was gone. She submerged so quickly that I could hardly believe my eyes as I looked at the empty sea with the curtain of fog beyond.

The ship was at last gathering way and as she did so ten charges were dropped set to explode at varying depths. But our distance from the submarine was too great to inflict a fatal wound, the best they could have done was to have shaken her, perhaps badly, with her negative stability. An enemy report was sent out on the wireless.

We ran away for a thousand yards or more so that we could place ourselves suitably for an asdic attack but when we came back we could not establish contact. We spent half an hour around the spot where the U-boat had submerged but failed to obtain the slightest indication of her presence. It was not that the submarine could have got out of range so quickly, it was a matter of water conditions. She was under a thermal layer which the asdic could not penetrate. We expanded our radius but still could find no trace of the enemy.

Her commander had evidently surfaced his boat not ten minutes before we had encountered her. The radar was obliged to shut down for five minutes every half-hour to cool the motor and it must have been during this interval that she had come to the surface. Had she not been submerged before the radar was switched off, she would have been detected. The German on the hydrophones obviously had not heard our propeller before she came up, and this may have been because it was turning slowly, although I would have thought that he should have heard it. Possibly he did not listen very attentively. I did not think it was a case of his hearing the beat of a propeller close to and the captain deciding to come up and torpedo the ship to which it belonged, in spite of the fact that our revolutions at this time equalled those of the average merchant vessel travelling at normal speed. Had this been his intention, we would have received the benefit of his idea. It appeared to me that he was taken completely by surprise and was intent on making a rapid escape.

Up to this time I had not known that a submarine could submerge without going ahead on her engines, which, with the hydrophones set to dive, would drive her down. I had never been told of this practice or read of it. But I knew it now. I found out afterwards, after much inquiry, that a U-boat could submerge without moving ahead if she vented all her tanks simultaneously, including her emergency tanks if a hasty descent was called for, but that this would not be done except in dire necessity. To this U-boat the necessity had been dire.

Now I knew for certain that danger lurked in the offing. If the fog lifted it would be very potent.

We had failed to sink the latest member of Admiral Doenitz' fleet, or even inflict damage on her. Could we have done either? Had I slipped up somewhere? Was it lack of preparedness? How many C.O's asked themselves the same questions during the war!

I thought about it for a bit, standing on the inevitable bridge staring into the fog. The only thing I could have wished was that the gun had gone off. It was a great pity the layer and trainer had been unable to bring the gun to bear, but it was not their fault. I knew that. They had to see to fire. I could not say I wished we had been in a different relative position because there was not a better one, unless it was 150 yards farther over and we had accidentally crashed into the boat. But our speed would have been too slow to have even cracked her pressure hull. It was not for want of skill or effort afterwards that the asdic ratings did not hear a submarine echo.

We would never find ourselves so near a U-boat again – or so I thought.

11. The Derelict

We resumed our patrol. Time passed slowly. The chief engineer had reported the bearing had cooled down. Sometime before dawn Black remarked it was the longest night he ever remembered. It was a summer night and a short one, but it did not feel like summer. The clammy chill of fog penetrated heavy clothes and the tension, the expectancy, made shivering easy, and the silence made its own sound.

Dawn started to show itself about 0430. Half an hour later I considered it light enough to move in though the fog was still very dense.

For some time we had noticed on the radar that one of the merchantmen had been slowly moving. The distance plotted between the two had been a mile originally, now it was four. We were nearer to the stationary ship, but it seemed wise first to investigate the one that was apparently underway.

She was making to the westward which was convenient as we could approach her from astern – the only safe way in fog. We slowed down as we came within half a mile; the radar was not accurate below this range. In a few minutes a dark, bulky shadow resolved itself into the broad stern of a big ship, a modern cruiser stern. Then her quarter came into view. She was a tanker with her funnel aft and we could see at once by her trim that she was well down by the stern.

'Must be flooded aft,' someone remarked. The part of her we could see looked so low and heavy I wondered how she could make any way.

We moved up abreast her bridge – she was certainly big, all of ten thousand tons. Her Plimsoll line was underwater. I put the megaphone I was grasping to my mouth.

'What speed are you able to make, Captain?'

After a moment the answer came back, 'I'm under tow. My engine-room and stokehold are flooded.'

I glanced forward at her fo'c'sle head. I had not noticed it but now I saw a heavy manilla rope leading ahead down into the water. So that was it!

The voice came again across the water, 'There's a corvette towing me and she's doing all right.'

'Good,' I replied. 'We'll probably stick around and lend a hand. What's your name?'

'*G. S. Walden.*'

With that we increased the revs a bit and pushed on ahead.

As we lost sight of the tanker, trimmed on so uneven a keel, the little corvette loomed up through the fog, her green and white hull blending with the fog and her single mast seeming very small in comparison with the huge up-canted bow behind her.

K129! I might have known. How could a tugboat operator resist it!

Her anchor cable was trailing out over her stern; they were using the strongest thing they had, nothing else on board would tow a water-logged ship like that without breaking.

We came abreast about fifty yards off. I recognized the captain standing in the starboard wing of the bridge. He had a white woollen toque covering his bald head. He waved. All hands seemed to be on deck looking at us as we jogged along almost hand in hand. Friends returned waved salutations.

'You've got a job on your hands,' I shouted through the megaphone.

'I've got her well fast. I reckon I'm making two and a half knots. Were you around us all night?'

'Yes,' I answered.

'I thought you were but I wasn't certain because I didn't hear anything after you first said you would screen us. Did you see anything?'

'Yes. We caught one fellow napping and gave him a good belt. May have sunk him.'

To my surprise a cheer went up from the men on the other ship's deck – they had been listening to the conversation – and it was so spontaneous that I felt a flush of pride surge through me, something I had not felt the night before. Then I had to spoil it by admitting failure in our second encounter.

'But there's another U-boat handy,' I shouted. 'We passed him about 0200 and missed him. How about the other ship still stopped back there, do you know what her condition is?'

'She's the *Loch Katrine*,' replied the captain through his megaphone. 'A total loss, so Knobby says. He stayed around last night long enough to take the crew off her – thirty-five, I believe. Then he beetled off to rejoin the convoy after telling me she wasn't worth towing.'

Knobby was in a four-stacker, one of the relieving escorts.

'In that case then I'll screen you,' I said. 'What's your course?'

'Two-nine-six. Thanks, I'll be damn grateful.'

'Two-nine-six. Aye aye, I'll keep ahead within a couple of miles.'

We drew away but had not gone a mile when the radar reported an object at extreme range more or less ahead. The radar soon identified it as a large ship and as we closed the distance it soon became evident that it was not underway. As usual we approached it slowly and with care, I did not want to collide with it.

A big black hull suddenly came into view two ships' lengths ahead. I glanced at her waterline. She was stopped. We turned and came parallel to the big freighter. She was deep in the water as though heavily laden, with her bow lower than her stern and a list to port of about ten degrees. She was obviously not old, in fact, fairly new but ugly; a war-built ship. Her stunted fore- and main-masts and thin signal-mast amidships made her particularly unattractive, and her untidy state did not improve her appearance.

There was no visible damage but it was obvious she was partially flooded.

We could see no sign of life on board, her decks were deserted, one boat on that side gone, the other lying hooked to her for'ard fall. A raft was drifting alongside. There appeared to be no one on the bridge, nor the usual familiar figure at the galley door. I picked up the megaphone again and shouted 'Ship ahoy', repeating it several times, directing my voice up and down the ship. My shouts echoed back in a flat, dismal way but there was no reply. She seemed empty and dead, a melancholy phantom on a lifeless sea overhung by mist.

We steamed slowly around her bow. The heavy paravane booms, formed like a bastard bowsprit, stood out at a drooping angle conforming to her low-lying fo'c'sle. The jaws of the wires which had passed through the boom and spread out beneath the water on either side, had, at one time, probably cut a path for her through some distant mine-field.

No damage could be seen on the other side either, but one of her lifeboats was still in its chocks on the boat deck. The other was lying water-logged alongside, still hooked on to the falls. A large raft lay farther aft attached by a long line to the main rigging.

As we rounded the broad stern, devoid of name or port of registry as was customary in wartime, one of the look-out men spoke and pointed away from the ship.

'I hear a cry out there, sir.'

We listened. Yes! There it was. A thin voice somewhere in the fog. Well, I thought, we will see about that presently.

We came up the starboard side and to our surprise saw a man standing on deck outside the 'midship accommodation. On closer inspection I could see he was a Negro. He had on an overcoat and a fedora and was holding two suitcases as though he was about to step down a gangway and go ashore. An odd looking rig, I thought, for a man in a sinking ship. I called to him through the megaphone.

'Are you the only man aboard?'

He shouted something that we could not hear, and when I said, 'What?' he put his suitcases down carefully, cupped his hands around his mouth and shouted, 'Yes'. I told him we would take him off.

I had already given the order for the boarding party to be called away and they were now in the boat gripping the life-lines. The water around the stern swirled and frothed as our propeller beat astern and the way came off the ship. The falls ran out and the boat went into the water.

I watched the party, seven of them, row over to the derelict, lay hold of a rope ladder which was hanging dejectedly down over the leaning side and one by one with considerable effort, for the lowest rung was well clear of the water, climb up and swing aboard.

With all the fickleness of the weather on the Grand Banks, the fog suddenly lifted, like a curtain being drawn back from a window in the early morning, and we could see a good five miles. This was unpleasant. To be exposed to the possible view of a submarine while stopped picking up boats and so on was not the best thing, and it seemed unkind in such visibility to be away from our friend and his tow which we could now see about four miles away. And just at this moment the asdic found a contact which took us a mile away in the opposite direction. It was a false alarm, however, so we were soon able to return and make over to a lifeboat which we had noticed when the fog cleared, a few hundred yards from the wreck and from which had come the cry we had heard not long before.

The lifeboat had a single occupant, another Negro, who seemed extremely happy, in fact hysterically overjoyed, when he saw he was going to be rescued, and sang snatches of something in a remarkably strong voice; it might have been a devotional song. It sounded in the stillness like a spiritual of some sort, but I did not recognize it. The tall Negro was unable to take his eyes off us as we approached slowly but broke off his song frequently to apply a few strokes to a hand pump, apparently as a matter of habit, his black head never turning away from us. The lifeboat was a large one and was more than half full of water. He waved with both arms and tried to go on his knees on the thwart but could not balance that way.

A man went down on a rope and helped him up. He was wet and very cold and quite exhausted. He said he had to pump a great deal. Then he shivered violently, collapsed on the fo'c'sle and wept.

We saw our own boat pulling towards us and went to meet it. I felt some relief. We were stopped no more than a minute while the boat was hooked on and hoisted clear of the water – their drills were of value now – and in another minute, with all hands manning the falls, the boat was at the davit head and its occupants scrambling inboard.

The navigator, who had been in charge, came to the bridge.

'Well,' I asked, 'what are her chances?'

'Fair, if the sea doesn't get up, I think.' He was holding a small square box by the strap which went round it. I recognized it to be a standard merchant navy chronometer box.

'Where was she flooded?'

'Number two and three holds are flooded and the engine-room and, of course, the stokehold.'

'She was in ballast, she must have settled fifteen feet.'

'Yes, sir, but I don't think she'll go down for a while if the weather holds like this; she might stay afloat for a week, she seemed steady enough while I was aboard.'

'What does the Negro say?'

'He says the ship was torpedoed on the starboard side and he was caught in the engine-room. When he got out the ship was abandoned. Put on his shore-going clothes because he thought he'd be picked up. Has three suitcases – rather a lot of luggage for a fireman, I'd say.'

His confidence in his preservation had been a lot different from that of his shipmates.

Leading Signalman West was on the bridge by this time and I asked him how he had found things.

'I have the confidential books, sir. Most of them were scattered on the deck of the wireless cabin. It looked as though the operator had put them in the steel box but upset them when he went to pick the box up. Probably he hadn't secured the lid. He was evidently in too much of a hurry to gather them up again and had left them all lying there.'

'Anything else?' I queried.

'Nothing of importance, sir. I picked up a few things, a couple of signal lamps, three pairs of binoculars and a telescope and a boat's radio set.'

'The telescope doesn't look a very good one,' I suggested, looking at the cumbersome thing which one of the signalmen had up to his eye and was trying to focus. 'But it may be useful to you. Let's have a look at the binoculars.'

'Yes, sir, this pair looks the best.'

I looked through each in turn at the ships astern and came back to the pair he had first indicated. 'These'll suit me.' They were an almost new pair of Bausch & Lomb.

We often wished afterwards that we had taken more gear off the ship. We would like to have had her pom-pom gun and her large floating raft. We had lost one of our custom-built ones recently when it was swept over the side. I also very much wanted another compass. We made good use of what we had purloined, though; the portable radio set, which was built into a fibre case, we eventually had fitted in the armoured shelter on the after gun platform to serve as an emergency wireless station in case of distress and the main equipment being put out of action.

It was a long time before the whole story of the derelict was revealed to me.

She was built as the *Empire Selwyn* in 1941, 7167 tons. After returning from Murmansk in the spring of '42 she was transferred from British registry to the flag of Belgium and was making her maiden voyage under the name of the *Belgian Soldier*. She had on board a crew of 53, 24 Belgians, 23 British, of whom eleven were coloured, 4 French and 2 Portuguese. Lifeboat drill was carried out at the Tail o' the Bank in the Clyde and she joined Convoy O.N.115 as Number 94, the fourth ship in the ninth column.

When the convoy made an emergency alteration of course ninety degrees to starboard, the Commodore turned his ships by signal, first forty-five degrees and ten minutes later another forty-five degrees, which was the customary method of carrying out this manœuvre. But the leading ship of the ninth column on the starboard wing thought a third signal had been sent out and made a further turn of forty-five degrees. The other three ships in the column followed in the wake of their leader, the last of which was the *Belgian Soldier*.

Though unknowingly separated in the darkness, all went well until just after 2300, when a colossal explosion occurred inside the ship. She was thrown heavily to port but immediately righted herself. At the same time a geyser of water shot up from the fore deck carrying with it the wooden hatch covers of number two hold. Water and broken hatches rained down on the starboard side of the bridge and boat deck.

The captain rang the telegraph to 'stop' and heard a faint tinkle from the bell in the engine-room but received no acknowledging signal. He picked up the telephone to the engine-room but it was dead. Although there was an emergency arrangement on the bridge to cut off the steam to the engines, this had not been connected when the ship left port. So no heed was taken of the device.

When the captain ordered the alarm to be rung, no sound came. But there was no need. Deck officers were on the bridge and the men were gathering on the boat deck. The ship was in utter darkness. An S.O.S. was sent out on emergency power but no reply was heard by the radio operator. During this time those on the bridge tried to ignite the rockets to indicate they had been torpedoed, but they would not fire.

On inspection, the chief officer found the torpedo must have entered the starboard side between number two and three holds, the latter a deep tank. The bulkhead was obviously destroyed, and water, though not much, was coming through the opening between the coal bunkers and stoke-hold, the watertight-door having been apparently left open contrary to orders for night steaming. The engine-room was full of steam, and water seemed to be seeping in from the stoke-hold. The dynamo was broken. The big reciprocating engine was still turning slowly.

Confusion seemed to possess some of the crew on the boat deck and it became contagious. The dark, moonless night made it worse; and they had already discovered that both starboard boats had been damaged by the falling hatches. The foremost of the two was hopelessly wrecked.

Without orders twelve men climbed into number two boat, the first one on the port side, and thirty-five men got into number four, the second boat on that side. Each was amply capable of holding them all. The first was lowered properly, but as soon as it touched the water it tipped over and six men were thrown out. Their cries were lost astern. Then the boat righted itself but was full of water and remained hooked to the rope falls. The other six men climbed back aboard by the falls.

The second boat was now lowered with the thirty-five men, black and white, sitting and standing in various attitudes flanked by oars and spars and kegs of water. It fouled the rope ladder on its way down but this was cut away. It went on down on an even keel until it was three feet from the water when the forward fall became entangled. When the man at the davit cleared the fall it took charge and he let it run out. The bow of the boat dropped, hit the water and submerged and unhooked. All the men were thrown out and twenty-two drifted away as the others had done. The boat, half filled, swivelled round and drifted, still hooked on to the after fall. Thirteen men had been holding the life-lines and up these they swarmed and got back on deck, among them the first engineer but not the fourth.

It was then that these men discovered that the *Belgian Soldier* was still underway. The first and fourth engineers had been on watch when the torpedoing had occurred and in escaping had left the main engine running. Perhaps the steam had driven them out of the engine-room.

157

Now the remaining men turned to the least damaged boat on the starboard side. It was lowered, but filled as soon as it touched the water and was left trailing by its falls, bumping against the black side of the ship as it yawed about.

Still no order had been given to abandon ship.

The two large rafts in the after rigging on each side were released and fell into the water properly and their little lights went on automatically. But they were secured to the rigging by long painters and were being towed too far out for the men to reach them. So they turned to the large raft in the starboard rigging of the fore-mast. This time they cut the painter. Twenty men tried to board it; they all made it but it was deeply laden. Unlike the rafts being towed farther back, this one hugged the hull of the slowly passing ship and it was with the greatest difficulty that the men pushed it off enough to bypass the trailing water-logged number three boat and then let it come back to pass inside the after raft. Clinging to the steel side as it dropped aft it was drawn in under the counter. The ship being down by the head the propeller was partly out of the water and was still turning! It cut the raft in two and threw it out of the small wake. Twelve of the twenty men regained the broken raft and hung on, six on each half. Of these, six died during the night.

Fifteen minutes had elapsed since the *Belgian Soldier* had been hit.

Those who were left on board, the master, the radio operator who had done his best with S.O.S's, and six men, went for'ard. They threw overboard several small floats, then launched the last large raft from the port rigging, cleared the painter and clambered in.

This one wanted to cling to the tall side, too, and the occupants also had difficulty in fending it past the wallowing boats still being dragged along. As they dropped back close to the stern they could not reach to shove off where the plating of the hull swept up into the curving counter. Suddenly a propeller blade came up out of the water and struck the raft. It was thrown up and the men spilled out. But they all regained it.

The captain did not know until then that the engines were still turning; he thought the ship was merely carrying her way. He saw the *Belgian Soldier*, apparently crewless, steam on alone into the misty night at three or four knots.

His raft picked up four men but could not reach some whose life-belt lights they could see and whose calling they could hear.

By and by one of our corvettes came on the scene and by 0315 had picked up the thirtieth man. Twenty-one were lost.

The boat from which we had taken the Negro was number four, the one which had half filled and swivelled round and was held by its after fall. He must have boarded it and cast it adrift when the ship came to the end of her run.

I was called to London later in the year to testify before an Admiralty board as to the condition in which I had found the ship; for she was never seen again, unless it was by a U-boat, in which case she would have been quickly sent to the bottom. A tug had been sent out from St John's following my signal to the effect that if the weather held she could probably be towed into port, but the tug, when it reached the position, was unable to find her.

The object of the Admiralty board was to determine who was responsible for her loss, whether it was the enemy or the master of the ship. The master was exposed to the accusation that he had abandoned his ship without due cause, which was a criminal offence. It was a crime which had my greatest sympathy, for many men lost their lives by staying with their ships too long. On the other hand, a large number of damaged ships, the value of which was inestimable at the time, were brought safely into harbour by the courageous efforts of their crews. What decision the Admiralty came to in this case I never learned.

We were now back with the *G. S. Walden* and the corvette towing her. Soon after we had taken up our station the fog shut down again. This damp, capricious element was usually referred to as THE fog because, to us, it always appeared to be the same one. It seemed to be like a vagrant, hungry animal; it just went away and slept for a while and then returned to hinder us again. But it often protected us from our enemies.

The captain of the corvette astern intended to tow the tanker until a tug came out from Newfoundland. It would take a tug about eighteen hours to reach us – the distance was now two hundred miles. We received word, however, that one would be dispatched later in the day.

My friend, I knew, would have liked to do the job himself and he could have done it. And I would not like to have stayed alongside the tanker nearly all night as he did, laying out his cable and making fast to the ship. He had not been at all certain that we were still screening him, and if I had decided to rejoin the convoy he would have been faced with the prospect of crawling along at no more than three knots and being severely hampered in his manœuvrability, a situation which he actually had faced before we caught up with him at dawn.

The captain of the British G. S. *Walden* was, of course, equally brave. The one object he had in mind was to save his ship despite the chance of being attacked again. Neither of the ships knew yet how close they had come to destruction. I realized it now as I thought it over and reconstructed the happenings of the night before.

We had just passed these two, one alongside the other, the bigger ship being clearly visible to us, when we came upon the first U-boat. His position in relation to these two ships was such that the tanker would have been visible to him, too. The submarine was stopped, his bow pointing towards her. A final blow was what occupied the mind of the submarine commander – or he might have seen us sooner.

We jogged along during the morning. We had to traverse the course line at wide angles even at five knots to keep from increasing our distance from the tow. We were really not of very great value as an escort as we had only seven depth charges left and they were all deep ones that could not be set to explode at less than two hundred feet. We could not lay down any sort of established pattern. But I did not care to ask to borrow any charges from the other corvette because she might need them herself after being relieved by the tug.

I went down to the wardroom for lunch. It seemed to have been a long time since I had seen the place, so much had happened since I had had my last meal there. It looked comfortable and the table was laid nicely – it always was except in bad weather. And it was somehow agreeable to be out of the daylight – the deadlights were screwed down against the ports to seal the hull. The electric light gave a pleasant impression of warmth.

I glanced past the framed ship's crest over the hard, leather-covered settee to the bell-shaped speaking trumpet above the door as I took my seat. It was comforting to know that I could be communicated with by the officer-of-the-watch if he wished to speak to me. I had been to some trouble to have it specially installed.

The conversation, as lunch started, was inevitably about our recent activities. But it did not last long; it was interrupted by Neil's voice coming out of the speaking trumpet.

'Captain there?'

'Yes,' shouted Black who was nearest to the trumpet.

'Hydrophone effect on the asdic, sir.'

That was all, and before we could scramble out of the wardroom the alarm gongs were ringing.

It was not often that an officer rang the action alarm before I reached the bridge but it was his privilege to do so at any time if he considered he was justified. In view of the several fruitless occasions I had recently called the men to action, I did not think the officer-of-the-watch would have them out on his own account unless he had a fairly sound reason for doing so.

I had a little difficulty climbing the only ladder to the bridge because I was caught in the tide of men rushing down to their stations, but avoided being thrown back as Burley had been. I was puffing when I got there but grasped what Neil had to tell me.

'It was red seven-oh – wheel's hard aport – should be nearly ahead now. It sounded like a fast-moving engine and it's not the other corvette because I checked it, her engines are much slower than this, anyway. Radar was shut down, it's just started up again. Sixty revs are on now.'

''Midships,' I ordered. 'One-one-oh revs. All right, go to your station, Neil.' Then to the navigator, 'Try the radar on either side of the bow. Steady the helm.'

'Hydrophone effect about green two-oh,' came the report from the asdic operator, 'loud and fast, but the arc's getting too big now to get a good bearing.'

'Radar says might be something in the ground wave, if so it's to starboard,' said the navigator.

'Steer ten degrees to starboard. Ring on one-three-oh revs.'

We were now placed in the most precarious of all positions, on a collision bearing with an invisible vessel who might be a friend; I did not know. Nor did I know her course precisely, but we stood a very good chance of ramming or being rammed and the latter would send us to the bottom, even if it were a submarine. We could see no more than a cable's length, two hundred yards, but we had to sight her if we could.

There was a shell already in the gun. My order was passed to load a full charge behind it. Into the chamber went the cordite and through the lock went a firing tube.

'Half cock!' I heard the breach-worker shout.

Not three minutes had elapsed since we had risen from the ward-room table; now I was craning my head over the dodger trying to see through the murk. My heart was beating fast.

A dark smudge appeared dead ahead. In three seconds it revealed its shape – long and low, high amidships. A submarine!

She was crossing our course with slight closing inclination going from starboard to port. Her bow wave made it evident she was making eight or ten knots.

'Hard aport. Full ahead. Open fire!'

The submarine was on the port bow now a little more than a hundred yards off. The ship was swinging to port – but not fast enough – the U-boat was inside our turning circle; we could never reach her. Would the gun never fire! Eighty yards . . . seventy only . . . broader on the port bow now.

At last!

With the gun on the depression rail and the ship swinging fast, it fired at point blank range, scarcely a ship's length away, two hundred feet, the enemy broadside on to the line of fire.

On that instant a gaping hole appeared at the base of the U-boat's conning tower, squarely in the centre. It was accom-panied by a hail of fire from the port point-fives and the Vickers machine-guns. The high explosive shell burst, ripping the near side of the conning tower out. I saw the pieces fly and then the yellow smoke of the projectile rising within.

She was visibly diving. Another round went out of the gun but went over; her bow was under water. A depth charge from the port thrower sailed through the air, fell with a splash into the water but was short of its mark. The boat went down fast and was beneath the surface before the fog closed over the place where she submerged.

We straightened out and steamed away as was necessary before making an asdic attack, and called our friend to slip his tow and join the hunt. The asdic was playing tricks on us. There seemed to

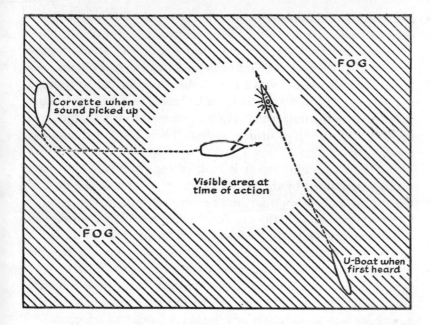

Corvette when
sound picked up

Visible area at
time of action

FOG

FOG

U-Boat when
first heard

be not one submarine but five, maybe six, surrounding us in all directions. It was one of the enemies of asdic – fish.

Fifteen minutes later the fog lifted. The visibility might have been four miles. There was the other corvette with a shackle of cable dragging from her stern. Her captain had placed a demolition charge along it so that he could release himself in a hurry and this he had fired when we called for his assistance. There, too, was the tanker about two miles away, lying still. The U-boat was not to be seen. We searched for two hours without success and then gave it up.

The question of whether the submarine survived would probably never be answered for me. If no German U-boat base witnessed the return of a submarine that August with the port side of her conning tower blown away, then the dive we saw her make was her last. Many of the crew said they saw her pennants painted on the side of her conning tower; most said it was U-26 but some said U-23. This seemed unlikely to be the pennants of this boat because these low numbers were supposed to be assigned to old boats and this one appeared to be a modern 740 tonner. Personally I was so intent on watching her movement through the water that afterwards I could only remember her size – she was longer than a corvette – and that she seemed to be painted pale grey or pale blue.

I estimated that the first shot had been fired about twenty seconds after she had come into view and that she had disappeared fifteen seconds later. It was a remarkable shot, for the layer could not depress the gun any further, yet he had to wait before pressing the trigger for the trainer to bring the gun on the target, which was difficult with the ship turning so fast. Their combined aim was good.

A U-boat's conning tower is built of comparatively light steel and is surmounted by the bridge. There is a hatch in the deck of the bridge and, below that another in the deck of the conning tower which is actually the pressure hull. When the boat makes an emergency crash dive the men on the bridge jump down the hatch and the last man closes it. They may or may not all go through the lower hatch down into the control-room and this hatch may not be closed. A U-boat was often conducted in her dive from a control position in the conning tower where the eye-pieces of the periscopes are located, in which case the lower hatch was left open.

If it were so in this case, the sea would have poured through the open hatch as soon as the gaping conning tower became submerged and the control-room would have been flooded. The U-boat would never have come out of her dive. Had it not been so, the bases of the periscopes would have been demolished, the bridge badly damaged and the conning tower hatch probably so badly buckled that it would not open.

The true story would probably ever remain a mystery, to me at any rate, and my curiosity unsatisfied.

12. Autumn 1942

The club was known as The Crow's Nest. Those who conceived it had apparently thought the name nautically appropriate for the top floor of a building which could be reached only by fifty-four stairs, mainly on the outside. The weather was cold and, from where I sat by the window overlooking the waterfront, the harbour of St John's had a dismal appearance. My mood was in keeping with the look of the harbour.

It was mid-November; the summer had passed and the fall was nearly over. It was really winter now in these parts. The surface of the water below me was grey and a watery sun was trying to shine through the partially overcast sky. But it was warm and comfortable in The Crow's Nest; a huge log fire was burning in the hearth and there was the friendly sound of ice being dropped into glasses at the bar. There were few people in yet; lunch would not be properly under way for another hour.

The question which had been nagging at me for the past few weeks was see-sawing in my mind again. Should I try to make another voyage? Was I justified in trying, with my nerves as jumpy as they were?

Symptoms of jadedness – some called it sea-fatigue – were beginning to show on the surface. There were always fears, of course. But these fears could normally be held in check, could be stowed away in the recesses of the mind. Now, and more frequently, they were pushing to the fore. They were vivid pictures of the ship breaking up under stress of weather, of getting in among the ships of the convoy on dark, invisible nights, as had happened, and being run down by a heavily laden merchantman, of being torpedoed and trying to abandon ship on a rough night.

The worst time was dusk, when the dull day was fading and another ominous night was bearing down. I hated the sight of the yellowish-grey light, the dun seascape, the cold, curling waves as the evening dissolved into blackness.

There were times when I had been unjustifiably irritable,

165

intolerant, which made me angry with myself afterwards – and probably angered others more. It was stupid, but there it was! Yet it was hard to tell how acutely I had been affected. I wondered how good my perspective was in judging my own nervous behaviour. I felt certain I had had enough.

I had spoken of it several days before to the captain of one of our ships, rather a friend, and he had tried to offer some comfort. 'Only one more trip,' he had said. 'Why not hang on?'

We had talked of the success of the Barber Pole Group. Only two ships lost in ten crossings. The tanker towed into port late last August was probably back on the high seas by now. I mulled over the past few months as I sat now before the window of the club.

We had two enemies; the U-boats and the weather. I often wondered which was the worst. The submarines had been very trying. There had been short periods of fairish weather but there had been a great many gales.

There was that dark night when we had been running in the Western Approaches before a high quarterly sea, four of us together in line abreast making for port after leaving the convoy. The ship was pitching and rolling deeply, slowly; too slowly – the speed of the waves rushing up behind almost synchronized with the speed of the ship. At times she rode like a surf boat before the rollers with her nose pointing down.

At 2000 the leading hand of the blue watch which was coming on deck found he was short of a man, a rating who had been taken ill, and requested a replacement. He was offered a radar rating and chose the one he knew could steer best. The man's first duty was after look-out.

At 2045 the stern rose high in the air and the ship rolled over fifty degrees to port and hung there for an interminable time until the great sea relented and ploughed its way forward along the keel. When the leading hand, making his rounds in the darkness, was able to get aft several minutes later, the look-out-man was not on the high gun platform. He made a quick search and discovered the bulwarks on the starboard quarter bent inboard. Going up to the gun platform above the boat deck again he found the protective plating around it almost flattened to the deck and the large raft on the port side gone. He struggled forward and reported to the bridge.

There was a grim search of the upper deck by all available hands,

166

but the mute evidence of damage told that the look-out-man had been swept overboard. The great sea rushing obliquely at the stern must have buried the whole after end of the ship. She had been pooped with a vengeance. The boy, hardly nineteen, may have been knocked senseless as the tide of water hit him and bore him through the obstructing spars.

We turned, all four ships, to search but realized the hopelessness of it. As we rose and dived into the steep seas we knew we could never find him. His close friend and ship-mate cried for days and nights afterwards.

We had encountered floating mines swept westward by the counter drift from the deep fields around The Faroes and Iceland. We had met water-logged boats, wreckage, parts of ships, stark testimony of tragedies, the details of many of which would never be known. These were the days when the routes over which the gasoline carriers passed were strewn with the bodies of their dead sailors. It used to make me angry when I thought of those people – few, I was sure, but nevertheless some – who obtained additional fuel for their cars by illegal or shady means to drive themselves around for pleasure or to add to their personal comfort.

This year was proving to be the worst in submarine warfare. U-boats were responsible for the loss of more than six million tons of Allied merchant shipping. And this November, the worst month, 117 merchant ships of nearly three-quarters of a million tons were sunk by U-boats.

We had worked hard to keep the enemy off the hundreds of ships we had escorted during the past three months. We had nearly failed several times. There was the occasion when our ship had been left behind to keep a U-boat down while the convoy pressed on. He had been sighted at midday and been forced to dive. We did not expect to find him, we had merely to make ourselves a nuisance by our presence. I was glad to leave the area after dark. I had felt the loneliness of it in the evening. Our small community, used to being a suburb of a vast metropolis of ships, alone on the oily ocean except for the waiting eyes beneath, gave me a sense of isolation and desolateness:

> *Like one that on a lonesome road*
> *Doth walk in fear and dread,*

167

And having once turned round walks on
And turns no more his head;
Because he knows a frightful fiend
Doth close behind him tread.

Such a position becomes rather personal. Each man knew that if we were seen he was pretty well finished. But he also probably thought that the captain knew what he was doing and let it go at that. I knew this – I had always been aware of this individual trust – thus it was a personal business.

It gave me some small conception of the feelings of the captain of a freighter who had fallen out of a convoy with engine trouble late one afternoon. In the early evening we went back to her. Asked if she would be ready soon to be escorted on to the convoy, she answered, 'No. Will be a couple of hours yet. Don't wait.' We could not. But she might have asked us to stay. As we left her her lamp blinked, 'See you tomorrow.' We wondered; especially when, somewhat later, our hydrophone picked up the sound of someone hammering in her engine-room. But in the morning she was back in her column. Was her master's nonchalance a true reflection of his feelings?

One of our destroyers encountered a lonely affair in late September and took a risk on a mission of mercy.

Plugging towards a feebly setting sun, still to the eastward of Greenland's Cape Farewell, we had watched the destroyer draw out and steam away. The voyage had been an active one, submarines having been heard and sighted and attacked. But stress of weather had added to the destroyer's problem. Her signal to Base on detaching from the convoy said:

Proceeding to St John's, Newfoundland, course and speed 237°, 13.5 knots for refuelling and immediate return to ON. 131. Shortness of endurance caused by sea-water leak in one fuel tank.

The day before the 11,000-ton motor tanker *Esso Williamsburg*, call sign *WTKJ*, bound independently for Iceland, had been torpedoed some 400 miles to the westward and the survivors had taken to a lifeboat. The lifeboat had a radio and her distress signals were picked up by a coast station. A series of signals then followed.

25/9. 1854 *From COAC – General*
Distress signal from lifeboat 53.10N. 41.02W.
1900 *From Destroyer to SO. Escort.*
Am steering course to pass through reported position
of lifeboat reference COAC's 1854.
2222 *From Destroyer to COAC – immediate*
Ask lifeboat *WTKJ* to transmit on 500 Kilocycles as
I am in vicinity.

Nothing was heard and nothing more could be done that night.
But at breakfast time in the morning hope ran high in the destroyer.
She had heard the lifeboat's signals, or perhaps some of them.

26/9. 0745 *From Destroyer to Lifeboat*
Keep transmitting we are trying to take a bearing.
0750 *From Lifeboat*
SOS. We were carrying navy fuel to Iceland when
struck approx. position 53.30N. 41.00W. SOS.
0758 *From Lifeboat*
In God's name send help quickly. We were swamped
yesterday and could not send other messages SOS
SOS.
0810 *From Destroyer*
Received your signals. Make Z and long dashes if
you can hear us.
0838 *SOS from WTKJ*
Have receiver generator still working please take
bearing 30 minutes past each hour.
0850 *From Destroyer to SO.*
Received lifeboat signals. Fuel situation improved
am now able to use contaminated fuel. Intend
searching to limit.
0930 *SOS from WTKJ*
Our approximate position 53.30N. 41W. we will send
30 minutes after each hour so you can get a D/F
bearing on us please hurry and get us in God's name.
1059 *From Destroyer*
Can you hear me please go ahead now. If you can
hear me call me with call sign *Abner.*

1200 *SOS Liifeboat WTKJ Williamsburg*
Badly in need of water and medical assistance.

1355 *From Destroyer*
We are coming to your aid. Keep sending. Our call sign is *Abner*. Can you hear me now?

1400 *From Lifeboat to Abner*
Yes and thanks to God old man to you we will send from here on the hour and 30 minutes after the hour as the men get very tired of cranking the generator.

1425 *From Abner*
I am going to drop a depth charge in five minutes. Let me know if you hear it.

1435 *From Lifeboat*
We did not hear your depth charge.

1545 *From Lifeboat Esso Williamsburg*
Will send again in 10 minutes.

1617 *SOS from Lifeboat WTKJ*
Need medical aid and water immediately will send again in 15 minutes.

1633 *From WTKJ Lifeboat*
The sun has just broken through to the west of us. We have a bright orange flag up from a 20 foot mast. We did not hear your gun fired or depth charge.

1718 The sun is shining and the sea is very slightly choppy. We have to use oars to keep from being swamped. The wind is blowing us outter (sic) to sea.

1730 *From Lifeboat*
We just sighted you north-east of us and coming closer. We are firing a flare in a few minutes.

1735 *From Lifeboat*
Flare pistol won't work but you appear to be steering towards us.

1740 *From Lifeboat*
The ship that we sighted was two to five miles away. Is that you?

1742 *From Abner*
Am going to fire a rocket. Report if you can see it.

1800 *From Lifeboat*
We are between you and the sun.

1810	*From Lifeboat*
	The ship we see has one stack.
1815	*From Abner*
	Did you see my rocket or hear my charge?
1828	*From Abner*
	Am I still steering for you?

Was she?

The destroyer searched the area but found only tossing, empty seas. She had been unable to pinpoint the source of the radio signals.

The last message heard from the lifeboat's transmitter, cranked by weary, numbed arms was. 'The ship we see has one stack.' The destroyer had two.

Why did the messages cease? Did the transmitter break down? Had the sailors in the boat passed the limits of physical endurance? Or did the little craft, her weakened crew unable to manage her, founder in the choppy seas?

The chapter closed in mystery and tragedy.

At the end of the next eastbound voyage we arrived off the north coast of Ireland in filthy weather and, while the other escorts went into harbour, we stayed on with the convoy for a while until we picked up the British coastal escort north-east of Inishtrahull. It was dark when we turned away and ran down to the entrance of the Foyle rolling to the heavy beam sea.

In my spare time during the long trip over I had waded through the paper which always seemed to come aboard in bales at either end, but particularly at our home port. It included a sheaf of navigational warnings. I had ticked off in red pencil those which affected us. Among them was the removal of the buoys that had marked the net which had at one time been laid across the River Foyle a little way in from the entrance. The net had been washed away in the strong tides but the buoys had remained. Now they had been lifted. I gave the sheets to the navigator so that he could correct the charts.

It was raining hard now and we had difficulty in picking up the shore lights in the vicinity of the Foyle as we approached. But we found them and eased into the shallow water clear of the big sandbank. It could not have been darker – or wetter. It was too foul for the pilot to board at the river mouth but the lighthouse on the farther shore ahead shone green. We were in its safe sector, in the centre of the channel. So we went on up the river, passing close to the wreck which had been leaning over on a rock for years, and presently rounded the bend where the left bank fell away to form the lower end of Loch Foyle. But the channel was narrow and we hugged the rocky right bank.

Up ahead several lights blinked through a damp halo. The ship was steady now in the river water but leaning a little in her light condition to the gale which swept down over the peat hills.

'We'll go to the tanker,' I told the first lieutenant. The wind held his dripping oilskin tight against his back and legs. 'Stand by to make fast. We won't know which side to the tanker till we get up to her. We'll take the pilot there, probably.'

He passed the order fore and aft and went down to the upper deck.

I remarked to the navigator that the ebb tide must be running fast. 'We're coming up very slowly, don't you think?'

'Seems so. But we've got a way to go to the booey yet.'

We were keeping a flashing light almost ahead, just a shade on the port bow. After nearly ten minutes I said, 'Damn strong tide! We seem to be making small way. Should be doing nine knots through the water.'

'Yes. Fast ebb, I guess,' agreed the navigator.

I asked the coxswain, who was at the wheel, the degree he was steering and then looked at Macgilligan Point Light and judged its rough bearing.

'Nip in and lay it off on the chart, will you,' I said to the navigator, giving him the bearing.

The wind fell away for a moment and I heard him blowing his nose in the asdic house. He was seizing the opportunity under shelter. He was not long.

'Should be up to the buoy by now, sir. It puts us almost abreast of it.'

'Well, we're not, are we?'

'No.'

'Flash every five seconds. That's it, eh?'

'That's the buoy,' he confirmed.

'Reduce thirty revs.'

Water ran off his sou'wester into the voicepipe as he lifted the lid and sang down to the wheelhouse.

'That'll give her five knots through the water. . . . I'm not so damn sure,' I muttered, half to myself.

The shrouds vibrated with a dismal two-note tune. The slanting rain alternately hammered against our oilskins and then swirled and sprayed. Canvas cracked now and then like a whip on the lee side.

'Can't understand why we haven't reached the bloody buoy,' I complained. 'Anybody'd think it was under way and going up ahead of us. Where's Moville Pile Light? Visibility's not that bad that we shouldn't see it. We can see the riding lights of the near ships at anchor.'

'We're pretty close up now, sir,' the navigator asserted, standing near me.

'Cripes!' I gasped.

I grabbed the lid of the voicepipe and threw it up. 'Hard aport,' I shouted down. I was looking at the faint outline of a beacon two hundred yards away fine on the port bow. The wretched light was blinking from the top of it.

'It's the bloody Pile Light, not the buoy at all!'

'Why . . . it is!' echoed the navigator.

Now we could dimly see the lattice spars comprising the framework of Moville Pile. And the ship had not swung off yet in response to the helm she had been given. But the coxswain had repeated the order.

'I think she's aground, sir.'

I glanced in the direction of the navigator's voice. He was leaning over the port wing of the bridge. As I came to join him I called down the pipe to stop engines.

Such as we could see of the water below us, pock-marked with heavy rain, was running slowly by, much as if we were at anchor.

Never having been aground before I did not know what to expect. The very word 'aground' had always made me shudder. I shuddered now but knew the bottom was sandy. I could picture the bank in my mind. We had been trying to get around the Pile on the side where Moville Bank almost dried out at low water.

I was back in the centre of the bridge. Looking along the

'mid-ship line of the ship between the mast and the bow I saw the mocking light was flashing slightly to starboard now.

'She's falling off to port, Pilot,' I announced with some fervour. 'Looks as though the tide's on the starboard bow.'

He watched, too. Then she swung off quite fast and in a matter of a minute or so the light lay broad to starboard. We put the engines slow ahead and the ship came obediently out into the channel. Soon we were alongside the tanker with oil pumping through the big flexible pipes into the almost empty fuel tanks.

The bilges, when sounded, were found to be dry but the asdic dome, which was like a three foot barnacle sticking to the keel, was gone. It had apparently sheared its bolts and now would lie in the sand of the bank for ever.

My feelings were rather mixed on the matter. However, this was the only damage I ever inflicted on any ship during the war.

Four months later I received, in a vast insurge of official mail, a copy of a memorandum to the Flag Officer, Newfoundland Force, and signed by the Secretary, Naval Board. It was marked Secret and referred to the former's submission enclosing my report of 'Collison or Grounding and relevant documents'. After stating that the Flag Officer's submission and the communication from the Commodore Commanding Londonderry were concurred in, it went on to state: 'The Commanding Officers of H.M.C.S. *Sackville*,' and it named three ships and their C.O.s, 'are to be informed that they have incurred the displeasure of the Department for not taking sufficient precautions to check their positions, knowing as they did, from QZH 368, that the searched channel had been altered.'

So two others had done the same thing as I had! But I had at least dug deep enough into the paper to find the QZH.

The copy of the secret memorandum was all I ever heard about it after making my tedious report, the day after it happened, in five copies with drawings.

Another voyage went by and then another. The U-boats came and went, appeared and disappeared, shadowed, reported and tried to attack us, but never a ship was hurt. We did our share of attacking the enemy, but he was elusive and we found no evidence of damage. He was using the Pillenwuffer, too, the bubble decoy. The ping of our asdic would be clear and hard on the hull of the submarine. Then it would grow soft and expansive and eventually disappear; no echo would come back. A chemical compound in a cartridge had been ejected from the boat far below which created a myriad bubbles and, for a while, sounded the same as the thick steel hull. The U-boat would escape behind it.

But sometimes we bore down on one another, mistaking escorts for submarines in the darkness.

There were the nights when you could not see. As the ship ploughed into the pitch blackness, eyes might have been tight shut for all the use they were in knowing what was before the ship. And then there were the nights of lesser blackness. I had been ashamed afterwards when I had come out on deck and had jumped as I caught the moon out of the corner of my eye; my pulse had quickened. I had thought, for an instant, it was a rocket from a sinking ship.

Yet one element had been avoided – ice. For some reason icebergs had not troubled us; they had not come down in the war years from Baffin Bay in their usual large numbers to make it more dangerous and difficult for the convoys.

It seemed silly to me that I could have arrived, after such a comparatively short while, at the state in which I now found my nerves; surprising that only three or four fairly intensive months could have replaced reasonable fearlessness by anxiety. Lack of sleep had something to do with it. I rarely seemed to sleep for more than three hours at a stretch, usually less; there would be signals coming in, the inevitable false alarms, and often the weather had to be watched and sometimes the behaviour of the merchant ships. But as soon as daylight came my worries left me and I was free again until dusk. Then I was back on that desolate ground once more. All night the wind would moan over the bleak, rugged, inhospitable hummocks, a directionless space, seeming treacherous at every step.

But I knew I was not the only one who felt it, or something like it; I could see the strain appearing in quite a few of the crew, particularly the chief engineer, and some of the officers, too.

So the question now was whether I should go on or not. Yet it wasn't really in question. I almost certainly had to. There was probably no captain to take my place. Then, I did not want to leave the crew, especially when I was quite sure that some of them were just as anxious to get ashore as I was. I certainly did not wish to leave the group until the job was done. The team worked perfectly. Moreover, I knew another captain who needed to be relieved more than I did; he was in quite a bad state.

The Crow's Nest was still quiet, so that I started when a voice behind me brought me back to my surroundings. It had once been a familiar voice. I turned round to find a big, burly, beetle-browed man standing with his hand outstretched. He was one of the men with whom I had joined the navy and who had been in command of a corvette nearly as long as I had. He was a New-foundlander and had sailed out of St John's years before in trading schooners and knew the sea well. I was glad to see him and he made a good companion for lunch. We discussed our problems at length which, as always, embraced the shore staff. They never seemed to do all we wanted to our ships, though we agreed that this was partly due to the heavy demands we made on them. It was generally a struggle, sometimes a battle, in a British base to get the shore engineers and shipwrights to do vital work in time for sailing.

Before I left the club that afternoon I said to him, 'I dread the thought of another winter voyage and perhaps another one after that.'

'So do I,' he replied feelingly. 'Don't we all?'

I went out and down the many stairs to the cold windy street and through my head ran the words, 'Don't we all.' So I was not alone! And if others dreaded it as much as I, then I could take it as well as they.

We sailed two days later.

The day before we left, the younger destroyer captain, the one whose vessel had so unhappily failed to find the lifeboat of the *Esso Williamsburg*, came into my cabin.

'Here's something I want you to have a look at,' he said presently, pulling out some papers from his pocket. 'It's a scheme I cooked up the other day and I'm thinking of giving it to the S.O. when he comes in.'

We laid the sheets out on my desk and studied them. It was an operation for foiling a U-boat attack. But it had to be carried out as the enemy was setting the stage and preparing to launch his torpedoes. I recognized it as an original idea and well worth having up one's sleeve, but also one that might never be applied because of the uncertainty as to exactly when one could expect an attack.

I told him I thought we should have it and that he must submit it to the senior officer on the latter's arrival.

But the senior officer never arrived. He had an accident coming from Halifax to join us. The new radar he had just been equipped with caused him to be run down by a steamer and he lost his stern.

In spite of this our group had the plan, for the captain propounding the scheme himself became the S.O.

Our new convoy had a rescue ship with it. These little vessels – usually ex-passenger ships from the British coastal trade – had been running with slow convoys for some time and went back and forth for no other purpose than to rescue men from the sea. They performed some very courageous acts and many outstanding feats of seamanship in pulling men out of the water in heavy weather. They carried doctors and nurses and were equipped with a hospital.

This rescue ship's services were put to use in this convoy quite soon. Before dawn on the third day out a great column of flame shot suddenly skywards. It burned viciously and then died down to a flicker about the deck of the torpedoed ship, with an occasional tongue of flame leaping up from inside.

The rescue ship dropped back and so did we, while the other forty-six merchantmen pawed their slow way on. As daylight came the fire went out and the rescue ship picked up half the crew and left. The rest, those who were not burned, stayed and tried to get the tanker underway. By and by she moved and slowly turned in widening circles. Then they repaired their steering gear and she straightened out.

She had made no reply to our inquiring signals – we were not close enough to hail, our job was to circle a mile or so off. Now we saw her blinker going.

'What is course to St John's?' she asked.

We told her 232 degrees. So they intended to try to make it!

Then she flashed, 'Is that the nearest port we can put into?'

An odd question! We just said, 'Yes.'

After a while the light blinked again. 'Steering 232. Making about three knots. Compasses not too accurate. All deck officers gone except one who is recovering consciousness.'

As we went ahead we passed close to the tanker's starboard side, and then we saw some of the damage which the torpedo had created. There was a great hole amidships and her upper deck was ripped open above it, the steel plates curled back like pieces of tin. In through her side washed the sea as the ship rolled gently to the swell, and now and then water shot up through the deck like vapour from a blow-hole. The after part of her 'midship super-structure was scorched and burned by fire. Even in this condition she was soon making five knots.

Two hours later an aircraft flew over and became the tanker's escort. We turned and left her. But our hearts went out to the few men who were working the tanker back to harbour. It was a dangerous undertaking. If air escort was maintained by relieving aircraft, she would be moderately safe from submarine attack by day but not at night, particularly during the early hours of the morning when the moon had gone down. There was also the danger of bad weather. She would not be able to withstand a gale in her present weakened condition.

I heard the fate of this American ship, *Brilliant*, 9,000 tons, carrying gas and oil, later that winter.

The great fire was extinguished partly by the phenomenon of steam being accidentally injected into the burning tank when the pipes were broken.

She made a good passage to Newfoundland, arriving in Bonavista Bay, eighty miles north of St John's, three days after we had left her. But she was obliged to remain at anchor there for several days while the wind blew hard and the sea beat against the rocks out-side the bay. She was too badly damaged to be repaired at St John's, a place where the port's shipyard was constantly occupied with emergency jobs and patching up casualties sufficiently to enable them to make their way to other ports where rebuilding could be done. So, like many others who had hobbled in, she was shored up and strengthened so that she could proceed on to the States.

Several weeks later she went out and down the coast, but was recalled when the meteorologists forecast a severe gale. She tried again when the weather appeared more settled, but it turned against her. The *Brilliant* was south of Cape Race when a storm from the north-west came out of the Gulf of St Lawrence; it was one of the worst of the winter. It struck her with its full force and she broke in two. A tug was at the scene but was powerless to help. Before the forward half sank the men tried to lower boats but they were frozen in; all were lost in the wild, icy water. But the after half remained afloat despite the raging sea and after two days those who were fortunate enough to have been in that part of the ship were rescued by the tug and a naval minesweeper. The two enemies of the Atlantic, submarines and storms, had ultimately won against a gallant crew.

When we returned to the convoy we took up a night station on the starboard bow.

'Bright night again, sir,' said Collins, who was on the bridge as we assumed our position.

'Yes,' I replied. 'It would be better if it remained like this all night.'

Collins was now the first lieutenant. Black had left us a month before when he had been called to a shore appointment in Halifax, and we were very sorry to lose him. His influence had been strong in the ship and it had left its mark. However, I was confident Collins would serve well in this new position.

Other changes, too, had taken place among the officers. The old chief skipper, who had been the navigator since the beginning, had left, together with his good chronometer, and had been replaced by Neil. He had assumed the unofficial title of pilot but was not very sure of himself yet; he had had no courses and knew only what he had picked up. Two new officers had joined, both sub-lieutenants, one of whom was very aggressive but very seasick. It had not been my wish to change officers but I could not prevent it. Fortunately we had very few changes among the ratings.

That evening radio bearings came in. The U-boat transmissions were picked up by one of the ships in the convoy regularly every half-hour, most of which were reported 'close'. I plotted them on the chart and soon realized that they were emanating from more than one U-boat, probably three or four. By midnight I was convinced there would be an attack but I did not expect it just yet.

I lay down on my collapsible bunk in the asdic house. I did not intend to sleep, just rest while I had the chance, and I did not take my boots off as I had in the early hours of the previous morning because I remembered how wet and cold my feet had become when I had turned out in such haste that I had failed to pull them on. Nor did I remove the cumbersome night glasses from around my neck and they were heavy on my chest as I lay in my narrow bunk.

The signalman had come to me twice with bearings which I had figured out without getting up. Soon after 0100 he came in again.

'Signal from the S.O., sir. "Expect attack after moonset".'

Quarter of an hour went by and he was standing over me once more.

'Operational signal from the S.O., sir.'

I told him to read it.

'"Preparative Operation Hoople 0325 executive 0345 fire two sweeps only at zero and zero plus five minutes. Turn outwards 60 degrees".'

So he was going to try out his new scheme. I was glad he had the courage to do it.

I got up and leaned over the chart table at the foot of the bunk; there were some pieces of paper scattered over the chart, one of which had the calculations of moonset on it. I found it and got the nautical almanac out again. I figured for a minute or so and confirmed my original timing – 0225. That would mean that we would have to wait an hour and twenty minutes after moonset before carrying out Operation Hoople. I wondered whether the enemy would wait as long as that to press home his attack. If I had been setting the time, I was sure I would not have had the patience to wait more than an hour after the moon had gone down.

An hour went by and the brightness of the night faded. The ship was on a zig-zag continuously, the helm never steady. I stood on the bridge for another hour waiting momentarily for the familiar sight or sound which would indicate that we were too late.

> *Yet, Royal, my comrade, before Fate decides,*
> *His hand stays, uncertain, like a sea between tides,*
> *Then a man has a moment, if he strikes not too late,*
> *When his soul shakes the world-soul, and can even change Fate.*

At 0325 I told the officer-of-the-watch to ring action stations. I was glad to have the men closed up at the armament. I felt we were in greater readiness for what must surely come soon. Then we turned the ship round and dropped gently back towards the ships, taking up a position close on the bow of the leader of the starboard column. We had executed our part of the preparative, the other escorts, too, would be closing in on the convoy in readiness for the operation.

'Let me know when it's a minute to, Pilot.'

'Aye, aye, sir.'

'I wonder how many of us know the exact time,' I said to the navigator. 'I doubt if any of our deck watches, after applying corrections, are within ten seconds of one another. Anyway, it doesn't matter much; the first up will lead the rest.'

I asked West to bring me the microphone and switch on the loud speakers. I put the little instrument close to my mouth.

'This is the captain speaking.' I looked into the darkness ahead. 'Submarines are close in on us but they have not been detected yet. Instead of waiting, all escorts are going to make a dummy counter attack. In other words we shall search for the enemy before he strikes instead of after. This will take place in a few minutes. Star shell will be used twice; if nothing is seen we shall resume our station. Be on the alert. That is all.'

Quietness reigned. We waited. I was impatient for the time to go by. Would the enemy fire first or would we beat him to the gun? This waiting was bad. It seemed we were always waiting.

'Minute to go, sir,' cried the navigator.

'Right,' I answered. 'Ring on a hundred and sixty-five revs – starboard twenty – load – steady on east.' Fifteen knots would be a handy speed.

In a few moments the navigator called out 'time' and I glanced around to see if anyone else had fired. They had not. I would not wait; my timepiece was as near as anyone else's. I gave the order to open fire.

'From green four-oh to red five-oh – star shell sweep – commence-commence-commence,' I heard Collins shout through his megaphone. The whistle began but was soon drowned in the boom of the gun. Then the first shell burst lighting up the sky and sea five thousand yards away to starboard.

'Other ships firing!' came a report close by.

I scanned the water beneath the falling row of lights – once

181

slowly across, back again. The sea was empty. The first star went out.

'Machine-gun fire on the starboard quarter!'

I turned round. There were tracer bullets flying in a low trajectory and bouncing off the water some distance away.

We did not wait but turned the ship towards the spot with the engines at full speed. The star shells from the corvette on the convoy's quarter were bursting outside our line of vision but in a few moments we were able to see from the light of our own which we threw up for the second time.

Disturbed water could be seen as we descended on the area which was still being marked by the little streaks of tracer light from our neighbour. A big splash went up; she was firing high explosive evidently. A shell passed close to our bow – we were coming into her line of fire.

A signal came indicating she had sighted a submarine. Then another from a corvette on the other side of the convoy. She had contact. It was our old towing partner.

We raced by but could see no object on the water, and as we wheeled round the other corvette was no more than a few hundred yards away. The submarine had gone.

We swept with asdic this way and that but could pick no echoes up: no sound of any sort came from beneath the surface. He had escaped us, perhaps had dived under the ships in the convoy; we never knew. Nor did the escort on the other side appear to have wounded her adversary. He, like the U-boat on the starboard side, escaped.

This was hard luck, but we at least achieved our aim – an imminent enemy attack had been foiled almost at the moment of its execution.

How many other U-boats were coming in or were about to launch their torpedoes we, of course, could not determine. There were certainly others in the neighbourhood. Whatever their movements were, they, with the two whom we came upon, kept away for the rest of the night.

Eight days and eight long nights followed before we came into the Western Approaches. We were constantly shadowed but never attacked. While sitting in my cabin at night I would sometimes feel a thud; the ship would tremble and my heart leap. Then I would grunt scornfully. It would be a wave hitting the ship awkwardly.

Fog hid us for a day or so, and the ships with the net defences – steel nets suspended from derricks thirty feet out and extending down into the water – took their unwieldly protective gear in. Tempestuous weather struck at us and the ship reared and plunged like a circus horse and pounded her keel as she sprang at the combers. One merchantman had draught trouble and heavy black smoke billowed from her funnel. Towards the end another ship had engine trouble, an old British tramp. She broke down under the heavy pounding of the seas and finally had to be towed.

By this time the Commodore was quite uncertain of his position. He asked all ships to report their latitude and longitude by dead reckoning so that he could pool them. Among those he received was one which gave the position by observation. This the Commodore could not understand. So he sent a signal to the captain asking how he had obtained an observed position. The Commodore had not seen the sun, much less any stars.

The reply came at once, 'With the aid of a sextant and thirty years on the Western Ocean.'

The master in question was a Canadian Pacific skipper.

At last we reached the coast. Except for one casualty, which was little considering the opposition, and the straggler who was under tow, we had carried out our standing instructions, namely, to ensure the safe and timely arrival of the convoy at its destination. I had a feeling of satisfaction as we parted company and made for the River Clyde.

13. Hard Lying

The speed of a convoy is the speed of the slowest ship. The speed of a British dockyard is the speed of its fabulous 'matey'. And the dockyard matey emulates the tortoise very well. In Londonderry the mateys seemed to work with a negative incentive, but in Greenock they had a more positive approach, they actively practised the avoidance of work. Shirking was hardly the word, I think, because it was not done out of individual meanness; it was the matey's trade policy. The phenomenon was to be found in most dockyards I was told, but Greenock certainly staggered us. It took two visits to the Scottish yard to have a new radar installed, in all about eighteen days. In Londonderry they had fitted them in some of our escorts in a week.

We at last left the dock with the tide at 0830 on the windy morning of the 9th December, and came down the last part of the Glasgow ship channel, past the desultory riveting sounds of the yards to the Tail o' the Bank, the Clyde's famous anchorage, from whence, only shortly before, the North African invasion fleet had sailed. Here we waited all morning for the compass adjuster to come off in his boat; a horrible waste of vital time, I thought, until the adjuster when he arrived pointed out that we could not do anything yet because the aircraft carrier a short distance away was lying at a mooring buoy blocking his view of the shore transits. 'That's why I didn't come off to you sooner,' explained the seemingly rather soured lieutenant. 'Captain (D's) office told me she wasn't leaving till 1400.'

A gale was blowing by this time and I suggested it was really a day's work to do the adjustments with the degaussing switched on and then with it off. 'Why haven't you a buoy we could secure to so that we could be pushed around and the adjustments made without our having to manoeuvre on every point of the compass in a congested harbour?'

'We have a buoy,' replied the lieutenant resignedly. 'I've been here nearly a year, and after fighting tooth and nail for six months,

184

I managed to get them to put down a compass adjusting buoy. It's over there,' he pointed to a small buoy between us and the shore. 'But when I asked them for a motor launch to swing the ships around the buoy they said I couldn't have one, so the buoy has never been used.'

'That sounds typical.'

'It is. I wish I was back at sea again, only I can't go. I was beaten up in minesweepers in the first year.'

We were standing in the asdic house hopefully watching through the front windows for signs of departure activity in the carrier. I glanced along the bridge at the unpainted wood extending from the deck to the rail. It still bothered me.

'New front,' I remarked. 'It was finished last night, though not quite.'

I told him how the front of the bridge, padded with splinter mats on the outside, had collapsed under the weight of a sea which struck it. 'It was leaning against the house here amidships. We asked for a new rail when we came in but they said they couldn't do it in time. I said we needed something to stand behind and they said they couldn't help it, they hadn't time, they could only straighten it up where it was possible and, as you know, that wouldn't have been much use. But we managed to interest a minor authority in it and at last had this solid wooden job built. Looks pretty good, doesn't it?'

'It does,' said the adjuster, eyeing the erection which extended right across the fore part of the bridge and along the wings.

'The dockyard mateys finished it at two o'clock this morning, or so they said. They had to be persuaded with cocoa and sandwiches to go on working and we had to provide them with oilskins before they would continue in the drizzle. And now look at it over here.'

I took him to the starboard side, grasped the rail and shook it. It wobbled back and forth. 'They didn't bolt this end down.'

'Umph,' murmured the adjuster. It did not seem to surprise him.

'But the gunnery officer obtained a very nice oerlikon gun, something we've never owned,' I concluded, looking for a bright spot. 'He tried to get a pom-pom but they said there wasn't time to find one and install it.'

At last the carrier slipped from the buoy and steamed slowly clear of the transits and the adjuster began his work. But there was less than four hours of daylight left.

The wind was so strong, blowing us across the transits, and the time so short, that the standard compass only could be adjusted, and on none but the cardinal points. The two compasses should both have been done on all thirty-two points twice, that is, with the degaussing belt – the energized cable around the ship for the purpose of counteracting magnetic mines – both on and off. But as I had the choice of one condition or the other and not both, I chose to have the adjustment made, such as it was, with the power on, as the degaussing had to be on in coastal waters and we were not obliged to switch it off in deep water. We would not have had the compasses adjusted at all had it not been for the new radar, the steel mounting of which upset the magnetic field entirely.

It was after 1800 and almost dark when the adjuster's boat came to take him ashore and he took a precarious leap into the pitching craft. We wasted no time in clearing the harbour; we were in a hurry.

The westbound convoy had already passed the Mull of Kintyre when we came out of the Clyde and we had to make 'Derry and get out again before it progressed too far. They could not fix our radio transmitter at Greenock either and we could not make the voyage without it.

It was pitch black when we arrived at the mouth of the River Foyle and I had to screw up my eyes and incline my head against the driving December rain to see the yellow light of the outer pilot station as we edged in. But he was there – the pilot in his small, white boat.

It was O'Connor. He seemed to have taken us up more often than any other pilot. Perhaps he worked the river more.

'Ye're alone, Capt'n? No other corvette with ye?'

'No. Just in for the night – I expect. Want the Base to get the radio to work.'

As the flash of Moville Beacon fell upon him standing near the telegraph his face looked deeply lined, almost scarred, like the craggy cliffs of Inishowan Head beneath which he lived. He was permanently bent and gave the impression of having spent his life gazing unflinchingly into a perpetual rainy wind from under the

186

peak of his cap. Periodically he blew his large nose and rubbed it vigorously with a coloured handkerchief.

He spoke little for an Irishman but he had told me once that he had gone to sea in sail in the days before boat davits were invented.

It was after midnight when we were alongside at 'Derry, snugly secured against another corvette.

'When'll ye be leavin' in the marnin', Capt'n?' he asked as he turned towards the bridge ladder.

'With daylight. Say seven-thirty – if all's well.'

'I'll be with ye, then.'

'Good! Thanks,' I said gratefully. 'But you'll have very little rest.'

He shrugged his rain-sodden shoulders. 'Makes no odds.'

I followed him below and gave him a good snort of gin before he went ashore.

Precisely at 0700, as the grey dawn was coming in, O'Connor knocked at my cabin door and came in. I was dressing.

'Had your breakfast, Pilot?' I asked.

'I have not. My daughter-in-law was not about when I got out of my bed. A good woman but not an early one.'

He wore a faded blue serge suit under his overcoat and when he took off his battered uniform cap – the only article which truly identified him as a pilot – his snow-white hair, silhouetted against the blue-black disc of the scuttle, contrasted startlingly with his weathered face and large, reddish-blue nose. His drooping white moustache further accentuated the purple runnels in his cheeks.

'If you go down to the wardroom you'll get a good breakfast. We've twenty minutes yet before we need to slip.'

'No, thank ye, Capt'n. I'll not have any breakfast. But I'd like a drop of gin if you have it.'

I said I had. I opened the wine locker and brought out a bottle and gave it to him with a glass.

He held both at eye-level, looking at the canted bottle for a moment, then filled the glass half way up.

'Help yourself to water out of the tap in the basin there,' I said.

But he evidently did not need any and I remembered then that he had taken his drink neat the night before. All he said was, 'Bless ye,' and swallowed it. O'Connor then applied the big green

187

banner he pulled from his overcoat pocket to his moustache and nose and carefully, gently wiped the corners of his blue eyes. All movements were synchronized.

'Thank ye, Capt'n,' he said, still standing.

We talked for a minute or two about the weather and the tide, then he picked up his cap from my bunk where he had laid it and said he would leave me.

He was on the bridge waiting when I got up.

He piloted the ship beautifully – dead straight on the reach which ran close to the high wooded bank below Broom Hall, and he took the curves with the ebb past Lyssahally as gracefully as an artist's pencil drawing the curves of a woman's body. As we came into Loch Foyle the wind came cold and damp across the open water and I felt sorry for old O'Connor. I asked him if he would not have a cup of coffee or perhaps cocoa.

'No, thank ye. I'll wait till we'll be at Moville.'

He looked chilled in spite of his hardy face. His overcoat collar was half turned up and he had the habit, while standing looking ahead over the dodger, of plucking at the lapel in an attempt to keep it close to his throat. But it always fell back as soon as he took his hand away. He did not seem to notice the fact. I was sure his coat was wet through from the night before. I never remembered him wearing an oilskin. I was also sure he did not know what gloves felt like.

On reaching Moville about 0830 we went alongside the tanker to top up with fuel. The pilot followed me down to my cabin to have his papers signed and when I suggested that now, perhaps, he would like some breakfast, he said he did not need any just yet, his old woman would give him it when he reached home, or he would have some in the next ship if he took one up soon. But he would like a drop of gin.

He took his usual liberal noggin, and after wiping his mouth and eyes with the inevitable handkerchief and emitting noises of satisfaction, shook me by the hand.

'Good luck to ye, Capt'n. Ye'll be havin' a good passage in spite of it bein' winter.'

The convoy went north of Rockall and nearly up to the 60th parallel. A group of merchant ships from Iceland was to join before sunset on the third day but they missed us and at noon on the fifth

188

day it was decided to turn the whole convoy round and proceed in the opposite direction as it had become clear that the Iceland contingent was directly astern but could not catch up. Four hours later we met them, took them into the columns and turned back on to our original south-westerly course.

High winds from the north-east had accompanied us at first, but behind us they did not hinder our progress; they may even have helped the merchantmen along, riding high out of the water as they were with little or no cargo. Then light variable winds prevailed.

Though many submarines were reported in the area, none seemed to have sighted us. The air cover we were receiving was very good, which may have had a lot to do with it.

The barometer had begun to fall on the fourth day and was still falling slowly when we met the Iceland section. An ominous feature accompanied it, a heavy, rolling swell. The next morning I was rather concerned to find the barometer was registering a little under twenty-nine inches. The swell, too, had become higher. At noon I asked one of the merchant ships what his barometer was reading. The answer came back, '28.87'. Ours was reading 28.90, so there was no pretending it was wrong.

'There's an old saying at sea about the glass,' I remarked to the officer-of-the-watch, 'which I can't remember exactly but its something like "Quick to fall, quick to rise; slow to fall, long to blow."'

'You mean you think it's going to blow for a long time?'

'Looks very like it.'

I was observing the water. The high, greasy swell rolled towards us from the west, and down its back we slid, gently, stayed a moment, then rode up its smooth front to an even keel on its rounded crest, there to hover in the windless calm and wait for another steep descent. But there were no waves, not even a ruffle on the water. This swell was the result of one of two things, either the wind had created a very high sea here only recently and then had died out leaving a swell, or it was the water which was being pushed in front of a high sea several hundred miles away. I discounted the former, it was almost certainly the latter, foretelling what we were steaming into.

The first lieutenant and I, with a couple of hands, went around the decks to make sure everything was secure. Collins was a practical man. We added lashings here and there, particularly to the boats, and set up the forestay a little tighter.

It remained calm that afternoon and evening but soon after midnight a north-west wind sprang up. The barometer had dropped to the lowest point I could ever remember, 28.74 inches. This was the real bottom of any weatherman's low. By 0500 it was blowing a gale, and so it continued all that morning; but being on our beam, it was not too bad. In the middle of the afternoon, however, it backed to the west and increased in strength.

We had ceased to zig-zag and now maintained the course of the convoy at a slow speed. I was glad to go slowly because it lessened our personal discomfort. The sky was a greyish yellow and the low clouds were moving fast. We edged in to about a mile from the starboard column of the convoy because the ships were becoming indistinct in the gloom and I wanted to watch their behaviour in the weather. But we found we were inclined to draw ahead of them; their speed was already very obviously reduced. By 1600 the wind had increased from a strong gale to a whole gale, and a signal went out from the Commodore to his ships to heave to.

The sea and swell had synchronized now; both were due west, and we headed the ship into it with the propeller turning at eighty revolutions which was equivalent to about seven knots, though we would not be progressing at more than two knots.

Collins had been with me on the bridge watching the rising sea.

'She rides nicely like this, doesn't she?' he remarked, watching the bow rise and fall.

'Yes,' I answered, 'corvettes are remarkable vessels.'

'The merchant ships will have a worse time of it than we will, I suppose, with their propellers coming out of the water.'

'In a way. They have so much of their hull exposed to the wind and so little gripping the water when they're light like this that it's hard for them to steer. We're fortunate there; our propeller keeps under pretty well.'

Presently we noticed through the misty spindrift the ships coming a little closer. We edged away. They would be carrying the wind and sea on one bow or the other rather than ahead as we were, and would probably have it on their port bow and so would work across the path we were following.

By 1800 it was much worse. It was dark, but not so dark that one could not see the great curling tops of the waves immediately before the ship. I estimated that the force of the wind was now over sixty miles an hour. The ship was plunging furiously, and she drove down into the trough so fast that it seemed incredible that her bow could rise before the next onrushing wave enveloped her.

The quartermasters had been told to steer very carefully to make sure they did not allow the ship to be thrown off the wind too far. It was very difficult steering because the compass was swinging violently with the rearing, corkscrew motion and it was hard for the helmsman to tell whether it was the ship that was swinging or the ill-adjusted compass card. As the sea came over the fo'c'sle head more heavily, we slowed down a little more.

Soon hard squalls came, accompanied by torrential rain driven at a furious speed into which one could not look with unprotected eyes. But the rain could be seen approaching. Its downward pressure temporarily flattened the tops of the breakers. Its hiss as it passed could barely be heard in the tumult of the crashing sea and shrieking wind. The long streaks of foam which stretched back from the broken wave-crests could be seen even in the darkness beneath the spindrift which flew like thin snow above the water. These I watched carefully, for they told me the direction in which we had to head the ship.

I knew the danger of not heading into the sea. If the ship fell off too far the wind would exert such pressure on the weather bow that she would soon find herself wallowing almost broadside to on her beam ends. That would be disastrous, she would probably be crushed and swamped. Time after time we were obliged to increase speed to keep steerage way, and that had its dangers too. The squalls came more frequently, every five or ten minutes, accompanied by vivid lightning, during which the wind blew with hurricane force, no less than eighty miles an hour, perhaps a hundred. The sea became steeper and more formidable in its anger.

I did not think to consider the height of the waves; they were the same as I had seen before, years ago, but never from the deck of

191

such a small vessel. Used as I was to bad weather, I was conscious of a sense of fear as the ship plunged down into the abyss of black spume-streaked water from the bottom of which reared a cliff of sea, its great white top curling and boiling above. How could her bow, only sixty feet beyond me, lift in time? And if it did, how could she climb the sheer wall of onrushing water? She achieved it again and again, but not without suffering.

Where the other ships were we had no idea. The radar could not tell us because it was useless now – the waves were as big or bigger than the ships, so it could not distinguish the difference.

At times the fo'c'sle was buried down under water, the fore deck submerged, the green seas battering the bridge. Spray thrown up by the pounding of the bow flew high over the funnel.

I knew the agony of the men below, the sickening torment as the bow plunged down incline after precipitous incline like a runaway roller-coaster. The noises would be constant – water rushing from end to end of the mess carying everything movable on its tide and crashing abruptly against the bulkhead; the penetrating scream of the wind outside, and the thud and crash of the ocean above as the sharp stem punched into the wall of water; the creak and groan of the frames and internal structure as the bow's flare struggled to lift the ship from under the sea.

Up on the bridge I could imagine what it was like down below. But no man spoke of it to me.

In the middle watch, the ship fell off further than usual. I must have neglected to notice it, or she may have been thrown off quickly.

'Is your wheel hard aport?' I bellowed down the voice pipe. Then, putting my ear right into the mouthpiece, I heard the faint answer, 'Hard aport it is, sir.'

'Eighty-five revs,' I shouted. I had been doing this so long now it was becoming monotonous. But this time she did not come up. I waited as long as I dared. She looked as though she were falling away more; she was nearly four points off the wind.

'One hundred and ten revs,' I yelled down the pipe.

'Watch her, Pilot, and tell me what way you think she's going,' I shouted in Neil's direction. 'I've let her go too far.'

This was bad. If she came round into this sea with revolutions for ten knots the sea would likely sweep the bridge right off her.

H.M.C.S. *Matane*, frigate. Her camouflage was also green and white.

H.M.C.S. *Saskatchewan*, destroyer. During the invasion she was painted two shades of grey.

But I could not afford to risk her going beam on. She rode beautifully like this as most ships do, because she met the waves with her shoulder instead of her sharp stem, half rolling, half pitching over them, though her rolling laid her far down. But while this was the best way to ride, a corvette could not be trusted to lie so; or that was my experience.

I was angry with myself; my nerves were tense and my body felt tired with the constant swaying, my fingers with the constant gripping. I felt insignificant against the might and power of the ocean which I watched so intently. It was borne in on me that the fate of the ship depended at this moment on the action of one man – me.

'Is she answering yet?' I asked the wheelhouse.

'Not sure, sir,' came the answer.

That was better than a negative reply. But I knew she was. The angle was less – at least no more.

Two minutes passed. Yes! She was coming! She could not be more than three points off now.

'I think she's coming up a bit,' shouted the navigator.

Then there was a small sound at the voice pipe. I put my ear to it.

'She's answering now, sir.'

'Keep your wheel hard over,' I replied.

I felt some relief. Sheets of water passed over the bridge. When I looked again the ship was barely two points from the wind.

'Stop engines,' I yelled.

Would her way come off? She was heading up more yet, nearly into it.

'Now steady your helm,' I called to the quartermaster. And the ship seemed to stay in the face of the storm.

'Half ahead. Seventy revs.'

The danger was passed! She dived, buried her stem and rose to the mountainous sea, shedding only normal water over the break of the fo'c'sle.

Dawn came at last, a grey, rack-driven dawn, dismal in the extreme, yet impressive, for the great sea had not decreased. As full daylight came, the visibility did not improve to any extent; spindrift filled the air so thickly that the waves themselves could not be seen five hundred yards away.

Damage to the ship became apparent now, though it was not severe. A boat had been smashed, its davits bent. Small fixtures on deck had been wrenched away; steel plates buckled. The starboard side of the lower bridge was smashed in, only twisted metal and tattered canvas remained. The first lieutenant reported much flooding below, mostly from water entering through hatches and doors on the upper deck. We had escaped lightly so far.

The morning wore on and the gulls also fought the storm, above the smoking water. But in the middle of the afternoon a lessening in the wind's force was noticeable and the squalls ceased. It was at this time that six depth charges came adrift; the racks in which they were stowed on the starboard side had sprung. I went aft with the first lieutenant and a dozen hands. It was an ugly sight. Charges weighing three hundred pounds were rolling round like marbles and solid water was pouring over the gunwale, filling the waist. Those who worked to secure them ran the risk of being badly hurt and of being washed overboard. While I kept the starboard side alee, Collins and his men did the job without hurt or loss.

But the charges had not been loose without effect.

'Did you notice any damage?' I asked Collins when he came forward to report them secure.

'I'm afraid so,' he said. 'The degaussing cable is cut in at least two places. I saw it fizzling when the scupper emptied once and when I saw a chance I felt one of the breaks. It was a deep cut right into the core of the cable and would have been burning if it hadn't been under water. I sent a hand to have it switched off.'

'That's right. But God knows where the compass will be now. It would happen when they weren't adjusted for the degaussing off! Damn!'

'It's a curse all right, sir, but we're lucky the charges didn't do more harm.'

I noticed that Collins was shivering. Looking at him I could see he had been under water.

'Well, get along below now, Collins. Take some rum. Good job.'

'The men . . . I'll give them a tot too, sir.'

'Sure.'

194

He went cautiously down the bridge ladder. I wondered vaguely if he would find any dry clothes; probably not.

The night which followed was better than the previous one, and I did not have to keep such a constant watch on the ship, though we were obliged to remain hove to. The barometer had risen very little and was still registering under twenty-nine inches.

In the morning the weather was comparatively clear and the wind had decreased to a strong gale. The fury of the storm was over but a tremendous swell remained and the sea was still running high.

The convoy was scattered – and hell's half-acre in this case was five thousand square miles. They would never reform; everyone was on his own. Our duty now was to find Newfoundland before our fuel ran out.

The old chief stood in my cabin as he had stood before me in our last ship when he was trying to get us to Iceland sucking at the dregs of his tanks.

'Seven hundred miles, Chief.'

'Seven hundred . . .' he repeated, looking at the bulkhead as if there were figures written on it.

'We're making about seventy miles a day.'

'And burning oil for two hundred, easy.'

'It'll improve.'

'It'll have to, sir.'

Lloyd sniffed and held tightly to the bunk board as the cabin tilted uphill. He was wearing seaboots for once, so the water washing across the cabin did not bother him. I was half sitting and half lying on my settee, my shoulders wedged between the padded back at the top end and the desk. With the pitching of the ship, I seemed to be alternately reclining with my feet higher than my head, and then bending over so that I tended to fall forward. My trousers were causing me some discomfort because, while they stuck to the leather upholstery of the settee, my stern slid up and down inside them, so that one moment my trousers were loose and the next exceedingly tight.

'Trouble is, Chief, we're trying to steer west, and it might be sou'-west or it might be nor'-west we're steering. The compass is all over the ocean; probably thirty or forty degrees out.

195

I don't know. Don't know where we are either; no sights for days.'

'Bad, eh?'

He reached down into the sloshing water and tightened up the rope which was securing the chair to the desk.

'Better get the steward to bale this place out, sir,' he said, straightening up as lightly as a feather as the ship pitched down.

'Yes . . .' I looked at the lined, unshaven face of the man I'd grown to like so much. 'You keep the fuel bill down, Lloyd, and it won't be bad.'

'That I'll do, sir.'

Four afternoons later we fell in with another corvette. We had seen her now and then in the morning when she had risen, like a toy boat, on top of the waves. Now, steaming along together, we compared our positions: we were seventy miles apart, theoretically.

She told us that all her search gear had broken down as ours had, but her compass was good. So we hung on.

It became colder and snowed, and the spray which flew across the ship froze. Next day the ice was inches thick, and the ship was losing stability with the weight of it on her decks and upperworks, and the empty tanks added to her tenderness. She rolled in a top-heavy fashion as the men chopped with axes at the soft salt-water ice.

That afternoon we saw what might have befallen us and still might befall our partner, who was even lower in fuel than we were. A large ocean-going tug was towing an old four-funnelled destroyer – her tanks were dry. The ten-day westerly gale had subdued at least one ship and the cold had added to her discomfort; she had neither light nor heat and the ice was thick on her topsides. We went on. Two minesweepers were escorting the pair, so they needed no additional assistance; not that we would have been any use.

We were looking for land the following dawn, a dirty, misty dawn. The cold wind still blew and the sea was rough. Where was the coast? We pressed on gingerly.

Suddenly a yellowish light gleamed hazily for a moment above us to starboard. At that instant we saw waves breaking against the foot of black, towering cliffs ahead in forbidding, foam-drenched confusion. Then the grunt of the fog signal above mingled with the

196

crescendo below and we saw the white finger on top of the high rocks. It was Cape Spear Lighthouse.

We turned together and presently were passing through the gorge-like Narrows of the harbour of St John's, the sea birds wheeling and crying overhead.

14. The King

When the ship that is tired returneth,
With the sign of the sea showing plain,
Men place her in dock for a season,
And her speed she reneweth again.
So shalt thou, lest, perchance, thou grow weary
In the uttermost part of the sea,
Pray for leave, for the good of the service
As much and as oft as may be.

Hammering of wintry seas against the Nova Scotia coast was lessening and brilliant days of sunshine were becoming more frequent when I took my leave in March 1943. The ship's overhaul and refitting were well under way in a Maritimes outport and the first draft of leave men was almost due to return, or disperse to other appointments.

Home had seemed so remote at times, so hopelessly far away; it had even appeared problematical sometimes whether I would ever reach it again. But I really was home now. And it was a vastly different life. It had comfort, security, no night watches – and my wife was in command. Moreover, I had the opportunity of studying my small daughter whom I knew very little. And after a while I began to know that my wife would not be the only one I would miss when I went away again.

But, I promised myself, I was not going away again – not any more. I went to Ottawa to make sure. A day would do it; I had only one person to see, the Director of Naval Personnel.

'I'd like a shore appointment, sir, please,' I said boldly.

'Shore appointment? You don't want a shore appointment!'

'I do, sir, very much.'

'Sorry, no.'

But this was said in a delightful way with the usual winning smile.

I was surprised to be so summarily turned down. After all I had been three years afloat and the war was three and a half years old. The man before whom I was seated had been our Captain (D) all the previous year in Newfoundland, and I was sure he would see my point.

One did not of course, argue. I did, however, put as much as possible into the few additional words I was permitted on the matter. Then what was called the frigate list was produced and I saw, among the few names that were already assigned, my own name.

'There you are,' D.N.P. pointed out, with a very determined finger, I thought. 'The first of the new construction will be commissioning in June on the West Coast, and you'll be out that month or in July with *Matane*, the first frigate in the East–your ship is building at Vickers in Montreal as you see. So you've got three months on the beach.'

It is amazing how a long-cherished ambition can so quickly be destroyed. I felt foiled, and knew that sharp disappointment would set in later. Yet, in spite of this, something had already crept in to mitigate my feelings of thwarted expectation. I would like to see one of these ships. I would like to feel one.

'What would you like to do in the meantime?' I heard D.N.P. saying. 'Have you been on the West Coast?'

I said no, I hadn't.

'Well, we'll send you out there if you like; it's a nice place.'

I told him I had heard as much from the people who came from the West Coast, but that I would prefer to wait in Halifax.

'Very well, then,' he said most kindly; and getting up, walked around to my side of his desk. 'You'll be relieved when your ship has finished her refit. Then see the Manning Commander at Halifax and tell him what you want to do. Do anything you like.' He held out his hand. 'Sorry I can't do better, but C.O.s, are still scarce and will be for some time.'

Skiing in the Laurentians with my wife finished off my leave; then we came home and I headed back to the yard at the outport. I finally left the little ship in April, with mixed feelings.

Nearly two months went by. I spent some of it in the dockyard picking up technical information and reading reports in the library but most of it I spent at home. As the summer came we would walk, my wife and I, wheeling or carrying the little girl, down the road to the North West Arm and sometimes across the water in the ferry to the delightful, quiet woods on the other side. It was my happiest time of the war. It may have been for my wife, too, but none of it was really happy for her.

Then suddenly one day, instead of enjoying the pleasure of lunch in a friend's ship in the dockyard, as had been arranged, I found myself sitting at the wardroom table of my own ship. How quickly life changed! But it was not really my ship; she belonged to a fellow who had been taken ill and had to be whipped into hospital. I, being in the way of a spare hand in the eyes of Captain (D), was hustled off at an hour's notice to Pictou, where the ship was lying, to relieve the captain temporarily. He was to be away only two weeks or so and as the ship was doing training exercises following her refit and would not be operationally employed for a little while, I did not strenuously object; not that it would have done any good if I had.

But the time passed and he did not return, and I became quite alarmed about him. The training was finished and a coastal convoy job done with the prospects of more ahead when, to my joy, something went wrong with the rudder. So we stayed in Halifax for several weeks having it rebushed and I was able to check the progress of the ship's rightful captain. But the naval hospital was renowned for holding on to its patients, and the rudder was repaired before the captain. We had made another voyage before he returned to the ship, fit and ready to let me step ashore.

The construction programme was behindhand, so despite the two months I had spent in this corvette, I still had ten days at home before going to the builder's yard. I had done very well really. And now I was going to a new command, a new ship with a new crew, both of which would have personality quirks to learn about and manage. My frigate was waiting.

Under the high, intensely blue sky, broken only by small white cumulous clouds which seemed to float, unmoving, just above the horizon, the frigate glided forward over a sea of even deeper blue. Oblique shafts of sunlight penetrated far down into the warm, clear water, stabbing at the ship's undersides as the long, sturdy hull gently rose and fell. Bermuda lay a hundred miles due west, the northern edge of the Sargasso Sea lay a little to the south, and the cold November weather along Canada's coast was pleasantly behind us, back on the other side of the Gulf Stream.

The sun reflected dazzlingly every now and then from a window on the flagdeck of the other frigate abeam of us, and we saw in her, as we steamed along together in the sub-tropical warmth, the picture we ourselves presented.

Lying low, she had handsome lines in a heavy kind of way, her upperworks rising steeply from the fo'c'sle deck in a broad-chested style to the bridge and the tripod mast abaft it. Beyond the stout-looking funnel the superstructure sloped down in steps to a long, low quarter-deck. She was a graceful vessel yet with a sheer that expressed weight. To me she was very easy to look at.

And what was to be our ship's fortune? She was to have her disastrous moment. But in the meantime she was strong and well-armed and perhaps well-manned.

Through the sunny days and warm, calm nights on the wide spaces of an unmolested sea we did our training. We went through all the manœuvres of shaking down. Then the two frigates turned towards the ungracious north.

Our first operational job came at once. It was in a sense un-important, small, but it was the first of a variety of duties in which this ship was to be engaged during the next eight months – until catastrophe overtook her.

The Atlantic tide had turned. The strength of the escort forces and air support had so increased in 1943, thanks to the decisions at Casablanca, that by the early summer the enemy had been all but swept from the ocean. But they were back again in the autumn, this time armed with new weapons, powerful anti-aircraft guns and acoustic torpedoes. Nevertheless, our weight in numbers and our own technical advances gave us the greater success.

So when we sailed from Halifax that December with three other frigates for the Flemish Cap to dig out just one submarine, it was perhaps understandable that we could be spared for the moment for such a meagre task. A U-boat was known to have established herself for the last month or so on this isolated bank in compara-tively shallow water, fifty miles by a hundred out beyond the Grand Banks, with the sole object apparently of transmitting weather reports to Germany. She transmitted regularly and molested no one.

We searched with, against and across the breaking seas for three weeks in the teeth of icy winds which cut our faces and made our eyes bloodshot. We only succeeded in stopping her broadcasts. Then we went south to Sable Island to hunt down another U-boat which seemed to have been on this beat for upwards of a year, on and off; it was thought to be a spotter station.

As we swept the waters on both sides of the low, crescent-shaped island we encountered only unpleasant weather. But we learnt to know how our shipmates acted, thought, worked and were prepared to live, in the bitter cold and salt-sticky wetness, in rain and snow.

There were a few, though, who already knew one another very well. Lieutenant Collins was still with me. He was first lieutenant, and between us we had searched the naval by-ways for old hands. We had found only a few: Signalman Burley – I could not go without him, this big, happy, wide-awake man – and Leading Signalman West, an officer now with his commission; the two stewards, one now a petty officer. I needed my old steward, Auclair; he was willing to serve with me in a third ship. There were one or two others from as far back as the wretched days of Gaspé and Jamaica. But beyond this nucleus a hundred and sixty officers and men were new. Most had been afloat, many in action, and of the six executive officers all but one had spent at least a year in a ship. The coxswain had been twenty years in the Navy, the engineer-officer, Lieutenant McNab, at least thirty in the Merchant Service (he hailed from the country you would expect, though long ago).

We were not in an encouraging region. As we backed and filled off the treacherous, low-lying island which no sailor ever wanted to see because of its hidden sandpits, the forces of nature froze the armament. This worried Leading Torpedoman Wood of the quarter-deck.

The very purpose of Wood's job was to keep his hundred depth charges ready to go over and explode at whatever depth was ordered, and to replenish those expended from the two hundred in the magazine below. But as the sea washed over the quarter-deck and broke against the racks and throwers, flinging its waters upwards like waves crashing against the rocks of a rugged shore, the locks and pistols of the weapons became sealed in solid ice.

Wood had seen this happen before when he was in a destroyer. But he had not been a leading hand then; it had not been his responsibility, except to chip at the ice with a hammer when he was told to. Now he took the matter more seriously. He informed the torpedo officer he could not keep it under control.

'You've seen them yourself, sir,' Wood argued. 'The depth charge parties of each watch spend their time chipping the ice away – when not jumping clear of the green ones coming over. Even if we could set the charges to "Fire" I doubt if they'd roll down the rails.'

The broad, six-foot leading torpedoman had thrown back the hood of his grey duffle coat revealing a thatch of sandy hair and was looking down at the diminutive French-speaking torpedo officer, whose equally youthful face seemed to register perplexity and uncertainty.

'Well, better just keep them at it,' he suggested.

'But we're getting nowhere, sir.'

'No.'

'It's not much use being here, sir, if we can't do anything when we do find a sub.'

'No,' muttered the torpedo officer. He stood looking out along the wet, glistening deck from the after passageway, his eyes screwed up against the wind. Then he said 'Thanks,' turned and walked forward, the heels of his rubber seaboots scuffing the iron deck as he trod.

We had a conclave about it – the torpedo officer had decided to tell me the difficulty.

It was an old problem and I resurrected a thought I had had before in a corvette which would not work there. We got McNab up to ask him.

'This ice aft, Chief,' I said gently. 'Is there any way you could get hot salt water on to it?'

'Hot salt whatter? On deck? Wherre is it going to come from, Capt'n? Hot salt whatter!'

'Well, Chief, I don't know, I'm sure. I was wondering if you could devise a means of pumping some up; enough to thaw the ice off the charges and rails now and then. They're gummed up properly. I know you can't get steam up there.'

'Steam? Certainly not.'

203

We were sitting in my cabin where it was warm and comfortable. The torpedo officer was reclining well back in a chair, his legs crossed, frequently tapping his cigarette over an ash-tray. He looked across as the chief engineer spoke.

'Whatter! Now you're asking for something that was never provided for.'

The old chief put a big forefinger into the bowl of his pipe and tamped the fine ash down on the dottle within. He sucked hard at a match, his cheeks hollowing, then took a good grip of the stem with his teeth and eyed me through his steel-rimmed specs. 'Circulatin' whatter you're talkin' aboot? Well, that would be difficult. You see, Capt'n . . .' and he explained the circulating system in detail. 'Of course, if you really need hot whatter . . . sure, I can do it.'

Leading Torpedoman Wood was relieved. This was something! It was glorious to see the steam rising as the water came out of the hose; it reminded him of the vapour which rose in cold weather from another stream more personal and familiar to him.

Tedious, cold and objectionable as this search was, with almost no hope of success, the ship offered warmth and comfort inside. The quarters were well lit and dry and you could go from end to end of the ship through passageways below decks. The motion was much easier than a corvette's and you did not have to contend with the cold unpleasantness in bad weather of having your behind washed as the sea gushed up through the plumbing while you sat on the seat in the heads.

When the signal came for our ships to return to Halifax, no one was sorry. We steered all night before a south-easter with torrential rain, and in the morning when we entered harbour we found that the rain had been snow over the land, the heaviest snowstorm of the winter. The bollards along the jetty had to be dug out before we could throw our mooring lines over them.

15. Support Force

It was now the beginning of February 1944. In two weeks we were ready to sail again. But conditions were different. Our ship was to be a unit of a support force, and we were to carry the senior officer. To be in a support group was handsome news. The Canadian Navy had never had such a flotilla before, but now two such groups were being created and the one to which we were assigned was to comprise six ships, two frigates and four corvettes – there were not enough frigates yet to make a group entirely of this class. We would take the designation EG9; there were apparently eight British groups of this kind either formed or being formed.

The word spread through the ship, and to most it meant something different, something which sounded intriguing. To those fresh to the sea it meant just more excitement. In the wardroom our appointment to such a group received less attention perhaps than the news that the senior officer was going to reside in the ship. This information was greeted with uncertainly, especially as it became known that the S.O. was not a Canadian but an R.N. Commander. To me it ran deeper than that. My feelings were not even mixed.

The very thing I had favoured, that of the senior officer not being in direct command of the ship he was in, had at last come to fruition. But it had descended upon me. This meant that it would be difficult sometimes to draw the line of responsibility and could be the cause of muddled and perhaps conflicting orders on the bridge; in some cases possibly interference, and that could lead to strained relations between us. It would be like having a high-powered elderly relative living with you. I foresaw it as being confusing to the crew.

Yet it could work. In the Royal Navy no senior officer was ever carried separately in a ship until the heavy formations were reached, such as a battle cruiser squadron where the admiral would be in a ship suitably appointed and commanded by a flag captain. The Americans, however, had nearly always carried commanders of small-ship groups separately. I had liked the arrangement since the time of my first convoy catastrophe, when I had had an opportunity to see the great task facing the senior officer. I had spoken out, in fact, at a conference in the depot ship in Iceland, following that event. The conference was attended by the local operational authorities and the captains of all the ships in Hvalfjord – American, British and Canadian. Brashly I had voiced my opinion. The British appeared to feel I had spoken out of turn. I learned only afterwards that this was the American custom.

On discussing it further with U.S. naval officers I also learned that, while they agreed wholeheartedly with the system, no one liked carrying the S.O. I did not visualize myself eventually being in such a position.

Some of the officers in our ship were a bit worried as to whether they would be retained to do the added duties of staff specialists. I was sure the signal officer and the navigator would be, because they were both fully qualified, but we would probably have radar and telegraphist officers added to our company; for one thing, we were to be equipped with a high frequency direction finder.

The senior officer was on his way from England. I had met him once or twice in Halifax when he had been in a destroyer, but I could not remember much about him. And I was not anxious to know him any better. I felt, as did some others, that we could have provided our own senior officers. From the point of view of doing the job we could have, but we did not have enough captains to separate any from command of a ship.

As to our appointment to a support group, this I was very pleased about, although its duties were rather vague. It was simply stated that we would wander around the ocean augmenting the strength of close escorts whose convoys were threatened with attack by submarines and to act as a striking force against U-boat concentrations. But this would call for searching, and as we all knew from experience searching was not very profitable; at least we had not found it so on our side of the Atlantic. But we were to be based on Londonderry, which might make a difference.

The remnants of the soggy snow still lay along the edges of the dockyard roads and under the big crane when the S.O. arrived. He immediately set about acquainting himself with the ships of his group who were now making ready to depart, and drawing up plans which would enable him to guide them through whatever adventures they might encounter. But he did all this unobtrusively.

He was a tall, slim man and very handsome, with dark wavy hair which was greying at the temples. He looked everything a naval officer should, and was possessed of that quiet reserve so common in Englishmen, though not so often found in naval officers. I saw that the captains of the other ships took to him.

When sailing day came, I felt certain that I was leaving Halifax for the last time, that I would not return until the war was over. This I estimated at about a year; less, I hoped. I tried to cheer my wife, as well as myself, with the thought that this was the last time we would have to part, but it did not make it any easier for me to say good-bye to her that cold winter morning as I left my house. But our little girl did not seem to feel it; a toy she held in her small hand was of more immediate interest to her, and I was glad in a way.

At noon we cast off from the jetty and headed up the harbour, then turned and steamed slowly down past the crowded wharves of the dockyard. They obviously interested the senior officer, who was standing close to me, and he asked about several of the ships. I told him all I knew of them – except one which had caught his eye. She was lying alongside Number One jetty, temporarily off her station as guardship in the Narrows at the entrance to Bedford Basin; I merely said what she was; I did not tell him the story of her more recent past.

She had been a big private yacht at one time and had been bought or taken on loan by the Navy at the beginning of 1940 with a number of other yachts to fill the role of coastal defence until proper vessels were built. She did valiant service for two years or so, and then one day, after a spell up the coast, she was ordered to Halifax. The signal from Headquarters directing her thither read to the effect, that she was to proceed at economical speed, etcetera, gave her E.T.A., and ended with '. . . on arrival the ship is to be de-ammunitioned and destroyed.'

Such a fate was sad but timely in a way. She had struggled out in all weathers, bearing a heavy gun on her flimsy upper deck but making, at a distance, a good silhouette of power and strength.

She had done her duty. Now she would be a small emporium of valuable salvageable material in an era of short supply.

The shipwright chiefs descended upon her and mentally tore her plank from plank. Then they went back to their shops and sent their workmen aboard.

The civilian foreman who had been servicing ships from constantly inadequate supplies saw, little though it was, material which had been lacking for years and which could now earn him a few quick shots of rum – brass ventilators, door handles, steel beams, anchor chain.

The dockyard engineers seized pumps and eyed the polished shaft and confiscated tools; and they arranged for a well-known merchant of Halifax to come and collect the boiler (which would in due time be sold back to the Government). The specialists took the movable stores – the lonely compass, the asdic oscillator, small arms, and were contemplating the big gun.

Almost as soon as the last wisp of steam had drifted from the pipe abaft her funnel the little man-o'-war was being gutted by the retainers of the dockyard. They were down below stripping her like miners hewing coal out of the walls of a pit. She was being destroyed.

Then a messenger arrived on the double at the Engineer Commander's office with a signal. At the same moment another messenger crossed the threshold of the shipwright's office. Telephone calls were going to others from the signal distribution centre. The Engineer Commander, the Shipwright Lieutenant-Commander, the base ordnance officer and the rest of the interested parties read or heard the message. And each issued an immediate order. Then they leaned back sadly in their swivel chairs. But they thanked their stars they were not the base signal officer.

In the signal office the slender fingers of a pretty Wren had been running lightly over cyphers to see if a fair sample of recent messages compared favourably with their decoded versions. Presently she came upon one which was not quite right, and when she looked at it again she saw that it made quite a difference. The message had come from N.S.H.Q., Ottawa, to the Base and was about an ex-yacht. The end of the decoded text read, '. . . is to be de-ammunitioned and destroyed.' But the Wren could see it should have read, '. . . is to be de-ammunitioned and de-stored.' She drew it to the attention of the duty signal officer, who wasted no time in passing it on before he had a fit.

As we passed close astern of the Halifax–Dartmouth ferry plying its way across the Stream, the signal yeoman reported that all the ships had warped out.

'Hoist "Line ahead, close order, ten knots",' the senior officer ordered. The yeoman passed the order to the flag deck below and I was glad to see the flags run up on the yardarm halyard in less time than would allow for criticism. When those astern of us had acknowledged the signal, the flags were hauled down and we set the speed at ten knots as did the other ships as they assumed their positions one and a half cables astern of each other.

Thus we sailed out of one of the greatest wartime harbours. The gate of the defence boom was swung open for us by the two vessels moored at latch and hinge. We went down the swept channel past the Thrum Cap, against the sands on which lay the pilot cutter that had been stranded there a few weeks before in the great snow-storm; on past Never Fail Shoal and the Inner Fairwat Buoy to the high cliffs of Chebucto Head. I glanced at the stumpy lighthouse which surmounted the headland, the friendly sentinel which I knew so well, and fervently hoped that the misfortunes of war would not prevent me from seeing it again as the landmark of my home.

'Nine red, G twelve,' the senior officer said to the yeoman, and with creditable smartness a string of flags went fluttering aloft. When the signal had been repeated down the line of ships, the senior officer ordered the 'executive' and we altered course ninety degrees to port, increasing speed to twelve knots, while those astern followed round in succession. We had turned our backs on the coast of Canada and were standing out to sea bound for the Azores.

The crash of the cold Atlantic rollers hitting the decks had the old familiar thud about them when, two days later, we were being lashed by the inevitable gale. I recognized then from visible evidence the superior power against the sea which this frigate had over the little corvettes steaming along on either side of us. While we were ploughing our way through the waves with comparative steadiness, though with sheets of freezing spray flying over the ship and green seas rumbling inboard and hissing venomously as

o   209

they crumbled and poured over the side, the corvettes were rising high, hovering on the billows' crests, then diving down into the trough almost out of sight. Yet I knew that they could withstand as hard a storm as we could, though they had to take greater care. The S.O. had already reduced the speed of the group, and now, after we had talked about it, he slowed down still more. Finally he had to heave the ships to.

Curiously enough, the second frigate in the group was the one with which we had trained and which had accompanied us on our more recent excursions.

To me there was another singular feature about the group. One of the corvettes was my old knave. I had not been on board her since the day I had given her up, had hardly seen her again until now, but I knew that it had taken nine months to put her back into service and I had heard that her engines had remained in a dubious state. Her name was known in every wardroom for her troubles, but I felt sorry for her now. You have a sense of nostalgia when you look at a ship in which you have once lived. Yet it is not altogether for her that your feelings run strong; it is the life you yourself had in her, like the memory of a life you once led in a house.

She was the slowest of the ships; her bearings would still heat if she were pressed; therefore the group's maximum speed was limited to hers. So once more she was slowing me down.

The captains of three of the four smaller ships were in command for the first time. Since the previous summer of 1943 volunteers who had started their seafaring careers at the beginning of the war had had the opportunity of taking command of minesweepers and corvettes. They had to pass through a 'command course' and qualify in navigation, and those who did so shouldered a responsibility which was considerable for men who had been acquainted with the sea for such a comparatively short time. The acquisition of ample knowledge of naval warfare over several years was not unreasonably difficult, but to be familiar with all the vagaries of the sea and to keep a ship clear of reefs and shoals in coastal waters beset with tides, to pilot her in and out of congested harbours in daylight, darkness and fog, and to so manœuvre her that she would not foul herself or collide with others, these things required seamanship. To older sailors, bred in ships from boys, seamanship is a kind of sixth sense, but to new sailors, taking to it later in life, that sense would not come easily, if ever. Moreover, could they co-ordinate fighting and seamanship at the same time?

So those officers of the R.C.N.V.R. who assumed command during the war deserve great credit for the fortitude with which they undertook it. It must have been hard going for them and not without worry. I do not doubt that after a year or so many looked back and wondered how they had managed to do it in the earlier months. I do not minimize their achievements. Though some looked back on a chapter of accidents, others looked back on marked success. Ultimately three-quarters of the smaller ships were commanded by them.

As the gale abated the six ships moved eastward, and presently we found ourselves emerging from the bitter cold into the warmth of the North Atlantic Drift. On deck coats came off, then caps and jerseys, and engineers and stokers came up from below to taste the clean air in comfort. Spread out in line abreast, sweeping our way to the Azores was no hardship after the Canadian coast.

Now we had a chance to tidy up and see that things were in first class running order. Stores came out and were re-stowed, but nothing to speak of was wet. The ship did not leak. The engineers tickled things up below and overhauled machinery on deck. The new bomb-throwing hedgehog* on the foredeck was greased and all the secondary guns were taken down and oiled and polished. The weather had at last lent itself to throwing the ship wide open and airing and cleansing her hitherto battened-down, over-heated interior. And one or two new aerials were rigged and fresh halyards rove to the signal yards as they swung beneath the warming sun.

My time, like that of everyone else, was fully taken up, and some of it, though really very little, was occupied with the S.O. This mostly had to do with orders which he gave the group.

As long as I could remember I had disliked in advance people I was forced to meet – since my mother used to take me to visit her friends whose nice little boys she wanted me to know. But I had been unable to dislike the S.O.

Before we sailed I had spoken to him about our relative positions. We were in his day-cabin, which was next to mine, a kind of

* A rectangular mounting containing twenty-four 50 lb. bombs, fired electrically in a pattern over the bow

office. His dark eyes looked at me gravely. 'I hate to say it, sir, but I think we'll both have to be very careful not to foul each other's flags.'

His mouth moved very slightly as though he were tasting a small peppermint. Then he said, 'I hope very much that we won't have any difficulties or differences. But I know what you mean. As a matter of fact I didn't want this job either. I would much rather have remained in command of my own ship.'

It was good to hear this, in a way, but it left me wondering if I had not spoken too abruptly. I apologized for having risked spoiling his welcome, but I did want to state my apprehensions clearly at the outset of our relationship. He obviously understood and we let it go at that. But I continued to feel something of a boor for having spoken out. He seemed to be a sensitive chap and I could not help thinking there might have been no need to bring the matter up at all.

On the second evening of our good weather I had dinner with him. He usually had his evening meal late and alone because he could not accustom himself to our supper hour. I had misssed supper this evening, as I had been busy in the charthouse with the navigator.

It was the first time I had talked to the S.O. on other than immediate matters. He told me something about himself, but not without my asking.

He had entered the navy thirty years ago when he was twelve. That was the starting age for officers in those days. 'I suppose I served in almost every class of ship,' he recalled in a soft, clear voice, full of inflection. 'But, like most of my contemporaries during that era when the Service was drastically cut, I was not favoured with rapid promotion.' He had not, however, been discharged like many others. Some of his later years, just before the war, he said, had been served in the Admiralty. I wondered whether his shy and retiring manner might have had something to do with his not having been employed in more spectacular activities.

He did not emphasize anything he had done and he was not very expansive when I asked him how he had won the Distinguished Service Order. After a hesitation he said, 'Crashed the defences of a North African port and put a landing party ashore.' I waited and then asked him more about it. He just said that in his withdrawal the destroyer he commanded was so badly shelled that she sank before he could get her back to Gibraltar. He made it sound very trivial, though there was a trace of sadness in its finale. I was sure that he was the kind of officer in whom, no matter how fear might assail him, the inbred traditions of the Royal Navy and his loyalty to it would stand fast in any hour of crisis and never allow him to falter.

We were interrupted for a few minutes by the leading signalman coming in with the submarine report. There was a fair number out, mostly to the north of us. My old anxieties about a situation report had largely disappeared and were replaced to some extent by pure interest.

We went on to speak of tradition. He said that in the R.N. tradition was a heritage of which they were very proud and in a sense was the moral backbone of the Service. 'You are not far removed from it yourselves, you know. You are a part of the Empire and much of your stock is British.'

'That's so, sir,' I acknowledged. 'But although we learned your customs and in fact were patterned after the Royal Navy, I feel, and I think most of us feel, that we have no direct right to your traditions. Nor could they apply really, because, what made them occurred mainly before we were in existence.'

A book lying on his desk, which I had several times seen him reading, rather demonstrated my point, I thought. It was Southey's *Life of Nelson*. 'Our tradition,' I suggested, 'is possibly being made now.'

Before we had finished talking, we were interrupted again, this time by the yeoman himself. He handed a signal to the senior officer and a copy to me. It read: 'Proceed with despatch to support convoy in position at 2000z latitude 49° 35' north longitude 41° 50' west course 067° altering to 074° at 1400z 6th speed nine knots. Report when rendezvous made.'

Having read it, we both stood almost simultaneously. 'This is where we start supporting,' remarked the S.O. as we made our way to the charthouse.

As dusk was approaching two days later, we were converging on the convoy from its quarter. Although we had been well to the eastward of it when we had received our orders, we had had to steer somewhat east of north to intercept it, as we had been far to the south and the convoy had been progressing steadily to the eastward into what the Germans called the 'Black Pit' – the central Atlantic region of least air cover. The prospects of a few days in the neighbourhood of the Azores, where we were to fuel, faded as we left these pleasanter waters to turn to our more familiar ground where turbulent seas and sullen skies prevailed.

The senior officer brought his group close enough to be clearly visible to most of the merchantmen, and then sent the others on towards the van while he ordered me to enter the convoy and go up between the centre columns. 'I'd like to show these fellows as much as possible of the strength they have protecting them,' he remarked as he took a pace nearer me – one of about three available to him on the cluttered bridge. As we forged our way past the heavily laden vessels, overtaking them at twice their speed, men on the decks of the near ones waved to us, a symbol which always gave me the feeling that I was glad to have the privilege of being with them.

The ships of this convoy were very different from those which had made up the convoys of earlier days. No broken down tramps these, no fifteen-hundred-tonners here. The day had at last dawned when America had once more lived up to the name of her tall statue which looks out to seaward from the harbour of New York. Liberty ships sailed out in their hundreds, and here was a fleet of sturdy steel-grey ten-thousand-tonners striding across the ocean where their frail but valiant predecessors had struggled against odds which were all but insurmountable.

We passed the Commodore's ship and advanced towards the destroyer which was moving in short zig-zags across the front of the convoy, the senior officer of the close escort. Signal lamps flashed, she straightened out on a steady course, and we came up alongside her, a hundred feet or so off. The gunner's mate on the forward gun deck rested the butt of a line-throwing rifle against the combing and pointed the muzzle towards the mast-head of the destroyer. One of his party stood by him with a bucket in his arms. At a word he fired, and from the wire-wound barrel of the rifle shot a steel rod invisible to the eye until the long thin cord which was attached to it, and which uncoiled itself from the bucket, was seen to hang over the destroyer, drift a little with the wind and then fall across her deck, to be seized by the waiting seamen. Thus between the two ships a tangible line of communication stretched.

Within a minute a wave and a shout came from the destroyer's deck and the gunner's party hauled away on the line. Across the intervening space came a sealed can bobbing up and down, well clear of the water, as the men in the one ship veered and the others pulled. As it came inboard we sheered off and drew ahead. The can, containing documents concerning the convoy and the disposition of the close escort force, was handed to the senior officer by the gunnery officer, who I heard complaining to the first lieutenant that the men in the destroyer had cut the steel rod from the line and kept it. It struck me that they were much less gentlemanly than we were in the business of replenishing depleted stores.

As we ran on ahead the S.O. examined the documents he had been given and began to dictate messages to the rest of the ships in the group. We then spread out in a great semi-circle well in advance of the convoy so that now any submarine who might try to approach within range of the merchant ships would have to penetrate two lines of defence. Moreover, if a U-boat were sighted by any one of us we would have no compunction in leaving our station and calling for the assistance of a neighbour to deal with him, for in doing so we would not uncover a direct approach to the convoy as the close escort would. We were here to protect, but also to roam within reasonable bounds and to strike if we could.

Next day we fuelled. The problem of endurance in trans-Atlantic crossings had largely been solved in the past year or so. No more making for port before the job was done, no more curtailment of speed. Though weather did not always make it possible, fuelling at sea had become common practice.

After our four corvettes had gone into the convoy in pairs and replenished their supply, the two frigates went in. The two tankers were somewhere in the middle, and as we entered the side of the convoy and threaded our way across the columns between the ships we looked for a red flag flying from a ship's yardarm. We spotted both tankers, and I chose one, leaving the other for the frigate which was coming in from the other side. They were ordinary commercial tankers carrying oil of some kind to Britain, but one of their tanks contained fuel for the special use of escorts.

We dropped into the tanker's column and worked up until we were within half a ship's length of her somewhat battered stern. In a few minutes the men in the tanker were paying out a four-inch buoyant hose and this we brought on to the fo'c'sle head and coupled to the oil fuel line in the eyes of the ship.

A large bight of hose formed in the water at the side of the ship so that no undue strain would be taken on it if the ship were allowed to fall back too much; steadying hausers had been dispensed with as so many had been broken.

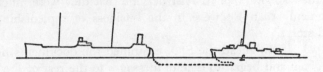

The oil commenced to run, warm oil so that it flowed easily, and the hose became submerged about ten feet. In this position, with the ship moving along at nine knots close up to the tanker's stern, we took on nearly two hundred tons of fuel in a matter of two and a half hours. You had to be constantly on the alert to prevent the weight of the ship coming on the hose, but this was made easier by keeping station on a buoy which was streamed from the tanker and which I kept as nearly as I could abreast the bridge. It was one of those curious buoys which sends up a tall fountain of water as it is drawn along, like the 'blow' of a whale; a very easy thing to see.

No matter how carefully a ship is steamed it is impossible to keep exactly the same speed as another for more than a few minutes without altering the revolutions of the propeller. This does not apply so much to high speed turbines, but it certainly does to reciprocating engines, even with large twin propellers like we had. In such cases as this and when manœuvring in and out of harbours I always had my old and trusty friend, Burley, at the wheelhouse voicepipe. I could then keep my eye on what I was doing and pass the helm and engine orders to him. His attention never wandered even though he might have to carry out this task for hours. I never knew him to miss an order – and I certainly would have known it if he had.

But in this instance my own attention wandered. Perhaps I had become a little over confident in the ship's ability to keep her station; it had been fairly easy up to now. Suddenly I realized that the guide buoy with its jet of water was opposite the forward gun deck instead of the bridge. I immediately increased the revolutions to catch up with it but not enough to increase the speed very much because I was aware of the difficulty of trying to settle the ship down once she had gathered too much way. But the wretched buoy still drew ahead. I increased the speed again. She did not seem to respond. Almost imperceptibly the ship was dropping back; or perhaps the tanker was going faster. I saw the bight of the hose grow smaller and then, to my horror, it came to the surface splashing as it tightened.

In a flash it happened! The end of the hose snapped, leapt like a whip over the fo'c'sle and spouted oil as black as ink over the white bow. With a final ugly fling it fell back into the sea, dead.

I was not polite to it.

The situation was seen on the tanker and word was evidently passed below to shut off the flow of oil.

I sent an inquiry down to McNab as to how much more oil he could take. Thirty tons was his answer. That decided it. I drew out and pulled ahead, remaining close abreast of the tanker while I apologized for what I had done. The chief officer, to whom I spoke over the loud-hailer, an Irishman without a doubt, was remarkably nice about it and told me two lengths had been lost earlier in the passage and now it was too short to feed any more escorts; I thought it had been on the short side. It occurred to me that he sounded quite happy at the prospect of not having to do any more fuelling for the rest of the voyage.

While I waited for the two chief engineers to agree on the amount of fuel taken, I was silently kicking myself for my disgraceful exhibition.

We stayed with this convoy another day and a half, then were ordered to part company and join another. After a day's run we fell in with it, a slow convoy this time which included the merchant aircraft carriers; MAC ships they were called. These were the principal answer to what remained of the hole in the Atlantic air umbrella. Having seen this convoy along what the Admiralty evidently considered the most dangerous part of its road, we moved over to yet another.

16. Distant Thunder

The weather had been variable but mainly fair. The wind held mostly to the east, which was common with the spring equinox, and at times blew hard, making it uncomfortable on the open bridge with its inefficient wind deflectors. Why the navy had approved the design with such poor baffling arrangements I never understood. The wind buffeted you all the time no matter where you stood.

When we reached the next convoy one of the close escorts, a Canadian destroyer, was away lending a hand to a ship which was on fire and had dropped out. The crew of the merchantman had abandoned the ship when the fire got beyond the control of the few hands she carried. But the destroyer captain, who was renowned for his many achievements at sea during the war, put a party of his own men on board the burning ship and, with the destroyer's fire pump and aided by some of the merchant seamen who returned, put it out after a hard struggle.

On joining, our senior officer had dispatched one of our corvettes to assist the destroyer. When the fire was finally subdued the three of them continued their voyage together and were not actually very far behind. They pushed on so well in the next twenty-four hours that they were only about fifteen miles on the convoy's port quarter by nightfall.

About 2100 that evening I was lying down in my sea-cabin hoping to sleep. With a little less thumping and a little quicker-sounding movement than usual on the ladder between the bridge and the wheelhouse which led down immediately outside my cabin, a signalman arrived at the door, knocked and thrust his head in. In an urgent voice, he said, 'Signal, sir.' He gave it to me and passed on to the charthouse where he expected to find the Commander. The signal was from the destroyer and read: 'U-boat sighted on surface bearing 025° 1.5 miles – diving.' Added to the signal was her position relative to the convoy.

With something of an effort I heaved myself off my bunk and

went into the charthouse next door. The senior officer, with the signal in his hand, was just throwing his legs over the edge of the settee as I entered. The charthouse served as his sea-cabin, which was very convenient for him, as he had the charts, instruments and everything he needed to work out his tactical schemes right by him. We both automatically went to the chart which was spread out on the large mahogany table. The table was built hard against the after bulkhead of the room and was of a height which made it comfortable to stand up against to work. Beneath its polished top was a series of long drawers containing folios of charts for all parts of the Atlantic seaboard.

'Looks as though he has a chance of catching him, sir,' I remarked, glancing at the signal again.

'Hard things to catch,' murmured the senior officer. He was fingering a pencil and absently gazing at the chart. Then, apparently having arrived at a decision, he reached for a signal pad and began to write. I watched his expression while he wrote, and thought again what a good-looking, intelligent face he had, with clean-cut features and very dark eyes; a clever man, though he seemed to underrate his own ability.

'I'll send the frigate,' he announced as he wrote.

It had taken him only a few moments to make this decision and in that time he had considered everything that was involved. I called the messenger from the wheelhouse and gave him the piece of paper to take to the wireless cabin.

'The frigate's the fastest, she'll be there in an hour from where she is now,' said the Commander, turning round and leaning back against the chart table. 'Our corvette should be giving the destroyer a hand in the meantime anyway,' he added.

He sat down on the settee and began pulling his boots on. I knew him well enough by this time to know that he wanted to go on deck.

'There's no need to go up, sir; all's well with us,' I said. 'Why don't you lie down again until more signals come in.'

'I'd like a breath of fresh air, I think, and I'll have a look at the weather.' His latter purpose I knew was an excuse.

'Wind's nor'-nor'-east, force four, fine and clear, sir,' I said. But he was probably as aware of it as I was.

He seemed to be a restless man. If there was anything going

on at all, or likely to happen, he would be on the bridge. I was sure this was because he was so accustomed to commanding his own ship. I wanted to try to persuade him not to; not that I minded; in fact, when he was talkative, which was seldom, I welcomed his company. But I wanted to get him into the habit of conducting affairs at night from the charthouse rather than the bridge. How difficult it would be for me though, if I were in his position, to refrain from coming to the bridge instead! His restlessness, I felt, was due to his comparative inactivity at times; there were periods when he had little to do really. His job was to prepare for and await action with the enemy, which was rather a more sedentary occupation than the active one he had known and become used to as a captain.

As he was about to leave the charthouse, another signal was brought in: 'Contact gained, attacking with hedgehog, corvette standing by.'

'Aha!' exclaimed the Commander. 'Sounds good.'

Almost immediately a signalman came in with a further message. This time it was from the senior officer of the close escort. He was on his way to join the action.

It was the plan that when a support group joined a close escort group, the senior officer of the close escort remained in overall charge, which was only logical. The Commander of the support force looked after his own ships but co-operated with the wishes of his confrere. The action of the senior officer of the close escort, an Englishman in an R.N. destroyer, in leaving his station, therefore, seemed rather unusual to me, even selfish, and I could not help expressing a word of surprise. My S.O., however, said nothing, though I gathered he did not approve either.

The S.O. stood thinking for a minute. 'That will make four of them; the senior officer will be on the scene before the frigate. Well, that's a fair party to deal with a U-boat. He was a phenomenally silent Hun; perhaps he didn't see the convoy.' With that he buttoned his coat, stepped through to the wheelhouse and climbed the ladder to the bridge.

Back in my sea-cabin I sat on the edge of the bunk. Normally I would have gone to the bridge first before lying down again, although it was less than an hour since I had been up there, but I had pains in my stomach and knew that I could not free myself of them until I had slept for an hour or two. These pains had been gradually getting worse in the past two months and had now reached the point where, after being awake for twelve or sixteen hours, I could no longer control them with hot drinks or food.

Auclair came in with cocoa and bread-and-butter which I took and then lay down. Before closing my eyes I pulled down the speaking tube from its retaining clip and pushed the button. As I did so the inevitable trickle of salt water splashed over my face from the mouthpiece. I wiped my face with a handkerchief and cursed the infernal drips. The cold, wet stickiness suddenly irritated me.

Through the tube I spoke to the officer-of-the-watch, and after checking a few things with him, told him I was going to sleep but to let me see any important signals and to call me anyway at midnight. After that I closed my eyes.

Twenty minutes later I was still awake. The wireless cabin was immediately beneath me and the ladder going down to it was outside my door. With both doors open I could hear the spoken messages coming over the loud-speaker of the radio telephone fairly clearly. I had only been half listening to them because, except for the name of the addressee and sender, I could rarely tell what they were about, as they were in letter code. Every now and then I could hear the phonetically-spoken letter groups drifting up and recognized by the code names the talking was between the ships hunting for the submarine. I half wished I could take my mind off it and go to sleep.

Then a signalman came down with two messages indicating that both the Canadian destroyer and our corvette had carried out an attack and that the two held the contact firmly. Interesting though this was, I closed my eyes again. I probably dozed off, because I seemed to come more sharply to my senses at the distant sound of a few words of plain language coming over the loud-speaker. What was it? Something about accurate attack ending with the corvette's code name. Then the buzzer went and I pulled the speaking tube down to my ear. 'Captain, sir?' came the gunnery officer's voice.

'Yes?' I had transferred the tube from ear to mouth – it did not drip this time.

'Several more signals in. The two ships have made four attacks, some with hedgehog and some with depth-charges. The last one by the corvette is claimed to be very accurate but I haven't the whole text yet.'

'What do the signals from the other two joining indicate?' I asked.

'The S.O., at least, is almost up to them. He had them fire a rocket to indicate their position.'

'Send every signal down to me now, will you please, as soon as it reaches you. I'll stay where I am in the meantime unless you want me; and keep your zig-zag frequent and irregular.'

I clamped the tube to the bulkhead beside me, turned my pillow over and relaxed again.

But I was wide awake. I listened attentively to the spoken signals, which were coming through louder now; they must have turned up the volume in the wireless cabin, everything was quite clear. There were two short messages the coded versions of which I recognized sufficiently to know that they were something to do with attacking; then there was an interval of about five minutes.

Suddenly a voice said: 'Submarine breaking surface – two miles to port.'

It was addressed to no one, obviously due to haste, but was closed with the code name of the destroyer. The ship had lapsed into plain language completely now, which was as well because, quick as code was, it was not fast enough for this situation. With a duplicate loud speaker on the bridge of each ship, the captains could obtain the information as soon as transmitted.

A moment later I heard another announcement; this time the voice was obviously English.

'Submarine surfaced to starboard of me – am closing.'

There was a lapse of about three minutes, then the same English voice. 'General chase – sub getting away on surface – am too distant for accurate fire control.'

I lay on my back with both ears clear of the pillow. The excitement of the battle had probably got into the blood of everyone who could hear.

The Canadian destroyer came on the air again: 'Enemy drawing away – am using what guns will bear.'

Immediately after this came a voice as yet unheard: 'Am engaging submarine ahead of me with gunfire.'

It was our frigate, who had evidently arrived on the scene as the chase reached its height.

Then from the senior officer in the British ship. 'Am barely closing – enemy has amazing speed.'

I had reconstructed the picture in my own mind. It was apparent that the U-boat had been forced to the surface by the severity of the underwater bombing he had received, or else the captain had decided, after an hour of these attacks, that he would have a better chance if he tried to escape on the surface. If he came up for the latter reason he had certainly misjudged the type of craft above him; despite the high speed he seemed to possess, he would never have attempted to outstrip a destroyer. The submarine's hydrophones should have been able to detect the class of ship as it passed overhead, but perhaps the hydrophones had been damaged by the explosions before the operator had had a chance to find out. Perhaps the slow hedgehogging speed had confused him. In any case he had surfaced, and for which ever reason he had done so he now refrained from diving.

Evidently the U-boat broke surface between the two destroyers, one more or less on either side of him, and had made off at a speed which would indicate that nothing was wrong with his diesels. His speed was so great that at least the English destroyer was taken a little by surprise, if she did not close the distance. In fact, it looked now as though the U-boat was getting away. The frigate seemed to have come in with her gun through being near the enemy's escaping course. The corvette had probably dropped out by reasons of her slower speed, but of course would be chugging along hoping to be in for the kill.

The signal officer came in to ask me if I was hearing everything satisfactorily. He said he had connected the public address system to the R/T receiver so that everyone in the ship could follow the battle.

The next signal which came in indicated that the enemy was returning fire with considerable strength.

Were the odds uneven? They may have been now but at the outset no odds were uneven with a submarine.

After a brief interval of silence the voices came on the air again in quick succession. It seemed as though each was waiting for a chance to speak.

BRITISH DESTROYER: 'Am closing now – report situation.'

CANADIAN DESTROYER: 'Range decreasing – now 2800 yards – am making 24 knots.'

FRIGATE: 'Maintaining distance – have enemy ahead.'

CANADIAN DESTROYER: 'Cannot see fall of shot but have his mark.'

BRITISH DESTROYER: 'Beware of diving.'

BRITISH DESTROYER: 'Report range.'

CANADIAN DESTROYER: '2400 yards.'

FRIGATE: '3000 yards – holding my own.'

Like searchlights the three ships' radars had the sub pinpointed.

I sat up in my bunk; I could rest no longer. I filled my pipe unconsciously, hesitating to strike the match in case I missed something.

CANADIAN DESTROYER: 'Believe scored direct hit – range 1900 yards – enemy fire fairly accurate if meant for me.'

FRIGATE: 'Assume direct hits also.'

Suspense for several minutes.

BRITISH DESTROYER: 'Closing more rapidly – keep star shell up.

CANADIAN DESTROYER: 'Sub's speed has diminished – am gaining fast now.'

CANADIAN DESTROYER: 'Another hit – sub slowing down.'

CANADIAN DESTROYER: 'Shall I ram?'

BRITISH DESTROYER: 'If he is stopping no.'

Evidently the Canadian destroyer was a good deal closer than the British ship, probably had been throughout the engagement, and was now almost upon his prey. Another message from him convinced his listeners that the U-boat's game was up. 'Sub stopped – crew abandoning boat – sending boarding party.'

We listened on and heard how the ships came up and lowered their boats; how, before the Canadian destroyer's boarding party could reach the U-boat, she was low in the water and visibly settling; all who could were pouring out of the conning-tower and jumping overboard.

As the destroyer slid past to windward of her whaler, the Captain, looking down from the bridge, saw a red glow in the conning tower as though there was a fire burning below, inside the boat. As the disc of illumination from her starboard searchlight moved jerkily along the sub's hull the havoc wrought by shell fire was starkly evident. The bridge appeared to be shattered and on the twisted metal lay several bodies. The last of the living crew had gone. The circle of white light moved along the foredeck. The gun seemed to have been uprooted and was leaning dejectedly towards the water.

The U-boat, now still and silent, deserted, almost awash, appeared large, larger than expected. Soon small whirlpools eddied over her deck and only the torn conning tower showed. Slowly, it too, disappeared beneath the black water.

The final episode of her plight was performed by the hands of her own men; she was scuttled like the *Graf Spee* at Montevideo.

Then the beam of light, joined now by others, turned on the survivors. The men in the whalers, having failed to board their victim, hauled the German sailors over the gunwales of their boats.

It was a valuable victory. She was of the larger, more noxious kind. The prisoners called her a sea-cow and said she was on passage from the coast of Newfoundland – where she had run aground at one point – to her Biscay base when she had been ordered to intercept the convoy. The ultimate intentions in her last mad dash were not clearly known because her captain was killed with the others on the bridge.

Several days after this we were ordered to make for port, our base at Londonderry, sweeping the paths which convoys followed.

In the latter part of March a tight patrol was established from the west coast of Ireland to the north of Scotland, a stretch of some four hundred miles. It was a blockade against the entry of submarines. A considerable number of ships took part, so that a substantial wall was placed across the western approaches to the British Isles. Assigned to the southern end of this patrol was E.G.9, and I was glad that it was not the northern end, for the region around Cape Wrath was not generally blessed with good weather.

We had stayed only a few days in Londonderry, and then went round the corner to engage in the endless perambulation of the north-west coast of Eire from Malin Head to the promontories of Mayo. None of us was very impressed with it, because for several

226

years submarines had rarely been known to venture as close to shore as this, although the authorities said there had been sightings recently. We did not know it at the time, but it became evident afterwards, that this scheme was a part, a prelude, to the gigantic naval operation which was soon to follow.

At the beginning of the ocean crossing, Leading Torpedoman Wood had been perhaps a little over anxious about his responsibilities. Life was not the light-hearted affair it had been when he was an able seaman. Also he had recently married, so that the dangers of an Atlantic patrol had gained a sharp double edge. Now he was happier. He could see the land nearly all the time and felt he had a much better chance if anything happened, in spite of the forbidding appearance of the coastline. Curiously enough the depth-charge crews, with whom he had been dissatisfied, had much improved. He found they could be alert and accurate. He laughed more too, showing the even line of his white teeth. It was the thought of the acoustic torpedoes he had hated. But here it did not seem to matter.

He was not the only one who shuddered at the mention of acoustic torpedoes, nor the only man who now felt safer. Probably all of us who had had our fill of the Atlantic had experienced that shudder. These weapons were designed to eliminate escorts and thus make convoys accessible. They were menacing indeed, these wandering torpedoes which attacked ships from behind, seeking their propellers.

Up and down the coast we went, criss-crossing our charted line every now and then, into the Bays of Donegal and Sligo, every mile of the area was covered. It was boring but we did not think it would last more than a month or so; surely something more exciting would develop. Anyway, there was the invasion coming along; when, no one knew, but it was coming. Once on this side we had heard talk of it which was really convincing. Training preparations were already under way and speculation was rife. We even feared the invasion might break while we were still examining the fossils on the cliffs of this barren and desolate coast.

On one of the trips I got a nasty shock. We had left 'Derry early one morning and were on our patrol ground in the early afternoon. The next day I was fairly all right but by the evening something went wrong. I could not see properly.

It was in the charthouse that I discovered it. I could not read the soundings on the chart! I was unable to focus on the little figures unless I stood back so far that they were too small to read. I looked at names on the coast printed in quite large letters. I made out Downpatrick Head but could hardly read Ballyshannon. Inishmurray Island seemed fairly clear, but then I was familiar with the look of these words. I looked at the title of the chart. That was easy.

Feeling a little frightened, I went into the wheelhouse and looked into the compass. Although I knew the course the quartermaster was steering, I could not distinguish one degree from another around the lit rim. The insignia at the cardinal points were all right but that was about all. I glanced through the magnifying glass used by the man at the wheel; that was not so bad!

Quickly I climbed the ladder to the bridge. It was still dusk. I looked astern. We were steaming away from the shore and I could quite clearly discern the mountains of County Sligo. Our consorts were proceeding along abeam of us in the usual way. I tried the binoculars on one of them. As clear as a bell! I noticed the clouds, the sharp edges of a line squall to the west; nothing was wrong with my long vision.

I asked the navigator to do what I had intended to do on the chart, but I could not confirm the figures he was reading off. When I took a pad of paper to scribble a small calculation, I could not distinguish what my pencil wrote.

In my cabin I picked up a Londonderry newspaper lying on my desk. It did not mean a thing! I thought of looking at my eyes in the mirror but that would not mean anything either.

Had I suddenly grown old? I had heard about people's arms becoming too short to read as they aged but I did not know it came so quickly. Well, as long as my intermediate and long sight were unaffected, which I thought had nothing to do with one's short sight, I could carry on for a bit. A sailor absolutely must have these, and I had always had eyes like a hawk for distance. In the meantime I had better watch my long vision.

My rest was uneasy that night. I went to the bridge often to look at the lights on the shore when we were close in, and sometimes just stood on deck outside my cabin and watched the waves when my eyes grew accustomed to the darkness. Another thing had been bothering me, too, that night.

When I went into the bathroom adjoining my cabin I had to stand for an inordinately long time before I could finish what I was doing. At first I thought nothing of it but in the morning when it was still the same I wondered if I was beginning to disintegrate.

I was not made happier either by being wakened after a short sleep at 0700 by a raucous noise coming out of the loudspeaker on the bulkhead. I had forgotten to turn the thing off the evening before after listening to a programme of records. The favourite tune of the man who put the records on had roused me like a sponge of cold water being squeezed down my back. It was the Pickens Sisters singing the 'Boogie Woogie Bugle Boy', in which the last word in each verse ended with 'reveille', pronounced by the Sisters to rhyme with Beverly.

The one bright spot was, however, that the pains in my stomach were not so severe.

When I went on deck I was thankful to know that I could see all our five other ships spread out abreast of us at two-mile intervals. I spotted the coast ahead as we came in from seaward as quickly as anyone else. But I had to use a magnifying glass, a spare compass magnifier, to read with. I had to admit it, too, to the senior officer and to the navigator. The S.O. was very sympathetic but had had no experience himself with ageing eyesight. I had to have the signalmen read all their messages to me and I had to remember much more than I was accustomed to.

But the problem which concerned me most was how I was to make an asdic attack against a submarine. This necessitated my watching an arrow of light reflected in the compass while listening to the reports of the operator, and aiming the ship – by compass – to intercept the enemy. How could I aim the ship when I could not see the lubber line or even the points of the compass, and only a very uncertain glimmer of the arrow of light? I could use the magnifying-glass but that would be a lot of use in the rain, which was a very common element in this region.

A solution came comparatively quickly. After almost three days of being much concerned, seeing even less, and still standing for far longer intervals than normally whenever I went to the bathroom, I suddenly found myself contemplating a pill I was about to swallow. I looked at the hazy outline of the little yellow pellet, then suddenly threw the glass of water I was holding into the basin. I put the pill back into the bottle and hurried to the bridge.

The other frigate was next to us a couple of miles away.

'Signalman,' I ordered, 'send a message to the frigate over there: "To the M.O. Could the pills you gave me affect my eyesight or any other part of my anatomy?"'

I listened to the clicking of the signalman's key. I was a bit excited and it seemed a long time before a light flashed across the water from the other ship.

'Sing it out as you read it,' I told the signalman as he stood ready to receive.

He did so.

'Stop . . . taking . . . pills . . . M.O.'

That was all. And it was all I wanted to know.

By the next afternoon I could read the minutest mark on the chart and I no longer had to stand around and wait until the lock gates closed, as it were, on the ebb tide.

When we returned to harbour the group medical officer came to see me; he was borne in the other frigate because we already had more officers than we could comfortably accommodate.

'Anything wrong with your eyes now?' he asked.

'What did you put in those pills you gave me just before sailing, Doc?' I countered.

He adopted a scientific approach. 'They contained a certain amount of belladonna which I intended should relax the muscles of your stomach and thus relieve your pain. But the belladonna obviously relaxed the muscles behind your eyes as well.'

'And the valve that shuts off the waterworks, too,' I suggested.

'Oh? How interesting! Did that happen?'

'It did, indeed,' I said, with some feeling.

'Yes. It could have done that. Anything else?'

'No. That was enough, I think.'

'Good. We'll have to try something else.'

'You needn't, thanks, Doc,' I said. 'I'll go along with my egg nogs.'

During these patrols I was again by with the simplicity with which our senior officer manœuvred his group of ships in these inshore waters. He could move them like a platoon of marines in any direction or inclination he wished without the least difficulty. The neatness with which he applied these manœuvres was, I thought, as I saw them from the leader, equally well carried out by our consorts. They had become well drilled and responded to orders faithfully.

The S.O. had grown on me; and he had grown on us all. He played the game perfectly. I respected his ability and admired his knowledge, yet I admired more his reticence in displaying it. He was a man of great sincerity with a fine sense of propriety. It had been a short acquaintance because now it was almost at an end. I could have served no finer officer – there had been no conflict, no differences.

17. The Ace

The frigate I had lived in for six months lay alone against the end of one of the pairs of short narrow jetties which extended out from the river wall in Londonderry dockyard. As I walked along the quay towards her my eyes admired her robust yet graceful contours; her sharp bow reaching up boldly in contrast to her long low stern, the profile of her upperworks giving a sense of stamina and potency. I noted with satisfaction that the guns were properly trained fore and aft and were at the correct elevation, that there were no unwanted ropes or fenders hanging over her trimly painted side. I came on board, raising my civvy hat in due respect to the quarterdeck and went to my cabin intending to relax in a bath before having a quiet supper.

I had had a glorious afternoon on the old and picturesque golf course on the hillside where grazing sheep kept the turf short and the fairways wandered with Irish individuality in strange directions defying the principles of any ordinary golf course architecture.

Wearily falling into an armchair to rest my limbs, which were unused to golf and cycling, I gazed unseeingly out the open scuttle thinking of the past few hours of freedom, the charm of the countryside. Then my eyes wandered to my desk on which, among other things, lay two signal logs. I reached over for them, and after some further thought about a lovely approach shot among many bad ones, I opened the confidential log which had been kept up to date in my absence. I glanced at the first signal, then sat up with a jerk and read it again.

Hell! What did this mean?

I turned it over and looked at the next signal, its counterpart. It was worse.

'Damn my luck!' I exclaimed aloud. 'At this time of all times.' Then I re-read them once more.

The first said: 'Senior officer is appointed to *Matane* in command and to combine this duty with that of senior officer.' The second read: 'Commanding officer is to be relieved by senior officer of group and is to return to Canada for new ship.'

I sat back again and thought, no longer of the pleasures of the country, but of the misfortune which had suddenly struck me. To leave this ship now, just when she was in perfect trim with all hands fully familiar with their jobs was a blow. The strongest ship I had ever had! To me the king of ships, and never a chance yet to use her to full advantage. Now I was to go home and start that hard grind all over again. And without the advantage now of being able to choose even one lieutenant, let alone any member of the crew. Another discomforting factor was that the doctors would probably catch up with me and put me in hospital.

There was, however, one advantage in returning. I had recently received a cable telling me that my wife had given birth to another daughter, so I would at least be able to see them.

Sitting in my bath and thinking it over further, I saw what had occasioned this sudden reversal of policy of keeping the senior officer separated from the direct command of a ship. They were short of captains. They would have difficulty in providing for all the new ships which would come down the St Lawrence as the ice broke up. But I knew of at least one man who would be pleased: our Commander. He was away on a few days leave in England, and he would be delighted when he heard the news. I was glad.

By the time I had finished my supper, I was resigned to my fate; I must accept this as I had accepted the better things the navy had given me; but the prospect of leaving such a company of people was wretched. The thought of losing touch with them and not sharing their adventures, achievements, their excitements and amusements, was depressing. My only consolation was that they would have a first-rate captain.

Next morning I was called to the Commodore's office. While I waited in the secretary's office I wondered what the matter could be. The secretary said nothing. Then he ushered me into the carpeted room. I was not the first to speak. It was not proper in the R.N. to speak to a senior officer until he had addressed his subordinate.

The man behind the desk put his pen down and glanced at me, naming me by the name of my ship. 'I suppose you saw the signal directing you to leave your ship?' he asked. As he spoke he stood

233

up and walked into the centre of the room, looking at the carpet. He was a short, stocky man with a round good-looking face, rather red, which was accentuated by his very curly grey hair. The bright ribbons clustered in several rows on the breast of his blue and gold jacket added to the contrast of colour He stood now as I had usually seen him, hands thrust deep in his trouser pockets, his shoulders giving the impression of being hunched up making his short neck look shorter. I told him I had received the signal and regretted it.

'Er, perhaps you do, but you're not going home.' His eyes had the humorous sparkle in them they always seemed to have. 'You're going to a destroyer which is due in here in several days,' he announced with a slight lisp.

He shifted his gaze from the carpet to a large blackboard which covered most of one side of his office, on which were inscribed all the ships under his command – the Londonderry ships – with their respective dates of arrival. He moved towards it and I did the same, curious to see which one he would put his finger on. My spirits had instantly rallied at his last remark. A destroyer instead of being sent home! This momentary suspense was almost pleasant.

'This one,' he said pleasantly, picking one out and naming it. I read *Saskatchewan* and repeated it as it would be pronounced at home. She was named after the prairie river.

'Due in next Tuesday,' the Commodore added. 'You will . . . er . . . you will take over on her arrival.'

'That sounds splendid, sir; I shall be pleased to.'

'You will be joining one of the two Canadian destroyer groups soon to be formed, I believe,' he added. He made some further remarks in his halting way of speaking and I thought he seemed pleased that he had been able to give me such good news.

Spring was advancing and the sun's rays penetrated the shoulders of my old blue, salt-stiff battledress as I sat in a chair on the bridge of the destroyer. The chair was an unusual one. It had obviously been made especially for the C.O. and had very long legs which made it resemble a heavy edition of a child's high-chair without the tray. It stood about three feet to port of the two standard compasses, which were in the centre of the bridge, and its feet were lashed to ring bolts in the deck. To mount it I had to step up on to the footrest. It was a very comfortable chair, with a convenient watertight box attached to one side for binoculars, and as I sat there my head came above the triplex glass screen eight feet beyond me which extended in sections across the fore part of the bridge. In spite of my head being higher than the screen, I felt no wind on my face; the breeze was deflected upwards and passed well above me – a pleasant contrast from the exposure I had experienced recently.

While I sat there in this comparative comfort, the enthusiastic young sub-lieutenant, Jason, gave me the history of the ship. She was nine years old and had in her prime been one of the crack destroyers in the British fleet. Nearly a year ago she had been taken over by the Canadian navy for convoy work. Her first commission was in the Mediterranean in 1935 and later she patrolled in the Bay of Biscay during the Spanish Civil War.

Within three weeks of the outbreak of war she had sunk a U-boat off the north of Scotland, and several days later helped another F-class destroyer to sink a second submarine that was attacking the battle-cruiser *Hood*. She was at Narvik in the spring of 1940. After that she went back to the Mediterranean covering the passage of reinforcements to Alexandria. She later took part in the operations against Dakar, where she sank a French submarine. She was damaged in 1941, and again in 1942 by aircraft, first at Gibraltar and then at Malta. Her starboard quarter was wrecked by a bomb, and consequently she still steered oddly, answering her helm quickly to starboard, but slowly to port.

She ultimately left the Mediterranean and in May 1942 took part in the capture of Diego Suarez. After this she went farther into the Indian Ocean against the Japanese fleet, before returning to help in the second and third landings at Madagascar. She was also in the East Indies for a time, and did some anti-submarine patrol work on the South African coast when the U-boats were active there. The chief engineer thought she had travelled a quarter of a million miles, but this was uncertain since the Ship's Book had been lost when she was bombed.

While Jason was giving me this history, Lieutenant Windram, the senior watchkeeper, pointed out that the ship had never once encountered the enemy during the past year, since he had been in her. He remarked that it was hard to keep the crew up to the mark when nothing ever happened. Being the torpedo officer he was particularly concerned about this.

We had sailed as a spare escort to a westbound convoy but it was not intended that we should go more than half way across with it. Early on the third morning we fuelled at a tanker; and this time I did not break the hose! At 1100 I received orders to return to base. As we turned into a gap in the columns and went down between the ships, I did not know that I was leaving the last convoy I would ever be privileged to escort.

We travelled back five hundred miles at thirty knots, not because we had to but because the chief engineer and I wanted to. We would give her her head. Her sharp stem cut the narrowest path through the rippling, moving sea and her bow wave arched high up her glistening plates like a rainbow until the graceful flare turned it away. She sped along with becoming ease on an even keel; her bow did not rise, her stern did not settle; she rode level except for the gentle lift over the swell. But her after deck shook and the boiling wake revealed the thrust of her twin propellers and the speed of their turning, driven by thirty-six thousand horse-power.

When we reached port, speculation on the forthcoming invasion seemed to be on everyone's lips; when it would be, where it would take place and who would be in it, what they would do if they were. For my part, I was soon to have a faint idea of our job; I received orders to attend a course in Liverpool and to take the navigator with me.

The two of us were given a lift across the Irish Sea and arrived at Western Approaches Headquarters at Derby House on the inevitable rainy, windy morning with mud-coloured gulls hovering about, to find many other C.O.s and their navigators equally curious to discover the score. Wrens, polite and knowing, conveyed us to an upper chamber where we immediately recognized the tall R.N. captain of tactics fame. If we had had any doubts before, we knew for certain now why we were here.

With remarkably little preamble our instructor came to the point as though he were just going to give another lesson on strategy to a class of pupils who had been attending his lectures for months. He turned his back to us and stood for a moment before a large blackboard. Then he drew a line across it, slanting up slightly from left to right. Then he added an upward curl at the left end.

'This,' he said, swinging round abruptly, 'is supposed to be a coastline.'

Then he made a mark with his chalk one-third the way along the line from the right. 'This is a port which I shall call Little Twittering-on-Sea.' He made another, larger dot near it. 'This is Greater Twittering-on-Sea.'

Then he drew his chalk along the blackboard below the line he had already drawn. It started fairly far from the first but drew closer to it to the right and had a sort of S in the middle of it.

'This is another coast,' he announced, stepping to one side so that we could all see it. 'Neither, of course, has any resemblance to any coast I know of. There is water between them, naturally; it might be called a channel.'

'Supposing,' he went on, 'you wanted to transport a great deal of material across from one coast to the other – people too, perhaps – you would probably want to take the shortest route, wouldn't you? Economical and all that. Yes, so would I. But these short routes aren't always sensible. Sherlock Holmes didn't invariably return to Baker Street by the quickest route. And, of course, the passengers wouldn't really benefit from the sea air on such a short passage as, say, twenty miles. It's got to be longer.

'Moreover, we were talking of an abundance of material. So, as Greater Twittering-on-Sea is a large shipping centre, that is the most likely place from which you would depart, particularly since, on the opposite side of this channel,' and he indicated a large indentation formed by the S, roughly opposite the Twitterings, 'the landing facilities here are most suitable.'

By this time we were phenomenally interested in his simple drawing. Some sat well forward on their chairs. No one made a sound. The poker-faced captain took a few strides back and forth and tossed his chalk. Then he blew his nose loudly, rubbed it vigorously with his handkerchief and faced us again.

'Now, if we were going to launch an amphibious attack on this coast,' pointing to the lower, crooked line, 'we might do it, for the sake of argument, between these two places. Mind you, we needn't. We might do it up here. But, for the purpose of illustration, I think we'll do it here.'

Now we were really into it! We were suddenly thrown into the greatest naval conception in history.

'One-way cross-channel lanes could be established and these could be buoyed the whole way across. Troop ships and smaller craft coming out of Greater Twittering-on-Sea – which could be escorted by vessels from Little Twittering-on-Sea – might be augmented by vessels from the lesser ports on the coast which could be brought along to the point of crossing. In fact, I see no reason why men and material shouldn't come even from around the extremities of the coast.'

He then pointed out how vessels such as E-boats and R-boats might come out of small ports on the farther shore and how submarines might conceivably try to work up this channel; that small naval vessels, such as ourselves, would be employed in different tasks and in various formations, and that our opponents would likely be aircraft, E-boats, R-boats and U-boats, increasing in importance in that order. In fact, he predicted, in the event of an assault, the first would disappear almost immediately, the second and third fairly soon, but the last, the U-boats, would persist until perhaps the principal part of the invasion was over.

During this discourse no mention was made of secrecy. There was no need to put it into words.

For several days after that we devoted our attention to tactics on the basis of what might be expected, and then the navigator and I returned to Londonderry.

The ship remained in harbour for the next two weeks, during which we worked and prepared and entertained.

On an afternoon two or three days before we finally sailed, Lieutenant Peters, the engineer officer, brought a guest on board. He greeted the middle-aged Wren officer at the brow; she had arrived on the wharf in a staff car. She climbed down the steep ladder leading from the quarter-deck lobby very nimbly and was guided into the wardroom by her host. The steward had already laid a small tea table by the settee for the chief and his friend.

There was only one occupant of the wardroom at the time, and he was stretched out in an easy chair with his feet on the bench which surrounded the hearth. Lieutenant Larose opened his eyes when he heard a female voice, an important thing in his life, and then rose slowly, straightening his tie and buttoning his jacket as he recognized his name being intoned by Peters which he sensed was an introduction.

As she held out her hand the Wren officer looked at the tall, handsome Canadian Frenchman and asked if they had not met before.

'Your face seems somehow familiar. It can't have been long ago. Now, where was it?'

Larose hesitated to speak because he knew that he had a slight French accent and it might help her to identify the occasion and locale of their last meeting. However, he could not remain completely silent. He searched for the fewest words he could use.

'Can't think. But I'm glad to meet you now.' He bared his teeth, but it could not have passed for much of a smile.

'Oh, yes. I seem to remember your voice, too.'

He could not have been particularly interesting to her, because the disparity of ages was a little too great.

At that point the first lieutenant came bursting in – he was a hustler. Bimson had to be introduced. This gave Larose the chance to excuse himself and make a semi-graceful exit reasonably quickly.

One late afternoon, only a week before, he and another officer had cycled over to the local Wrenery, Broom Hall. They had been received most cordially, both being very amiable characters, and were entertained in the mess and in the gardens where shrubs were in blossom and the perfume of flowers filled the evening air.

Later the party developed, and hospitality became quite lavish. However, Larose's companion got clear before midnight and said afterwards he had ridden back without undue difficulty. But Larose had stayed on, and by and by grew sleepy.

Perhaps he had been a bit muddled, because when he was wakened by a loud female whisper and a hand shaking him, he found he had been resting on a cot in a small cubicle among a lot of other small cubicles in the upper part of the establishment. He was asked some pretty rugged questions by the low-voiced Wren officer who, he hazily realized, must be the officer-of-the-night or something, and the single electric light bulb hanging from the ceiling hurt his eyes. He wisely answered the questions in French while pulling on his jacket, and, having thus explained himself to at least his own satisfaction, he felt free to tell her, in English, his voice attuned to her quiet speech, that he too felt it was about time

239

he returned to his ship, though to which one he did not say. He was then ordered to walk quietly so that his manly footfall would not disturb the slumbering inmates of the Hall, and the officer accompanied him.

During the journey along the long corridors and down the spacious staircase he attempted once to voice an apology but was stopped by the raised hand of his guardian.

Lieutenant Larose had not remembered having a door held open for him by a lady before; but once outside he was unable to find his bicycle. He was sure he had left it against a pillar at the foot of the wide steps. But no . . . and then he became conscious of the eyes of the *pro tem.* proprietor. Strangely, there was amusement in her voice as she said, 'You can walk. You're used to that on the bridge.'

My last ship came into Londonderry again and dropped her four corvettes, replacing them with frigates. The corvettes from the group were split up and I was delighted to see the old knave booked for the invasion. This honour for a ship of her age should surely vindicate those unhappy traits which had marked her as a dubious character. (They were vindicated. She carried out her duty nobly throughout the invasion, plodding back and forth to the beaches.)

Before I had left the frigate I had asked my successor, the senior officer, if he would grant me the favour of allowing me to take my steward with me, and he had cordially agreed. I would have liked to take a good many other people from the ship, but of course it would have been foolish to think of such a thing. However, as the frigate had sailed just before my new ship came in, I left the transfer until later because I wanted to provide a replacement. But now when I came to complete the arrangement, the poor steward hesitated. Auclair's usual cheerfulness was gone when he came to me to report that he was going to fetch his gear aboard. Seeing an unhappy look in his eyes, I asked him if he did not want to come with me.

'Why, yes, sir,' he said, but there was a flatness in his tone.

'You don't seem very certain about it.'

'No, sir?' He tried to grin but it was a feeble effort. Then he feigned professional interest. 'You got a nice place here, sir.' He glanced around the big cabin.

'Yes.' I knew he was trying to skirt the issue. 'Speak the truth Auclair. You don't want to transfer?'

'Well, sir . . . You want me. Sure, sir, I'll come.'

I nearly let it go at that. I had no need to pursue the question. I wished afterwards I had dropped the discussion there and then. But I did not know – we never do – that it was a life and death matter for him.

'What is it? The ship?'

He looked down at the rug and did not answer.

'Well?' I persisted.

'Partly, sir. But if I didn't come it'd be a long time I wouldn't see you again.'

'Perhaps.'

'Yes, sir.'

'What else?'

'My friends. They're good, sir.' He named several, one in particular – the P.O. steward he had always sailed with.

'You know,' I offered, 'this ship has been hard run and I don't think her engines will push her for long without being refitted. That would be at home. By coming here you'd probably see your family sooner than you would if you stayed in the frigate.'

'I suppose so if you say so, sir.' But he showed no enthusiasm. I knew his friends had always meant a lot to him.

'You've looked around the ship, of course?'

'Yes, sir.'

'And you don't like your quarters, do you?'

'No, sir.'

I could understand that. I was shocked myself when I first saw the dingy hole right aft where the stewards lived; a sea had filled it a couple of trips previously. His quarters in the frigate were sumptuous by comparison.

The upshot of it was that I did not take him. I had not the heart to insist, sorry as I was to lose him. It was not only for his stewardship that I was sorry. He had had the faculty, by reason of his quiet cheerfulness and bright disposition, of having often lifted me out of despondency on coming into my cabin, even for only a few minutes. Besides, he had been with me always, longer than anyone else.

I never saw him again; he was killed.

While we waited at 'Derry, one after another of Canada's nine River class destroyers came in, until all but one of us lay at the jetties; the missing one was still under refit at home. As the ships congregated there was a great foregathering of old friends, though I was rather out of it because I had never belonged to the destroyer sphere. So I spent a fair amount of my spare time playing golf and visiting friends up the steep hill above the river. We walked into the country or rode bicycles, the only other mode of locomotion. It was really a blessing to get away from ships for a while and enjoy the spring countryside with a companion who was not a sailor.

Towards the latter part of May, either by coincidence or design, the senior Anglican naval chaplain overseas visited Londonderry and conducted a Sunday morning service at a church to which the navy used to go. I confess I was not a regular attendant, but on this occasion I went, partly because I wanted to and partly because I counted myself something of a friend of this particular padre. He used to take divine service in ships long ago in Halifax and it was then that I had been attracted to him. I used to like it when he took the service on the jetty on summer Sundays for the crews of the ships alongside; I never knew a man who could bring into one's heart a desire for goodness and love of God and one's fellows in less time and in fewer words than he could.

He did not disappoint me on this occasion when I attended with several officers and a contingent of men from each of our ships. I could not help thinking that this might be the last time I would be in church perhaps for a long time and I rather wished that I had gone more often in the past. One may not have had the time or thought to pray when in immediate danger; we did so, more naturally when danger was impending, but there was certainly no excuse for not thanking the Lord for deliverance from it when one had the chance.

The service was well known to me, almost routine; I followed it automatically, picking out this line and that as particularly appealing; but too often my mind wandered, thinking of what was to come, what the outcome would be, whether I would survive. Self-preservation seemed to be a not uncommon feeling of mine, yet I think it was less selfish than unselfish; there were those who would need my support for many years to come. I was not free and independent. Then a prayer would take me back to where it had impressed itself on my memory most, a church otherwise forgotten, a ship where a reverend voice had intoned it so many times that I could hear it in the background now.

Like any captain, I prayed for the success of my ship and the protection of her men, for the defeat of our enemies. I listened attentively to the brief, simple sermon in which the chaplain asked his congregation to be, above all else, men, upright, honourable, helping others, men of conscience and of loyalty, not only to their ship but to their God on whom they could depend for their destiny.

The sun outside lit up the colours of the stained glass windows on the south side of the church and brilliant beams streaked in as the voices of two hundred men sang their hymn of protection:

> *Eternal Father, strong to save,*
> *Whose arm doth bind the restless wave,*
> *Who bidd'st the mighty ocean deep*
> *Its own appointed limits keep:*
> *O hear us when we cry to Thee*
> *For those in peril on the sea.*

It was not being sung without thought or feeling, most of us had lost friends. Moreover, we wanted to be preserved ourselves.

> *From rock and tempest, fire and foe,*
> *Protect them wheresoe'er they go:*
> *And ever let there rise to Thee*
> *Glad hymns of praise from land and sea.*

I felt better as I left the church and watched the men falling in and marching off down the street to their respective ships; I hoped they felt glad, too.

At 1000 the next morning we cast off from the jetty, turned in the narrow river and slid downstream. To the strains of martial music issuing from the loudspeakers on deck, we rounded the first big bend to pass close to the river bank, beyond which, up the sloping meadow, stood Broom Hall. Heads popped out of windows, girls lying on the grass stood up and waved their handkerchiefs, as did those at the edge of the water. The signal of friendship was returned by the men on deck, some of whom probably did so with more feeling than others.

18. The Invasion

An amazing document! I closed the book, fully two inches thick, and lay back in my chair gazing into the fire with eyes tired from reading. *Operation 'Neptune'!* It was positively stupendous, it seemed to me, both in its conception and in its development.

It had arrived that morning, labelled Top Secret: orders covering the part to be played by the allied navies in the greatest invasion in history. It was midnight now, and I had hardly put the book down since it had been delivered to me along with another large book dealing with signal procedures, and a number of sealed envelopes containing numerous corrections made since these publications had gone to press three months or more before. A description of the entire Normandy operation was disclosed here, the routes to be taken by the landing-craft and convoys, their destination. Detailed diagrams of the beaches with their artificial harbours, photographs of the shore defences and the orders for razing them. Every naval vessel to be engaged in it was named and placed. Bombardment objectives were described, patrol and mine-sweeping areas designated, the system of air protection outlined. Charts showing the progress of the seaborne movement of the invading forces were drawn at six-hour intervals from the time the pre-D-day contingents set off until hundreds of thousands of men would be on the farther shore.

The whole vast secret was here, the plans of the much-heralded, long-awaited invasion of Europe from the north. On the second page of this momentous volume was listed a number of dates with a code against each, odd dates somewhere between the end of May and August. One of these would be D day. Until the day approached we would wait, remaining at anchor here in Lough Foyle.

Rising at last, I lifted the cushion of the settee and pulled up a little trap door beneath it. Opening the safe inside the locker, I placed the book in it and carefully locked it. Then I switched out the lights of my big after cabin and went through a sliding door into my sleeping cabin.

On 2nd June we received orders to raise steam in readiness for immediate departure. That evening I was called to a conference in the senior officer's ship. As the motor boat moved down the Lough stemming the strong flood tide, I glanced around at the ships riding to their anchors in the clear light of the waning summer day. There were still perhaps thirty left: frigate groups, our two destroyer groups and a number of corvettes, considerably fewer than there had been two days earlier; an equal number had already sailed.

I was piped aboard and taken by an officer to the captain's cabin. One of the other two C.O.s, was already present, and then we heard the pipe again, heralding the arrival of the captain of the fourth ship of the group.

The senior officer was a small man of about forty-five with a rather cherubic face, though somewhat weather-beaten, and a lower lip which stuck out a little, providing a feature of determination to his otherwise innocent appearance. I had met him briefly in 'Derry but still only know him by reputation. He was an R.N. Commander but had been on loan to the Canadian Navy during the past year, where he had been the senior officer of one of our close escort groups, and from what I had heard from time to time, a very good one in every respect.

The other two captains were young, about twenty-eight, a good age to be in command. The fearlessness of youth had probably not yet been replaced by the caution of years. I knew only one of them fairly well, a straight, good-looking man, an anti-submarine specialist who had been in charge of the asdic school at Halifax at one time, where I had first met him. Both had been in command for nearly a year, and were permanent service officers. They had done ten years active service already. R.C.N. officers rarely served in ships smaller than destroyers, because there were so few of them and because they were trained for these and larger ships. The reason I was in command of one was that there were no more of these men available.

The senior officer was businesslike. 'As you see from your reading of 'Neptune' we are going to be in the Channel. I am not going to burden you with any standing orders; your own knowledge and common sense will tell you what I want. I don't propose to lay down any tactical schemes; we know those which are advocated in Liverpool, and we shall adhere to them unless situations demand changes. You all know the value of your armament and detectors; use them to advantage. And your familiarity with ordinary destroyer tactics and fleet manœuvres will prevent you from going far wrong.

'We sail for Plymouth in the morning,' he went on. 'As we have known for a day or so, D day has been set for 5th June. I intend to enter Plymouth some time on the 4th so that we can re-fuel and get out the same night; I expect to pick up my final orders at the same time and we shall probably be informed of the the latest intelligence. Have you all everything you require?' he asked. We said we had. 'Then weigh anchor at 0500.'

We drank a toast to the success of the invasion, and after chatting for a short while returned to our respective ships before it was dark.

At first light we were drifting gently on the ebb, the ship point-ing towards the narrow entrance of the Lough, engines stopped, anchor home, the leadsman in the chains. We watched the move-ment of the shadowy forms of the other destroyers getting under-way. The haven would be empty today except for the old tankers. When the sun came up we were passing down the North Channel between Scotland's Mull of Kintyre and Ireland's Fair Head from which the Antrim Mountains rose, blue in the distance.

We were all happy, at least everyone seemed to be. The first lieutenant was in his element, his fresh face alight with intensity. 'I'll have the anti-aircraft guns manned,' he said, when he was setting the watches. Lieutenant Bimson seemed to be rather partial to A.A. guns. I had seen him directing A.A. defence one night in 'Derry during an alarm and had been impressed by his competence; it was obvious that he had been under air attack more than once.

Bimson was slim and lithe with a strong mouth. And he dressed the part. He wore a special type of steel helmet, not the regulation kind – it may have been German – and a heavy belt over his blue battledress with a pistol in a holster. A large sheath knife, a whistle and several other things hung from the belt. He presented rather a swash-buckling appearance, but his accoutrements were un-doubtedly practical.

In the opinion of one of his earlier captains, whom I had met recently, Bimson was the best ship's first lieutenant in the Navy.

246

He was a permanent officer, had been in the Malta convoys and the Sicily and Crete campaigns, in one of which he had been mentioned in dispatches. I was not quite sure whether his nerves had been affected by his experiences in the Mediterranean but he was undoubtedly a highly strung fellow. He seemed to me to be in several places at once sometimes, he moved about so fast. He was only twenty-two but for his years had an excellent power of command. His darting mind, however, made it difficult at times for his petty officers to carry out all the work he assigned to them; but although he might have been a little confusing, he accomplished a great deal.

It was quite delightful, I found, to have three R.C.N. officers on board. These permanent force men were definitely an advantage. They knew many wrinkles with which the others were not familiar. I did not under-rate the value of R.C.N.V.R. officers, but they had not received the all-round, intensive naval training the R.C.N. had, and therefore were not as versatile, and were less flexible.

The four ships, one behind the other, sped on, passed the Isle of Man and farther down the Isle of Anglesey, behind which my erstwhile frigate was lying at anchor, guarding with her consorts an aircraft carrier which they were soon to take to a strategic position somewhere south-west of Ireland.

The chief engineer came to the bridge once. His face registered the same contentment and pride it had shown on the day we travelled the five hundred miles at near top speed. Peters said little, being a Scotsman, but implied that there I was, if I wanted speed he could give it to me. And he could, in spite of condenser trouble. He could get as much out of her as other engineer officers may have done when she was a much younger vessel.

We crossed Cardigan Bay in the late evening and during the night negotiated the swept channel which ran from Milford Haven to Hartland Point. A minefield had been laid long ago from the southern part of Wales and England to the Irish coast to block the approaches to the Irish Sea. This channel provided the passage through the field.

Towards the end of the channel we overtook a convoy of about a dozen vessels creeping slowly through the darkness in a long line, their dimmed navigation lights no brighter than candles. The invasion fleet was underway! As dawn came in – and to me, who had watched it so often, this stealthy approach of light which so gradually yet perceptibly brushed away darkness and opened one's vision, never ceased to seem a miracle – another convoy was to be seen hugging the north Cornish coast, and beyond it, farther along, the masts of yet another.

Now came the famous signal, brief but momentous, surely almost terrifying for those who had had the responsibility of making it. The invasion was postponed a day; the waves on the beaches were too high to risk the initial landing.

But provision had been made for such an eventuality; nothing had been overlooked in Operation 'Neptune', though it added to its already complicated precision. For our part, we steamed on, but would stand off the south coast for twenty-four hours.

As we drew close to the convoy whose masts we had seen at daylight, I found myself looking at the most pathetic group of ships I had ever seen in my life. Large merchantmen, light and high out of the water, obviously without cargo. But that was not it. Their upperworks had an unusual appearance. I looked at them through binoculars. They were stripped! Booms, derricks, running rigging were gone, top-masts were down, decks appeared to be clear of everything. They looked derelict, as old as the cedars of Lebanon.

What was that at the stern of one of them? An anchor! I looked at the others – yes, they, too, seemed to have stern anchors. Then I remembered. Blockships. The 'Neptune' instructions had told me about blockships and described their purpose. They were to be sunk in shallow water – six to twelve feet at low tide – at the five assault points to provide immediate beach shelter for smaller landing craft and ultimately would become a part of the breakwaters protecting the Mulberry harbours. An honourable grave, indeed, for ships which had already done their duty.

The high cliffs of the rugged coast of Cornwall lay black against the blue June sky; a moderate following breeze was barely keeping pace with us, which made the air delightfully still on deck. Few were below, only those who were obliged to be; everyone seemed to be interested in what was to be seen. And now another strange armada hove in sight.

Heavy masts with fighting tops came up over the horizon and soon developed into bulky battleships and heavy cruisers accompanied by the inevitable fleet destroyers. The battle squadron bore down, the sun glinting on the damp armour-plated sides, a picture of towering strength.

The general interest had attracted most of the officers to the bridge and now they all seemed to be up. As I sat in my tall chair – I did not stand a great deal because of the dull pain I usually had – I listened to the remarks which went between them. Jason, the historian, was calling out the names of the ships to the first lieutenant. This was an interest which they naturally had in common. 'That's *Rodney* or possibly *Nelson*,' I heard him announce confidently as he examined one of the on-coming ships through his glasses.

'Anybody'd know that,' Bimson answered sharply.

'The inshore one is a County class cruiser,' Jason reported again.

And, so it went on. They were enjoying this almost unique opportunity for ship spotting.

But now, as this great squadron drew abeam of us, we suddenly realized that another was following close behind. It was instantly apparent from the very shape of the ships that they were American. They, too, were beautiful; a little higher freeboard but massive. And their destroyers, spread out in their protective fashion, were larger than the British and our own. Here were the lions of the great armada and the flags of two nations bent together. I had never seen them quite that way before. As they ploughed on past, up the north Cornish coast into the head breeze, I lost any feeling of doubt I might have had for the success of the invasion, at least as far as the sea-borne operation was concerned.

We put into Plymouth on the eve of Normandy to fill our fuel tanks and I seized the opportunity to write to my wife.

Monday, 5th June '44. 9 p.m.

I have only a very short while in which to write this, so it will be very brief. A chance of putting a letter ashore developed this evening but I may have to push off before I can get it away.

I am feeling better now and haven't had a pain for a couple of days. I think I'm pretty well O.K. The ship is going along very nicely and I'm quite enjoying life, that is, as much as I could in the circumstances.

It is a week since I had your last letter. Am looking forward to another in a few days.

I have no news whatever so don't know what to say. Have been very busy lately and wish I didn't have so much to read. I never saw anything like the navy for producing reams of orders. . . .

The next day we were off England's south-west coast. It was warm and bright and calm. It was the 6th of June.

We did not know how others were faring; we only knew our own small world. Quietness reigned on board, broken occasionally by a shouted report from aloft. Sometimes we came near the rocky Channel shore and could see here and there a white beach and, behind it, green fields.

We talked now and again, the officers-of-the-watch and I, as they kept their vigil and I sat in my chair, sometimes getting down to obtain a view astern or to look over the side at flotsam passing by. But I could see most things from where I sat; the bridge chart was on the table in front of me which was set into the bulkhead; the electric log was to one side of it, its hands showing the speed of the ship and figures on its face showing the miles run as they ticked by; an indicator showed how much helm the man at the wheel was applying, and by leaning over towards the binnacle I could obtain a long view of the compass and also see in it the reflection of the asdic beam. If I turned my head and looked up at the main radar tower I could observe the direction of the surface search, and by dropping my eyes I could see on a panel the state of readiness of the depth charges. It was certainly a well placed chair.

During the day, we had seen one little convoy after another, escorted by two or three corvettes or trawlers, passing along the coast, all bound up-Channel. We were standing guard at its western entrance. It was our job to prevent U-boats from attacking the convoys as they rounded Land's End and to stop any from getting into the Channel.

Now the four of us were gliding along in line abreast, listening for the sound of U-boats beneath the quiet sea. It was like drawing a net through the water, stretched tightly between the ships, so that it would snag the big fish while letting through the small, unwanted ones. But the net did not always hang down as it should; temperature gradients sometimes interfered with it.

There were others besides ourselves searching the sea. Now and then we could see the masts and perhaps the hulls of the ships of another group working to the south of us, and beyond it would be another. Spread across the mouth of the Channel from the Lizard to Ushant was a number of anti-submarine vessels – destroyers, sloops, frigates and American-built destroyer-escorts – sufficient, in theory and in fact, if their asdic equipment was working well, to block any attempt on the part of the U-boats to enter. A little farther up-Channel, acting as half backs, was another line of ships waiting to catch the enemy if he should slip through the forward line. Away out to sea beyond us aircraft carriers were stationed so that their satellites could watch and try to detect any eastward movement of under-sea craft. Roving overhead and sometimes skimming the water were land-based aircraft. These planes, with their white-striped markings, a special design which they had adopted for their own protection in this operation, covered every part of the Channel at intervals of twenty minutes.

The 7th of June was a repetition of the 6th, quiet and peaceful, like a summer excursion, until the evening when, a few minutes after 2000, a low rumble was heard, the unmistakable sound of an underwater explosion.

As I came to the bridge from below I asked what it was.

'Don't know exactly, sir,' the officer in charge answered. 'No one hoisted the attacking flag but actually the sound came from over there.' He pointed beyond the port quarter. 'It didn't seem to come from the ships and it was louder than usual.'

Strange, unanswerable things had often occurred at sea in the last few years; unaccountable sounds, lights appearing at night and then disappearing, erupting water, shadows, even ships, like the *Flying Dutchman*, but I had long ago given up trying to solve all the mysteries. Yet there were some which we had to discover if we could. This one, for instance. It was broad daylight, the sun had not yet set; there were only ourselves, the four ships.

The senior officer was flashing. While the signalman answered we saw one of the others turn out of line and hoist a flag indicating she was listening to an underwater contact. The S.O.s message suggested the sound might have come from a torpedo exploding on the bottom. Five minutes later the other two were nosing around more or less together at slow speed while we opened out to make a wide circle around them at a higher speed in accordance with the order just received from the leader.

We went to action stations. This was an evolution which was not so simple in this ship. Nearly two hundred men took their places for battle; the magazines in the bottom of the ship, both fore and aft, were opened up, tackles rigged and parties assembled to pass the ammunition. Seven men stood to at each of the three four-seven guns. The depth charge crew took up their position, torpedomen turned out their tubes amidships and lined up their instruments, the men at the hedgehog stood by on the fo'c'sle head to the rear of the foremost gun ready to remove the caps from the bombs. The fire-and-repair parties mustered, closed water-tight doors and hatches, laid out hoses and primed the downton pump. From the radar tower aloft to the engine-room below the men were ready for action.

Ten minutes elapsed, then a sharp cracking was heard, like a burst from a heavy machine-gun, and almost immediately numerous little splashes appeared just ahead of the ship which had recently gained contact. Twenty-four bombs had left the hedgehog mortar. They had been fired in such rapid succession that they fell in an elliptical pattern almost together.

Nothing happened. The three destroyers continued to move this way and that, opening out from one another and closing again. Twice the yeoman reported ships flying the attacking flag but on each occasion it was hauled down without an attack being delivered.

The asdic officer, Sub-Lieutenant Coyne, stood beside me gazing at the ships; he watched their movements, their flags – the asdic cabin was a few paces behind him.

'I think the Channel is not going to be an easy place to locate submarines,' he said after a while.

I said it looked rather that way.

'In the few days we've been in these waters,' he elaborated, 'the H.S.D. and I have been watching the sound effects and so on of the asdic and they're very confusing. Fish appear to be very plentiful. The tides may have something to do with it. To my mind

the outlook isn't particularly bright. The way those ships are be-
having now is an example of it.'

'Yes,' I agreed, 'there may be difficulty.'

Coyne sounded rather disconsolate. But there was plenty of
optimism in him really. There always was in asdic people. He was
young, the junior among the officers; humour normally hovered
around his eyes and mouth. He and the asdic ratings were aching
to find a U-boat. But it was not going to be easy. 'It's not like the
clear water of mid-Atlantic, sir,' he said. 'There's the place for
good asdic conditions!'

My own thoughts were suddenly interrupted by the sound of a
heavy, half-muffled blast. The ship shuddered. It was like the
violent tremor of an earthquake.

Almost immediately the sea opened no more than a ship's
length abaft the port beam and a solid column of water shot a
hundred feet into the air.

No one spoke. Then, as the thick column broke and fell like a
cataract, its myriad splashes tinted with the pink of the sunset, a
gasp went up from those on deck.

As we looked at the still pool whence the eruption came, dark
against the white encircling foam, we saw puffs of yellow smoke
lying close to the water. And as we watched, the puffs seemed to
change colour or were followed by a thin cloud of blue smoke
which soon lifted and drifted away on the breeze.

A torpedo had exploded just a hundred yards from the ship.

We increased our zig-zag and searched.

Perilously close as extinction had come, the ship had probably
been saved by a defective torpedo. That this fast-moving, fish-like
machine had destroyed itself when it lacked but four seconds of
travel to wreak havoc in the bowels of its target was certainly a
miracle.

We could now make the assumption that the torpedoes being
used were electric and not air-driven because the latter would have
left a track of bubbles in its wake which would have been seen on
the calm sea. Moreover, their erratic behaviour led us to think
they were not the old reliable kind. This meant that they would
most likely be the acoustic variety since only those driven by
electricity were fitted with the acoustic device, or so it was generally
believed. In that case the submarine would not be more than three

miles away and probably a good deal closer, for the effective range of these torpedoes was not thought to be very great.

Each of our ships carried an ultra short range radio telephone on the bridge with a loudspeaker. During this episode, the loudspeaker had been switched on but nothing more interesting than a continuous hum had come out of it so far. But about eight minutes after our miraculous escape there came forth a piping voice from one of the ships working together. It simply said: 'Torpedo just passed down starboard side running very shallow leaving slight swirl behind it. Heard on the hydrophones. No explosion.'

I looked over towards the ships which were separated more now. They seemed to be doing nothing, which is an impression an observer often gets when ships are hunting. A few minutes later a short report came from the same ship indicating that she had picked up several contacts only to find they were fish. We were encountering the same thing. But the third ship met something different.

She was turning slowly to starboard to investigate an asdic contact when the top of a periscope suddenly appeared out of the water close abeam to starboard. Guns which could be brought to bear opened fire but the slender spike disappeared. The contact fizzled out too, a voice on the telephone told us.

Twenty minutes later it was the leader's turn. A swirl was seen ahead. The asdic operator reported the sound of a submarine blowing tanks. The captain increased speed and set his depth charges. Then he sighted a periscope on his starboard bow; it was moving to the right making a little feather as it went. He applied full helm but could not swing his ship around fast enough to intercept it. As he slid by, his guns peppering the water fruitlessly, the tiny object submerged and several seconds later he let go his depth charges. But the U-boat was out of range. Again no underwater contact was made.

I was still looking through my glasses towards the disturbed water created by the leader's charges, hoping to see the object of the attack appear, when the ship shivered again and my glasses shook before my eyes. Almost instantly I heard the roar of an explosion.

As I turned my head in the direction of the sound I saw a great pillar of water rise out of the sea, dead astern. When it reached mast-height it mushroomed and, almost slowly, collapsed.

I knew this time that it was a torpedo and, sure enough, the spot was soon marked by wisps of smoke.

The column of water had appeared only a hundred yards astern but it did not give us the surprise its predecessor had, partly because it was a repetition of an earlier experience and partly because the proximity of the explosion to the stern was more understandable. We realized immediately that we had, ourselves, caused the torpedo to detonate before reaching the ship. It had been an acoustic torpedo; and our catcher had caught it. The anti-acoustic torpedo device which we were trailing from the stern had interrupted it on its run towards the propellers and actually made it go off. It seemed like a close call, but it was not altogether.

We had some reason for satisfaction. We had proved the value of the device. The Admiralty had not accepted our CAT, the Canadian counterpart of the British catcher design, as affording much protection and had said that, while working under their authority, we could use it if we liked but at our own risk. Now they would know that we were justified in sticking to our own model.

Where was the enemy who was so persistently endeavouring to sink us? Where were the other U-boats? We had not the slightest idea except that we knew the one who had attacked us was probably within a mile or so. The asdic would pick up nothing except useless echoes. It was extremely aggravating. Here was a submarine almost below us and here were we, a modern anti-submarine vessel, quite unable to find it. However, I had looked for U-boats and failed to find them for long enough now to know what I might expect.

A little over a year afterwards, when the surviving U-boats had surrendered, Naval Headquarters in Ottawa received the following communication from London and a copy was sent to the ship.

I am commanded by My Lords Commissioners of the Admiralty to refer to the Commanding Officer, H.M.C.S. *Saskatchewan's* signal 161005 June 1944 and the senior officer, 12th Escort Group's report of proceedings of Operation NEPTUNE dated 18th June 1944.

Evidence obtained from captured documents confirms that two GNAT torpedoes were fired at H.M.C.S. *Saskatchewan* on 7th June,

1944, at about the times stated in her signal. The first appears to have prematured, and the second was almost certainly captured by the ship's CAT gear which was destroyed when this torpedo exploded. The attack data was as follows:

1st Attack

Time	2100
Range	10 hectometres (1100 yds.)
Angle on bow	40 Red
GNAT setting	W.S.
Depth set	4 metres (13 feet)
Enemy speed allowed	12 knots (actual speed was 15 knots)
Time of explosion	48 seconds after firing

2nd Attack

Time	2136
Range	9 hectometres (1000 yds.)
Angle on bow	180 (right astern)
GNAT setting	N.S.
Depth set	4 metres (13 feet)
Enemy speed allowed	10 knots (actual speed was 15 knots)
Time of explosion	6 minutes 30 seconds after firing

Both attacks were made from periscope depth, and after the second attack the U-boat crash-dived to avoid attack by other ships of E.G. 12. It was considered that the ship had been sunk.

Soon after dawn the next day we were sweeping north and south in line abreast. At 1930 there was a deep underwater explosion at the far end of the line and five minutes later another one was heard. The position of the second was indicated by the almost simultaneous appearance of a waterspout between the third and fourth ships.

We saw one of the ships turning off her course and at the same moment heard the urgent voice of one of her signalmen coming over the loudspeaker of the radio telephone.

'Torpedo passed close to port – lookout!'

Then: 'Contact ahead – attacking with hedgehog.'

Half a minute later we heard the ripple of bombs exploding. But louder and heavier by far was a single blast which then occurred. This was followed by a great gout of water which shot up midway between ourselves and the leader next to us. It apparently marked the end of the run of the torpedo whose approach we had been warned about.

Again the voice: 'Periscope ahead.' Then the sound of charges. The destroyer was forging ahead and close astern of her, uncomfortably close it looked, pyramids of water rose.

A few more minutes passed and we heard her captain calling the senior officer.

'Thought the bombs hit the target but it was probably the bottom.' I recognized his voice. 'Periscope did not belong to the object first attacked. This sub could not have been the one which fired the torpedo. Depth charges none too accurately placed. The concussion has upset things aboard. I was hardly going fast enough for a shallow pattern. Will report shortly if anything serious is wrong. Out.'

If any of us had been uncertain last night that there was more than one U-boat in our neighbourhood, no one was this morning. And they seemed to be taking pretty frequent looks at us – to their surprise sometimes, I was sure, when their proximity to one of us was closer than they would have deemed healthy.

But if we were forefeiting our unusual opportunities through wretched water conditions and the unique situation of being too close to the enemy – of all things – they were failing equally to benefit from their strategic position through having rotten ammunition. The U-boat captains must have been cursing their unpredictable projectiles as much as we were cursing the sea and the fish.

All four ships searched for the rest of the morning but it seemed hopeless. Five attacks were made but the only result was dead or unconscious cod rising to the surface.

At 1700 an aircraft flew overhead and reported sighting a U-boat on the surface about eight miles to the eastward. Having had no success where we were, we set off in this direction but instead of meeting the submarine we fell in with a group of six British destroyers. Being all together, it was decided that the two groups should combine forces and sweep as a body of ten ships.

We were all in line abreast and our own senior officer was at the extreme right flank. My ship was next to his a mile and a half away. The sky was overcast but the light drizzle which had been

R   257

falling had now ceased. While there was good visibility ahead and to port, a rain squall which was passing to starboard prevented one seeing more than three miles in that direction. As it slowly drifted away the view cleared somewhat and as it did so there appeared on the edge of the squall, on a bearing about sixty degrees on the starboard bow, a column of smoke.

I pulled my glasses out of the box on the side of my chair where I kept them when it was wet, and levelled them on the smoke to see what sort of ship was emitting it. I could not see the vessel and concluded that it was hidden by a part of the squall – the range of vision could be deceptive in drizzly weather, especially with a calm sea like this. I paid no particular attention to it for a minute or so and then had another look. Still I could see no vessel.

'Wonder where the ship is,' I remarked to the officer-of-the-watch. 'That smoke hardly looks as though it's coming from beyond the horizon and the squall seems to be well passed.'

'Looks to me to be about five miles away,' said the officer.

'Yes, or a little less.'

The smoke was rising in a very ordinary manner. I knew, however, that the ship to starboard of us would be scrutinizing it, and since she was nearer than we were it was her responsibility to identify it. If she gave it no apparent notice I would assume she was satisfied. But at that moment it received her attention. I saw a puff of white smoke rise from her fo'c'sle deck and then came the boom of her gun.

On that instant I knew what she was firing at. I altered course towards the smoke and rang for twenty-five knots as I saw our neighbour turning too. A minute later the smoke had dispersed and nothing whatever was to be seen.

What we had observed was a new German invention in operation, an invention with which we were acquainted but not familiar. It was the snorkel, or what we termed 'snorter'.

Prior to the invasion, British Intelligence had learned that U-boats were being fitted with an underwater breathing apparatus. It was believed to be essentially for use in coastal waters and particularly in the case of an invasion. But it was evidently such a precious secret that it was not used in the meantime. Intelligence made an extremely accurate report of it. The snorter was described as being a long rigid pipe extending vertically from the deck of the U-boat, close to the conning tower, to a height beyond that of either periscope when fully up. It was capable of being lowered flush with the foredeck. It was trunked through the pressure hull to the engine-room and served as an intake for air and an exhaust for the diesels. The boat could then remain submerged for a great length of time and operate on her diesels instead of her electric motors, providing, of course, she could keep the top of the pipe above water. She could even charge her batteries in this manner. There was a radar antenna on top of the pipe so that the submarine could be warned of the approach of an aircraft or vessel. They were believed to have an arrangement which prevented the top of the pipe offering much of a radar target to us.

It had not occurred to me that a snorter would smoke. The engineers in the submarine possibly did not know they were making smoke; they certainly could not see it. Whether or not the ship next door to us realized at first what it was, I did not know, but she finally saw the pipe sticking up and, remembering what they had been told, fired at it. The submarine either detected her by radar or heard her propellers, probably the former, and thereupon switched over to her electric motors, closed the trap of the snorter and went down deeper.

On our way to the position where the smoke had been seen, which had been recorded on the automatic plotting table in the wheelhouse below, we passed through a thin patch of diesel oil which tended to confirm the situation. Both ships reined in as we approached the spot and searched and, in a few moments, we had contact with what the asdic officer assured me on the telephone was a submarine. We slowed down more and the hedgehog crew were ordered to stand to.

Coyne, in his series of reports, sounded sure.

'Moving slowly left and opening, sir . . . Sub's speed three knots . . . Still moving left.'

I peered into the compass, telephone to ear, watching the beam of light moving, and altered course to intercept.

'A little woolly, sir,' came Coyne's voice over the phone.

'You're still sure?'

'Y-e-s, two knots now, opening.'

259

Had doubt entered his voice?

'Moving slowly left,' he reported again.

'Off caps.'

My order was immediately passed down by phone to the hedge-hog. A few moments later word came back, 'Caps off.'

'Still good, sir. Stand by.'

I was listening carefully to the asdic officer and watching. I was feeling confident I had made a suitable allowance.

Brrrr. The projectiles were away! I relaxed. I had only to wait and see.

The answer came back – a deep thrum, too distant to be explosions on anything but the sea floor.

Such was our luck in the Channel. When we thought we had a bead on the elusive enemy we could not hit him, or did not think we had. They were probably using their pillenwuffer decoys – the chemical which they ejected from a submerged position and which produced an area of bubbles that gave an echo on the asdic almost identical to a submarine. Behind this the U-boat would escape and it was only as the bubbles dispersed that the echo sounded untrue. This ingenious lure was still hard to beat.

That evening we received a disturbing report from an aircraft. It informed us that nine enemy destroyers and two mine-sweepers were off Ushant and steering towards us at twenty-five knots. This speed I did not take seriously because aircraft estimates of the rate of travel of ships were often erroneous. As we were only thirty miles off the French coast, this meant roughly that half an hour's steaming, if we went towards them, would bring us together. I saw afterwards a note in the S.O's report in which he said: 'As it was not my idea to engage Narvik and Elbing destroyers in daylight and as the submarines we had been attacking might have been mauled sufficiently to have to surface soon, I decided to withdraw to the northern edge of the area and patrol in close order.' (Close order in case of enemy destroyer attack.) We raised steam on our third boiler for full speed as we withdrew, just in case.

The four of us were separated from the British group now and our fire power could not have matched Narvik destroyers, which were Germany's largest. But at night it would be worth a try. However, before this chance was offered us, the Commander-in-

Chief, Plymouth, despatched his Tribal destroyer force – which included Canada's Tribals – to engage them, which they did with effect. The next night we passed through an area where the water was covered with oil and beneath it lay the wreck of an Elbing.

The next twenty-four hours were equally fruitless and seemingly wasted hours, yet they were probably not. We were unquestionably harassing the U-boats.

Our own aircraft began to bother us at night. They would come in low and illuminate us brilliantly with their search light, often before we even heard them. They would not extinguish their light until we had displayed our recognition signal which I sometimes thought was quite unnecessary, for our identity must usually have been obvious to the aircraft. We wanted to remain concealed by the darkness; it was one of our best chances. But no! They had to show us up to any submarine which happened to be looking. And it was always a scramble to get hold of the pistol and fire the recognition cartridge in time. The silence on the bridge would be suddenly broken:

'Signalman. Fire recognition!'

'Recognition, sir.'

Suspense. Scuffling noises.

'Come on! Fire.'

'Aye, aye, sir.'

'Pistol! Where's that bloody pistol, signalman?'

'Coming, sir.'

'Godamn the bastard's light! Fire!'

Muttering. 'Blast the mechanism!'

'What the hell's . . .'

The crack of the pistol would at last relieve the tension and a green light would appear a few hundred feet above. The searchlight would go out as the plane roared over the mast.

Our radar, of course, could warn us of the approach of an aircraft, but they were so plentiful that the indicating bell took on the features of a five-minute alarm clock and jangled our nerves to the point where we had to plug it.

At 0200 on the fourth night a small surface radar echo was observed by the rating in the tower. It was bearing due south so we turned and headed towards it. It was over four miles away and the

261

radar operator had plenty of time to study it as we approached. We did not go very fast because I did not want to make the bow wave noticeable.

The echo gave every indication of representing a submarine, though the operator at times had difficulty in holding it; it had a tendency to fade. As the distance decreased, I was obliged to alter course to port gradually to keep up with its movement and this made me quite confident of its genuineness. When Jason, the navigator, reported that it was making twelve knots in a south-easterly direction, I was still more confident and increased speed somewhat to catch up with it more quickly. The leader, with whom we were in telephonic communication, had broken away from the others and was following us.

The two forward guns were loaded and all was in readiness. Everyone on the bridge who was not otherwise occupied was staring ahead. It was a perfect night with a low moon, wind nor'-west-by-north, moderate. Nothing, however, was visible by the time we had reduced the distance to a mile but that was not out of the way. I stood behind the binnacle, the light in the gyro-compass dimmed down so that I was not blinded from seeing ahead yet could see the figures in the compass and the lubber line. The gunnery officer, Lieutenant Everleigh, stood close by my side, his ear phones on his head and his chest transmitter close to his mouth. I could hear without difficulty the radar reports coming through the voicepipe.

'Bearing 135, thirteen hundred yards.' We were steering 135° – south-east.

Twice I had heard the warning voice of the S.O. coming out of the telephone loudspeaker: 'You are standing into the minefield, don't go much farther.'

This was backed up by a report from Jason below who urgently informed me that we were on the edge of the field. Out of the corner of my eye I could see to starboard the flashing light of a buoy off the Brittany coast. It was from a bearing of this buoy that Jason had checked his position.

A thousand yards – half a mile – and still no one could see it! Yet it was clearly displayed on the radar screen. Was it lying as low in the water as all that? The dark little waves gave an undulant

262

appearance to the water so that the back of a U-boat might not be so readily recognizable.

'Eight hundred yards . . . seven hundred . . . six hundred . . .'

Nothing visible.

'You're in the minefield!' exhorted the mechanical voice.

'Fire port and starboard snowflakes!'

As suddenly, two brilliant balls of flame threw a pool of light ahead and around us.

'Balloon! Balloon!' came a chorus of voices.

'Balloon!' I said to myself, half aloud.

There, in the light of the flares a couple of hundred yards ahead and about seventy feet above the water, hung a small balloon, two or three feet in diameter. Its mooring rope went down to a wooden float which could be seen moving briskly along the surface of the sea, dragged by the balloon as it was being blown to leeward by the wind. Either attached to the mooring rope or to another line suspended from the balloon were a number of pieces of tin foil which glinted in the brilliant light.

A radar decoy! We had been balked again – magnificently fooled.

It had been released from the deck of a U-boat to throw us off his scent; he had gone off in another direction.

These things had been used for some time and I knew all about them though had never encountered one before. I had been warned and I had often reminded myself of the warning, to be suspicious of radar echoes which showed movement directly to leeward at half the speed of the wind. This had not occurred to me while we were chasing it – it had actually shown a faster movement than half the velocity of the wind – but now I remembered that there had been some fluctuation in the strength of the echo; it had been inclined to fade. But I think I would have followed it, anyway. It resembled the real thing too nearly to be waved aside as an obvious decoy.

'Disengage to the north,' was the terse reply when I told the S.O. what we had encountered. I was doing that.

We swept and hunted all the rest of the night and the next day. We investigated oil slicks, aircraft reports of submarines in every conveivable state – rising, diving, snorting – and examined innumerable underwater contacts which seemed to emanate from everything except submarines. Then, at 0500 on the morning of 11th June, we were ordered to return to Plymouth.

At breakfast time we were off the Lizard and in the buoyed channel which skirted the coast. The long, narrow convoys were still moving east but now there were the empties coming back from the beaches.

19. Inside Ushant

As I sat at my desk in my after cabin I could hear the evening rain pattering down on the still water outside the half-open scuttle. It was July and this was our third two-day stay in Plymouth since D-day. Though these relief periods were short, they were long enough. They enabled us to sleep ourselves out and drink our fill and sometimes go ashore. But there was always work to be done.

Occasionally the varying tones of a different sound, mingling with the rain outside, drifted in. They were singing in the wardroom. It was distracting and contributed to the hardship of having to write a report when I did not feel like it.

Finishing the thing at last I pushed my chair back and gazed into the glow of the electric fire which was partly burning.

We had achieved no individual success, yet it seemed we had not done badly. It was considered by Operations that only a handful of U-boats had negotiated the Channel, perhaps three, perhaps five, probably fewer. One was believed to have reached the Channel Islands. Very little damage had been inflicted on the convoys, but then, fewer submarines had evidently attempted to get through than I had expected. I had thought that at least a hundred would have sought to enter but it was believed that only thirty or forty had tried. Perhaps there were not a hundred left. The blockade was looked upon as very successful and although few submarines seemed to have been sunk by ships, a good many had been destroyed by aircraft and some by mines. But the ships must certainly have damaged quite a number and nearly all must have turned back when they found their progress was made too slow and difficult by the opposition they encountered.

Going back to my report I read what I had written. Then abandoning my cabin I went up the ladder into the lobby and down through another hatch to the wardroom.

There was an atmosphere of conviviality and visitors. It looked cheerful and bright in the glow of the lamps and the more austere aspects of the place were softened by the green carpet covering the hard steel deck. Although it extended across the width of the ship the room was hazy; the wet air outside seemed incapable of drawing the smoky warmth out through the open scuttles and absorbing it.

The place was crowded, all in the everlasting monotony of blue, relieved only by white collars and cuffs and splashes of gold. A group was sitting at the end of the mahogany dining table leaning across it, talking earnestly, the pack of cards and dice discarded. Some were sitting on the bench around the fire-place laughing; two leaning against the mantlepiece. Others were standing in groups in the middle of the room talking and sipping their drinks, and behind them at the piano several were singing 'Roll Out The Barrel.'

I found Peters with the chief engineer and first lieutenant of a neighbouring destroyer, talking to Bimson and our M.O.

''Evening, Capt'n,' the chief said. He used a Merchant Navy term.

'Gin, sir?' Bimson asked as the steward worked his way towards us.

'So you're going home, sir,' said the visiting executive officer. 'In a month or so?'

'Ask the chief,' I answered. 'I don't know. It's up to him and his engines.'

'Now, I didn't imply it would be that soon,' said Peters, looking at the other. He spoke with a slight Scottish burr. 'We'll all be through here before long, anyway.'

The M.O. said he thought it was far too soon to be going home. We hadn't done anything yet. Why, he had had no business at all. 'I've done nothing but censor letters.'

'And talk incessantly,' said Bimson.

'I haven't. There's been damn all to talk about except the lovelies running the picket boats in the harbour here.'

The difference in age was probably too much to keep us together long. The two first lieutenants and the medical officer carried on with their own topic, a popular one, while we discussed other matters.

Behind us on the bench, beside the fire, Jason was using his hands to illustrate a tactical theory. He was always keen to convince.

From what I could hear of the snatches of conversation going on among those standing near the open forward scuttle, Everleigh was telling his friends from the other ships how it was they saw at our bow the open-mouthed muzzle of a pom-pom leaning out over the water like a figurehead. It had been an old ordnance friend of his who had got it for him, as well as the rockets for the gun-shield of the forward four-seven – all contrary to regulations and not in the books.

Presently the group behind the chief merged with us and a base lieutenant-commander, related an amusing incident to do with signals that got mixed up. He had the wit which made him an acceptable visitor from ashore. A paymaster began to describe a mess dinner he had once arranged, a formal affair, but no one was interested.

The torpedo officer hammered out something fast on the piano, and Larose, with one of the subs and several visitors standing around him in the brave attitude of those who are not going to let lack of talent prevent them from singing, launched into another song. Windram's fingers flew over the keys and his head moved slightly as his eyes watched his hands. The glass on the end of the keyboard vibrated and its contents bubbled.

A quartermaster came to the wardroom door to make a report and two more visitors arrived. But several left and, with the exchange of guests, the piano and singing stopped.

Unobtrusively the piano began again, quietly, then grew, but songs were not being played. They were the more difficult pieces; a change, pleasant in a way. The charm of this music no doubt brought to some the thought of home – particularly those who were married – and to others, younger and freer, the feeling of being braver than usual and proud of what they had done. But it also made them wonder why they had not seized that past chance of being more heroic; it could have been done more dramatically.

Presently the piano went back to a song. Windram played a few bars of 'The Road to the Isles', then stopped. It was the signal! When the lilting tune began again every voice in the wardroom started to sing what had now become almost a shanty in Canadian ships, written by a surgeon-lieutenant who had been in the Barber Pole Group:

It's away! Outward the swinging fo'c'sles reel
From the smoking sea's white glare upon the strand.
It's the grey miles that are slipping under keel
When we're rolling outward-bound from Newfoundland.

From Halifax to Newfiejohn or 'Derry's clustered towers
By trackless paths where conning towers roll.
If you know another group in which you'd sooner spend your hours,
You've never sailed beneath the Barber Pole!
It's the grey seas that are slipping under keel
When you're rolling outward-bound from Newfoundland.

So beware! Harbours that berth the Barber Pole,
If you'd keep the situation well in hand,
After grey seas that went slipping under keel
When we wallowed outward-bound from Newfoundland.

Drink a whisky or a navy rum or drink a gin-and-lime
Let inebriation be your final goal:
Pick a lady you've selected for a short and merry time,
There's merry men beneath the Barber Pole!
After grey seas that went slipping under keel
When we wallowed outward-bound from Newfoundland.

It's away! Astern of us the Western Islands die,
There's an ocean lies before us to be spanned.
It's the grey seas where sullen icebergs lie
When we're rolling inward-bound to Newfoundland.

From Halifax to Newfiejohn or 'Derry's clustered towers,
By trackless paths where conning towers roll.
If you know another group in which you'd sooner spend your hours,
You've never sailed beneath the Barber Pole!
It's the grey seas where sullen icebergs lie
When we're rolling inward-bound to Newfoundland.

The next night we sailed for our usual haunt, the coast of
Brittany. On arrival we relieved a group who were due to go into
port. We resumed our hunting, moving this way and that, slowly at
times, faster at others: line abreast, line ahead, line of bearing:
straight courses, zig-zags, listening and watchings, more or less

the same routine but never quite the same. The day was bright and clear, the sea nearly smooth with only a slight swell. We saw several bodies in the water at different times that day. We had not seen many previously and I did not know why we should now particularly; two were obviously airmen.

The steward brought my supper up to my sea-cabin from the after galley at 1800 as usual. He carried it in a sort of lunch pail, a wooden box with a handle on top which I had had specially constructed to keep a complete meal hot. I removed each course from its shelf in the box as I wanted it and placed it on a napkin spread out on my desk. Beside my plate lay several signals which were causing me some thought. I had received the latest just before supper and this had made me refer back to another which had been handed to me on sailing the night before and which was addressed to all ships in the western part of the Channel. I read it again to make sure I had considered everything. It ran:

Operation "Dredger". Information: Air reconnaisance shows enemy is accustomed to escort U-boats with up to five M-class mine-sweepers between Brest and a point about ten miles south of Ushant. Rendez-vous appear to be made about two hours after dark. Intention: (A) To destroy the escort with a striking force of destroyers before the rendezvous is made. (B) To destroy the U-boats with a support group assisted by the striking force. Execution: (A) Date will depend on air reconnaisance and D/F activity. (B) The striking force will be routed outside shore radar cover to approach enemy's effected track from southward. (C) The support group will keep clear to westward until ordered by S.O. striking force to close and assist in hunting U-boats after surface vessels have been disposed of. Warning: Attention is called to enemy minefields. Executive order: The operation will be put into force by signal: Carry out operation "Dredger".

When I received this signal I had read it only casually, thinking it would not fall to us to execute its purpose. But I was wrong. The latest signal addressed to us read:

Carry out operation "Dredger". Striking force E.G.12. Support group E.G. 14. Date: night 5th/6th July.

The signal then contained a lot of figures which concerned the positions through which we were to pass and also the statement that the U-boats would probably be inward bound when encountered. A further injunction added that if nothing were met we were to resume our patrol.

This last order was the one I thought was the most significant. I had no confidence at all that we would meet this enemy. I had carried out so many fruitless search schemes ordered by one authority or another. I had not even given instructions to the officers to prepare for an engagement. After supper, however, I did.

The navigator was told to lay off on the chart the courses we would take, then I sent word to the chief engineer to have the third boiler lit up for 2200. The first lieutenant and the gunnery and torpedo officers foregathered and we discussed the whole project. It was arranged that we would come to the first degree of readiness for action at midnight. All hands were then informed and the officers went off to check final details with the chief petty officers of their departments and lay any particular plans for the operation.

At about 2000 I received a message from the senior officer outlining his mode of attack. I had been waiting for this; I knew he would provide us with specific instructions.

Night intentions: Area will be swept in line ahead at about twenty knots. Blue turns (turns together) may be carried out to close or to avoid torpedoes but line ahead will always be reformed. Tides start setting to the north at beginning of operation and may reach three knots by 0230. Rear ships are to sweep for new targets rather than opening fire on each target already engaged. Generally speaking I shall seek to engage leading ships on parallel courses and rear ships on opposite courses. I intend to use high-explosive-delayed-action shell with flashless cordite. Radio telephone only will be used after silence is broken. Except during action, fire should not as a rule be opened without signal. Radar policy – main surface set only, "friend-or-foe-indicator" to be silent until after action is joined.

This gave me the impression that the S.O. at least thought he might be lucky enough to find the enemy.

We checked among our confidential books to verify the type of armament an M-class mine-sweeper had. But we could not find it; in fact, we did not have the book. Larose, the signal officer, then remembered it was one of many secret books we had left behind in Plymouth the day before when we had been ordered to retain only several simple and less important code books and land the rest. We no longer even held the instructions for Operation 'Neptune'. We were reminded by Larose, in what sounded very like official language, that this sort of thing happened when there was a likelihood of being stranded on an enemy coast or sunk in shallow water. A pleasant thought!

However, by pooling our resources of knowledge we satisfied ourselves that M-class mine-sweepers mounted two five-inch guns, one forward and one aft. Since the main armament of three of our destroyers consisted of two four-point-sevens, the enemy would be slightly stronger in fire power. Our ship, on the other hand, carried three, so we would have the edge on a single mine-sweeper. We also had a forty-millimetre pom-pom.

Sometime later, lying in my cabin but still awake, I heard the distant hail, 'Lay down from aloft'. Dusk was descending – no use for a look-out in the crows-nest now.

I could really raise no enthusiasm for this project. I felt vaguely annoyed that I would have to stay up all night. I was tired and had that gnawing pain. At this time I could no longer keep it away with cocoa or milk or food and it was not only in my stomach, it had reached round to my back, like a pair of interior claws, and gave me pains between the shoulder-blades. The only relief would be sleep. This was one of those evenings when I knew I ought to sleep and waste not a moment in going off. To add to my discomfort I was suffering from an idea of the M.O's. I was off smoking. I had not smoked for two weeks and time did not make it any easier. I was definitely bad tempered.

The reason I had not given in to my ulcers was that, firstly, I was fairly sure I could live with them if I had a moderate amount of sleep and took milk and eggs and things like that every two hours or so; and, secondly, I did not want to find myself in a hospital on this side of the Atlantic. I was really afraid of hospitals, but like most people I felt I would be safer in a hospital at home if I ultimately had to go to one. Moreover, of course, I knew we were short of C.O.s, and I had been anxious to see the invasion. Anyway, my plan was to hold on until we went home, which I thought would not be long now.

At 2300 I gave up trying to sleep and got up.

At 2340 we were passing the pre-determined starting point,

steering 128° by gyro, speed twenty-four knots, with approximately forty miles to go. The Commander's ship was leading as usual and we were next in line at a distance of three cables; the other two destroyers followed at similar intervals. The support group, E.G. 14, lay fifteen miles to the westward but would be moving slowly east. The wind was very light from the nor'-nor'-west, making only small ripples on the water, and such swell as there was made the ship rise and fall very gently and gracefully. To make the night more perfect, the diffused light of an almost full moon shone through the light cloud cover which hung two or three thousand feet above.

Windram and Coyne were keeping watch together; they would be on until midnight. The first lieutenant was also on the bridge. He had seen that all was well on deck but could not go back to his cabin or the wardroom; he was too interested in the forthcoming adventure, for adventure it was to him. He had his steel hat on, the pistol in its holster strapped around his waist and his sheath knife on the other hip. I did not doubt he had a hand grenade in his pocket.

'Hope it'll be a close engagement, sir,' he was saying. 'We'll be on them in less than a couple of hours, won't we?'

'We'll probably see nothing, Bimson,' I answered.

'Oh surely, sir, Intelligence wouldn't make a mistake like that.'

'Have they never barked up the wrong tree before?'

'Perhaps; but they can't be wrong this time.'

We talked for a while about the preparedness of the ship. I thought there was little need to really, because we were supposed to be able to make ourselves ready for fighting in a matter of a couple of minutes. I knew we could, but since we had so many hours notice this time everyone seemed to think it right to make doubly sure that the ship was in absolute and complete readiness. It was an advantage too in some respects, because we were able to bring up an extra supply of high explosive shells to the guns and return the armour piercing stuff to the magazines. Also an opportunity was given to outline the scheme to the men so that they would know what was coming. And Peters had ample time to get more steam up.

At midnight we went to action stations. At 0015 course was altered to east-by-north, sufficient southing having been made.

Five minutes later there became visible on the starboard bow a triple flashing light which, after watching it for a minute and counting off the seconds, the navigator and I concluded was the main light on the Chaussée de Sein.

'That's rather extraordinary, isn't it, sir,' Jason remarked, still looking at the intermittent appearance of the little pin-point of light.

'It is indeed. I certainly didn't expect to find the character of the lights unchanged.'

Jason took a compass bearing of the light and went down to the charthouse to lay it off. He was up again in a minute to report that we were on our dead reckoning position.

'This is going to make it easier for us, Jason,' I said. 'If the other lights are burning like that one is, navigating will be a cinch.'

'It's marvellous,' he answered in his enthusiastic way. 'We'll run foul of no rocks at this rate. I must admit it lifts a load off my mind.'

This light – a group of three flashes every twenty seconds, being precisely the same as that shown on the Admiralty chart – meant that it had not been changed since the war began. We knew its brilliancy had not been cut down either, because we had sighted it at seventeen miles and the range of its visibility was recorded as fifteen miles at fifteen feet above sea level. If the rest of the coastal lights were on we would know our position at all times. The senior officer had a special radio navigating instrument after the fashion of loran, with which he was able to establish his position very accurately, and as it was our duty to follow him we should normally have no worry. But it was also our duty to know where we were. To ground because the leader stranded was no excuse to my mind and moreover we might have to part company. So I was glad we were likely to have lighthouses to guide us; the drift of the tides could easily set us beyond our calculations.

I went below with the navigator to look again at a reference in The French Coast Pilot book about tides. As we came in from the rear of the wheelhouse the picture in the semi-darkness was one I had often seen. The dim outline of men; the central figure of the coxswain, his back towards us, arms spread out from his body grasping the spokes of the wheel; a man by his side, another by the telegraph; and adjacent to the wheel at the port side the bent shoulders of the navigator's yeoman leaning over the plotting table. Advancing, I noticed the yeoman's rapt expression as the light coming up through the glass top of the plotting table lit his face.

It seemed warm, almost stuffy, and there was a faint smell of rope and bunting. I glanced at the chart on the plotting table and saw the course line which the stylo was automatically recording. Then I reached for the pilot book which was placed handily at the end of the table-top and held open by a heavy shoe laid across the book at a page announcing 'Approaches to Ushant'. I moved the shoe and read two paragraphs which were roughly familiar to me:

> Between Ushant and the mainland to the south-east there is an archipelago of islands, reefs and shoals which it is imprudent to approach without local knowledge.
> Mariners approaching Ushant should be on their guard against the dangers of being set eastward of their reckoning and must exercise the greatest caution on rounding it. This island is surrounded by dangers; rocks are numerous and some lie far from the and; fog and thick weather are not uncommon; the tidal streams are strong, and the extent of their influence seaward undetermined. No dependence can be placed on seeing the lights, although they are very powerful, nor of hearing the fog signals, in thick weather, and when such prevails the island should be given a wide berth.

Ouessant in the Breton language means Isle of Terror. Well, it was not foggy!

I put the shoe back and, shifting to the middle of the wheel-house, looked into the compass. The coxswain kept the little graduation marked 078° dancing on the lubber-line. The speed made the compass vibrate. But everything was vibrating, the wheel, the man, the deck, the ship, and every so often an extra quiver would send a rattle through the wheelhouse like the thrum of loose rigging in a gale.

My sight became fixed on the lubber-line and my eyes drew relief from their steady staring. When I dragged them away I had resolved one thing: I would break the pledge.

'Who's got a cigarette?' I asked quickly.

Three or four hands appeared simultaneously. I accepted one from the rating beside the telegraph. After a couple of pulls I

274

felt giddy, but it disappeared in a moment. It was delicious! But satisfying as it was, I wished it could have been my pipe; I had parted with my tobacco.

We ran on for another ten minutes, then reduced speed to sixteen knots, the object being to render the bow waves and wakes of the four ships less visible. We were now coming into the Iroise, a bay bounded by the mainland of Finistère to the east, the Chaussée de Sein to the south (a fourteen mile chain of rocks commonly called the Saints) and the Chaussée des Pierres Noires (the Black Stones) to the north. Brest lay sixteen miles in from the Black Stones, in through the narrow Goulet de Brest, to seaward of which a minefield was sown so that it extended to within three miles of the Black Stones. Through this field there would be a passage somewhere known only to the enemy.

All at once I began to feel the attraction of the exploit. The very fact that the Germans had not put out the French lights, had not even reduced their power nor altered them to mislead the foe, was an indication that they had not expected their enemies to come within the precincts of Brest. And yet they had big guns on the extremity of land pointing out to sea. As far as I knew we were the first allied ships to enter the approaches to the famous U-boat base since the fall of France. I was warming to the prospects ahead, though I did not consciously notice my change of spirits.

At 0040 the red flashing light of Les Pierres Noires became visible to the north-east. This marked the southern edge of the mass of rocks and islets which lay between the Island of Ushant and the mainland. Jason took a cross-bearing.

The leader could be seen quite plainly ahead in the diffused moonlight and I could have seen those astern had I looked, but I was not at the moment concerned with what was astern of me. I was standing behind the gyro-compass. Attached to the binnacle were three voicepipes, one to the radar cabin, one to the coxswain at the wheel, and one to the navigator at the plotting table in the wheelhouse. Thus I had direct communication to three vital stations. Beside me stood Everleigh, wearing ear-phones and chest transmitter which kept him in touch with the three main guns. Larose was keeping the bridge with Sub-Lieutenant Coyne, so either could take over from me if need be. There were probably fifteen ratings on the bridge as well; there were the yeoman and

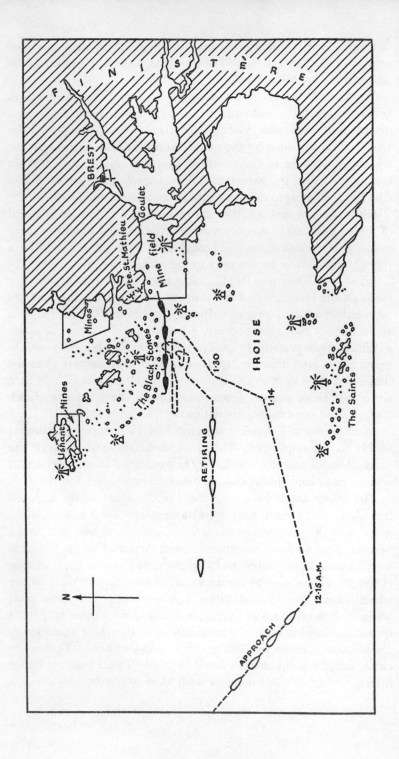

several of his signalmen and a telegraphist; look-out men; two men manning the big searchlights; the oerlikon gun director and his communication rating at the telephones and several others at telephones which connected with the torpedo tubes, engine-room, damage control parties. There were more on the bridge than I would have liked but I could not reduce them. The officers were fairly well dispersed. Apart from the three on the bridge and the navigator in the wheelhouse, the first lieutenant was on the iron deck, the torpedo officer amidships at the tubes, a lieutenant at the forward guns, and a sub-lieutenant aft. The chief engineer was in the engine-room and the engineer sub probably around the boiler rooms. The surgeon was below at his medical station. Chief petty officers were well separated.

Suddenly the scene altered. The log was to show:

0112 Radar echo thirty degrees on port bow, eleven miles. Signalman passed information to leader by telephone. Leader has echo, too.

0114 We alter course in succession to nor'-nor'-east to close. Beams from several lighthouses glimmering intermittently.
We are well in – almost as far as judicious. Now approaching from south as directed.

0126 Navigator, from plot to bridge: 'Enemy's estimated course, west; speed, nine knots.'

0128 Four distinct objects in radar, six miles, dead ahead. Radar: 'Vessels in line ahead, close order . . . first larger than other three.'

0130 We turn in succession to north-east – getting behind them – good!

Guns were trained to port, and I watched the sea on the port bow, levelling my eyes just below the red flash of the Black Stones light. I also watched the leader, dark on the dark water. Our slender bow was cutting her silver wake like a knife. The breeze which occasionally touched my face was cool and pleasant. All was still on the bridge. I felt curiously content and alive, yet tense as I listened to the reports from the radar P.O. Jason below, who was also in contact with him, would be listening, too, and with his yeoman plotting the course of the enemy vessels. They were three and a half miles away. We were working in towards their rear and towards the minefield.

I gave the order, 'Stand by to open fire.'

'All guns . . . salvoes,' Everleigh ordered in turn.

The ship was ready – ready to engage. She would respond on the instant to whatever word was given her. I had no fear of a blunder. In this moment before battle I had complete confidence in the ship.

The port look-out's voice suddenly broke the stillness. 'Red three-oh, light flashing, sir.'

'Aye, aye,' Larose acknowledged.

He and others saw it simultaneously but the port look-out was quick to report.

The slow deliberate flashing ceased.

'What do you make of it, Yeoman?' I asked, without looking away.

'Challenge, I s'pose, sir.'

'There it is again,' said Larose abruptly. 'It's a challenge, sir.' He muttered something else in French.

'S.O. to all ships, sir – thirty knots – executive.' The announcement came from the leading signalman who had it from the signalman at the phone.

'Three hundred revolutions,' I called down to the wheelhouse. This would put us beyond the point of critical vibration and make shooting easier. I put my binoculars up again; the flashing had not been repeated a third time. But now I saw the vessel which had challenged us and received no reply. Two and a half miles was her distance. She was heading west. We were still steering north-east.

The destroyer ahead made a slow turn to port. We kept on in her boiling wake and turned where she had turned. Now the turn was quicker; the ship leaned over to starboard. West by north now, and still we swung.

All at once I saw them, four dimly silhouetted vessels in a neat row one behind the other; the gap between the third and fourth, however, was somewhat greater than between the others. We would, when we came on to a parallel course to theirs, be on the port quarter of all except the last one.

At 0146 all destroyers were heading west and had the enemy broad on their starboard bows.

'Lay on the second ship,' I told Everleigh.

He indicated the target to his gunners.

Then the signal came and at the same moment the leader opened fire.

'Flares!' I cried.

With hardly a second's delay, six rockets left their mountings at 'B' gun, soared up over the second ship of the enemy's line and burst, leaving vivid flares suspended beyond her.

'Open fire!'

Then the roar began.

My attention turned to where we were going. I could leave Everleigh to his target for the moment: all guns were bearing.

Through the hot waves of concussion and gun smoke I looked up the short, solid silver path. We were dead astern of the leader. But I was shocked to see what was happening to her. A stream of fire was coming from the ship in the van of the enemy force and was falling directly into her. The lighted tracer – every bullet a tracer – came across the intervening mile like high pressure water out of half a dozen hoses. Arched up, the jets looked like streams of liquid fire.

Have we got to go through that, I thought. The leader will never get through it herself!

But we were receiving the same thing from the ship we were engaging. I had hardly realized it. I could not see her heavy guns firing because the enemy, like ourselves, was using flashless cordite.

We had been rapidly overhauling the ship we were opposing and now were drawing abeam. Lit constantly by flares, she appeared to be a vessel of about 250 feet long. As I looked I saw her hull below her main mast hit by a shell from our main armament. Her sides glowed as though red hot.

'Stand by torpedoes!'

Larose jumped to the torpedo control sights. Now I would use the weapon that had been so often used against us. But I could not bring myself to part with three torpedoes at once; there was another ship yet to be engaged.

The noise of the guns was so great that I had to leave my position

279

in the centre of the bridge and take several strides to the wing and shout into the sighter's ear.

'Fire one only . . . not the whole salvo . . . Fire when ready.'

A minute later he reported one torpedo fired. But I saw no result, so concluded it was a miss.

The noise was terrific; the four-point-sevens were firing at upwards of ten rounds a minute, and between the heavy boom of these could be heard the continuous deep-throated grunt of the bow-chaser and the high-pitched rat-tat-tat of the three starboard oerlikons. The one on the lower bridge was deafening.

As we sped on beyond our target I saw another hit, this time square in the enemy's fo'c'sle. Her bow surrounding the point where the shell entered seemed to cave in, glowed a little inside, then millions of sparks flew outwards. Even amid the din I could hear a cheer go up from those on deck.

The oerlikons were out of range. 'A' gun would no longer bear; we were too far past.

'Shift target, take the leader,' I shouted.

'Cease fire, shift target,' Everleigh said, speaking into his transmitter, and a moment later as the abrupt lull came, he gave the guns the range and lay of the next ship. His order ended, 'Rapid independent – shoot.'

With 'A' arcs open, the full broadside fired.

The engagement had thus far lasted four minutes and the enemy had returned a great deal, or so it seemed to the eye, but not apparently as much as we had given. The leader had disengaged with all but her after gun. I did not know what the destroyers astern were doing. We were overtaking our opponents so rapidly, by about twenty-two knots I judged, that it must have been rather difficult for them to hit us; a number of their shots must have passed astern. I kept an eye on the leading destroyer, always unconsciously judging our distance from the white mill-race coming from her low black stern. And I thought of the possibility of her speed being suddenly cut down by damage and lying unmanageable across our path.

As we overhauled the enemy in the van, I ordered another torpedo to be fired. I was beside Larose while he aimed and had to stop the oerlikon fire because our tracer blinded us to the target. Besides this, the smoke from the forward guns was blowing back and badly interfering. Again there was no visible evidence that it struck its mark.

By the light of the flares I could see that this ship was much bigger than the other, perhaps it was an M-class mine-sweeper, but I did not debate this now; I was merely conscious of it being fairly large.

Our ship was shuddering under the recoil of the guns; the roar was deafening. The men passing the ammunition up from the magazine would be worked to the limit by the rate of fire. They would be hot and sweating, and the guns would be hot, too.

Our new adversary was laying it on more heavily than her consort did, I thought. Occasionally the rattle of shot made me aware of the closeness of her fire to the bridge. I could not differentiate between a shell hitting us and the concussion of our own firing, so I assumed that if we were hit I would know it quickly enough in another way. Yet I wondered why I had not yet been informed of damage below. Surely Bimson would have sent word; we could hardly be escaping unharmed.

For nearly three minutes the vessel a mile away received the full force of our fire power; then we were obliged to break off.

A signal came: 'Turn to port 180° and attack again.'

For a moment I thought, 'Surely not!' I did not want to go in again.

For the first time fear struck me. I had not felt it in the heat of those seven minutes, nor earlier. But now I realized with a sharp sense of awe what we had come through. There was no time to dwell on it, though. I saw the senior officer turning.

I applied ten degrees of port helm as we reached the foaming silver curve, a wake now broader with the turn and smooth on the outer side, like the glassy sleekness of water before a tide-rip. It was rather more helm then a destroyer should have at thirty knots, but her old sluggishness in turning to port demanded it. And as she felt the full effect of her rudder she leaned over to starboard and stayed so. My eyes were on the leader. If I cut the corner we would finish too close to her; if I made too wide a turn I would make the gap too great and partially destroy the close order of fighting. As we came on to the opposite course the ship righted with the release of helm and I caught sight of the fourth ship of our line just starting the turn. Then flares fell over the first of the enemy ships. The S.O. had started again.

We opened fire too. Our immediate opponent had turned away to the north-west but I knew she could not escape in that direction. We had the flotilla hemmed in against the Black Stones; there was less than a mile between them and the treacherous rocks, which was the reason we had not turned to starboard and attacked them from the other side. Moreover, the tide was setting all of us fast towards the Stones.

It was then that I was told by the navigator that this vessel was no longer underway. Jason could see it on his plotting chart. As we slipped by I saw, through my night glasses, two heavy shell hits. She was sinking by the stern.

The S.O. turned to the north-east, and as we came abreast of the second ship the range was no more than eight hundred yards. She also was stopped. The third torpedo was launched, this time in local control, but with no greater success. It mattered little, for shell after shell crashed into her hull and split her superstructure apart. We were close enough this time as we passed to see her heavy forward gun firing valiantly. Black smoke was billowing up from her when I took a last glance back.

'Don't go any farther to the nor'ard, sir,' came Jason's urgent voice up the voicepipe; I caught what he said between the last salvoes.

'How much room is there?' I shouted down.

'Less than half a mile from the rocks. Turn east, sir.'

I did not fail to heed the navigator's warning. Without looking up I shifted my mouth to the coxswain's voice pipe and gave an order which swung her off. Looking up I saw that the senior officer had also turned away, so by the time we were heading east we were still astern of his ship.

'Ship to starboard!' came a look-out's ringing voice. In the lull between firings, voices sounded different.

Yes, there she was, the third ship of the enemy's now irregular line, the one which had been the third destroyer's opponent and which had been subjected only to her onslaught and that of our fourth. What our leader had actually done was to cut through the enemy's line between the second and third ships, risking the rocks, to attack this one from the north. She took the full force of both our broadsides, but as we passed beyond her not four hundred yards distant she pounded us with fire that we had not experienced before – at least as far as I could judge. Shot and shell fell fast and heavy in the vicinity of the bridge. All heard it, and most fell on their faces, as ordered. I crouched behind the binnacle, unconsciously putting my hand to my steel helmet. But I could not stay in this position for more than a few seconds; I had to watch where we were going and I had noticed the leader turning to starboard.

Only our after gun was firing now; the others would not bear; and as we had to avoid hitting the destroyers astern who would be coming close to our line of fire, I ceased using live shells with this remaining gun and sent up a spread of star-shell for the benefit of those following. There was no need. Before they were in the sky the ship who had bombarded us so heavily burst into flames.

As we continued the turn, I looked to the eastward for the fourth enemy ship but could not see her. We headed west once more, and then came a signal from the senior officer.

'Am withdrawing to westward with damaged steering gear. Second division take over.'

The three of us turned again, but I was late in doing so, and by the time we were around I could not see my companions. Actually I had not seen them for the past ten minutes I had only sensed they were there.

'What ship can you see on either bow?' I shouted through to the radar.

'None, sir,' came the response. 'Radar's broken down.'

Cursing, I instinctively looked up at the tower behind me. In the dim light of the moon I could see the big lantern was half shot away.

The aircraft radar was in readiness in case the main set failed. I passed the word to switch it on. In four minutes it was reported jammed by the enemy, so was turned off. They at least had the frequency of one of our sets.

On our way back we saw one ship only, the burning third, and although we passed close to her I could not bring myself to fire on her. She was silent. A feeling of pity ran through me. I felt for a moment desperately sorry for her crew and for the men of the other two ships which I thought were either sunk or sinking. Perhaps they had had their one chance, like *el toro* in the Spanish ring. Was it weakness on my part to hold such feelings for an enemy who had been guilty of bringing such devastation upon the world? No. These Germans were sailors, they were men of my own cloth, my own profession.

Presently we found the other two destroyers coming away from the Black Stones and together we bore to the westward, having exchanged signals sufficiently to assure ourselves that two of the enemy were probably sunk and the third ship, as we could all see, was a burning hulk. As for the fourth, none of us had seen her again. She had evidently turned back and escaped with little or no damage.

Had there been any submarines present?

That was a question I could not answer. Two of us had seen no sign of any. But one of our captains had. In fact, he had been fired at by a submarine. He and the last destroyer of the line believed there were two, which could have accounted for the gap between the third and fourth escorts. They doubtless submerged during the attack or turned with the last ship and escaped into Brest.

We wasted no time in getting away – we were all aware of the four eleven-inch guns on Pointe St Mathieu eight miles away. It was 0230. The last shot had been fired at about 0212. The battle itself had lasted twenty-five minutes. Our ship had expended 280 high explosive shells and 2,400 rounds of smaller ammunition.

Twenty minutes later we considered it safe to reduce speed to twenty-five knots.

Shortly after this I went below to the charthouse, which was next door to my sea-cabin. I halted as I was about to pass my cabin; a blanket covered a still form lying within. I entered the open door and, bending down, drew back the blanket to reveal his face. It was the face of one of the cleanest cut fellows I knew on board.

I was strongly affected. As I looked at him, dead now but so much alive so short a time ago, I had a sense of sorrow, yet a sense of pride in this man who had had to pay while we lived. I felt a bitterness towards war.

I covered him up and went on to the charthouse.

Seven wounded and one killed. Those were our casualties. I was surprised they were so few but thankful they were no more.

The man who died was shot while firing his oerlikon gun on the lower bridge. When he fell his loader carried on single-handed.

The doctor had found it necessary to cut off an arm of one of the wounded. He came to the bridge to ask me if I could slow down to avoid the rise and fall of the ship in the swell, but I could not. I followed him down to the messdeck to see the man before the operation. He was a fine big fellow of Polish descent from a farm in Manitoba, and he looked at me as he lay on a table as though there were almost nothing the matter. Yet his arm, I was told, was in ribbons. I said something futile in an effort to cheer him and then watched him go under as Coyne, under the guidance of the surgeon, applied the anaesthetic. I stayed no longer. The amputation was reported to me afterwards by the naval hospital ashore to have been a first class job.

As the three of us headed for Plymouth, we heard from the leader, but not from the Commander himself. He was seriously wounded. A four-inch shell had struck the bridge. He had had to give up as he broke off the fight, though he was the kind who would have probably gone on had his steering trouble not dictated otherwise. He had more casualties than we; the other two destroyers had fewer.

I had the highest admiration for this senior officer now. In my report of the action I could not forbear to express some word of praise, however distasteful its reading might be to the unemotional authorities.

'Complete confidence was felt in the senior officer's leadership,' I wrote. 'At no time did I have any doubt as to his intentions and every manœuvre was made quite clear.'

Little enough to say but I could hardly say more of a senior officer in an official report.

At 0700 in the morning we were entering Plymouth Sound – all four of us. Though there were scars visible on the ships, internal damage was minor.

It was all so different from the U-boat warfare of the Atlantic. Here we were able to reach home within several hours of an engagement, whereas if we were hurt in the Atlantic it might take weeks to get home; more likely we would never get there. Looking back on it, I felt that I would prefer this kind of thing at any time to the long-drawn-out, anxious nights of the submarine war.

20. Homeward Bound

When a seaman sails from his native shore and he is young, he is embarking on adventure; if he is neither young nor old he will have an ache in his heart; if he is old he is used to both. But when his ship is homeward bound he is happy no matter what his age.

Most ships which sail away come home again. Most sailors do, too. But not all. As I sat in my chair on the bridge, looking at the ocean I had grown to hate, I thought about one who should have been with me now.

It had been early in the evening of 18th July. We were somewhere off Portland Bill. About sixty miles down the Channel E.G. 9, the frigate group, was on patrol. As dusk advanced several Junkers flew over and presently launched their glider bombs. One came in towards the leader – still under the command of my old senior officer – and, while deflected by a gunner, struck the top of her after gun-house. Its 300 mile-an-hour glide carried it through the upper deck, fortunately obliquely, and out through the ship's side. Its delayed action fuse prevented it from exploding until it had entered the water. When it burst it blew the side of the ship in, flooding the engine-room. The ship did not sink, however; both engine-room bulkheads held and she was towed in.

But my old steward, Auclair, was blown to pieces. He had been standing on the port side of the gun-house passing ammunition. With him went a signalman. Two others were killed in the engine-room and several were wounded.

The war had taken a number of my friends but this one man's death affected me peculiarly. He seemed so much to be the type of person who did not deserve to die. He had spread cheerfulness and warmth wherever he had gone.

We were half way across the Atlantic, without convoy or consorts. This was the first time, in the war, that I had crossed alone. Although the engines were still perfect, the condenser had given out. It had become troublesome due to leaking ferrules on old tubes, brought about by constantly changing speeds. We were un-

286

seaworthy in this respect and as the ship was overdue for refit and the British yards could not accommodate us, it was decided that we should go home. Towards the end of July we left the Channel and my last patrol. Now I had only four days before me.

She travelled fast to the end. Twenty-five knots down the coast, guided through the fog by radar, loran and soundings. At last the denseness, on which the sun glared but could not entirely penetrate, thinned, parted into rolling banks of mist and then suddenly lifted. The ship slid out into warm, clear sunshine. There, over the dazzling water, lay Chebucto Head topped by the squat white lighthouse – the symbol of home.

Around the fairway buoy, past the pilot cutter, up the buoyed channel to the boom and through the gate, the ship stood on into the harbour of Halifax as though no rein would hold her. And then the scent of the pines came down from the slopes of the North-West Arm – I knew I was home.

And as she glided up the Stream on that hot Sunday afternoon in August 1944, a military band played through the speakers on her upper deck. To the eyes of those who saw her, tall, slim and eminently graceful – crew-men of other ships, passengers on the crowded ferry, strollers along the shore – she was only another naval vessel entering a naval base, more dramatically than most perhaps. But to her officers and men she was a triumphant destroyer returning home from the wars.

At sunset the shrill call of the bosun's pipe sounded. Those of us who were on deck faced aft and saluted. As the white ensign slowly fluttered down, I knew that it had been lowered for the last time in a ship of mine.

Seeing my distress, the first lieutenant, who was standing beside me, asked, 'Do you really think you will not come back with us?'

'I'm afraid not, Bimson,' I answered after a pause during which I saw many things. 'I'm destined for the big house on the hill tomorrow,' I added, nodding towards the tall hospital building above the dockyard. 'I shall be able to sleep there without a voice-pipe at my ear. No, I shall never go to sea again – and I'm not sorry, fond as I am of ships and men.'